Becky Wicks is the author of two previous humorous travel memoirs, *Burqalicious: The Dubai Diaries* and *Balilicious: The Bali Diaries*. She's been gallivanting around the world since graduating Lincoln Uni in 2001 and has lived and worked in London, New York, Dubai, Sydney and Indonesia. To earn a living she's sold her soul to the advertising industry, written credit card copy for banks that wouldn't give her a credit card, been a morning radio show sidekick and sold jello shots in Manhattan. She's currently Bali-based, where she's freelancing, working on fiction, and awaiting the next adventure. Becky blogs most days on travel and random ridiculousness at www.beckywicks.com. Twitter: bex_wicks

Latinalicious

THE SOUTH AMERICA DIARIES

A true story of travelling the
world's sexiest continent

Becky Wicks

HarperCollins*Publishers*

HarperCollins*Publishers*

First published in Australia in 2013
by HarperCollins*Publishers* Australia Pty Limited
ABN 36 009 913 517
harpercollins.com.au

Copyright © Rebecca Wicks 2013

HarperCollins*Publishers*
Level 13, 201 Elizabeth Street, Sydney NSW 2000, Australia
Unit D1, 63 Apollo Drive, Rosedale, Auckland 0632, New Zealand
A 53, Sector 57, Noida, UP, India
77–85 Fulham Palace Road, London W6 8JB, United Kingdom
2 Bloor Street East, 20th floor, Toronto, Ontario M4W 1A8, Canada
10 East 53rd Street, New York NY 10022, USA

National Library of Australia Cataloguing-in-Publication entry

Wicks, Rebecca.
  Latinalicious : the South America diaries / Becky Wicks.
  ISBN: 978 0 7322 9641 4 (pbk.)
  Wicks, Rebecca – Anecdotes.
  Women travelers – South America – Description and travel.
910.4

Photographs by Rebecca Wicks
Cover and internal design by Natalie Winter
Map by www.ianfaulknerillustrator.com
Typeset in 11.5/17pt Minion by Kirby Jones

For Mary Wicks

Acknowledgements

'To the nights we'll never remember and the friends we'll never forget.'

I read that on a hostel wall somewhere in Chile and I thought it summed up my travels perfectly. There were so many people I met along the way who changed the direction of my South American journey in one way or another. Some of them changed my entire life. You know who you are and I thank you.

Huge thanks to my fab agent Margaret Gee, publishers Katie Stackhouse and Jeanne Ryckmans at HarperCollins, and Kim Swivel, my editor, for smoothing out the manuscript when my eyes were bulging from reading it too much. Massive thank yous go out to all the hotels, travel companies and tour guides who enabled me to have so many amazing experiences, too. Oh, and the hostels for the ever-humbling nights amongst snorers.

I hope you love this journey as much as I did.

Ecuadorean addictions and ash clouds …

As Rosa rolled the hard-boiled egg across my forehead I wasn't as disturbed as you might think, even though I was sitting on a plastic table in a five-star hotel bathroom in my underwear, being chattered at in Spanish by a lady I'd met only the day before in the herb and flower market. The truth is, I've probably done stranger things in hotel bathrooms.

The idea of a South American 'Limpia' treatment — an ancient Andean ritual intended as a means of energy equilibrium restoration — appealed not just because I was feeling pretty short of breath at 2800 metres in Quito, but because I'd had a night of debaucheries just twelve hours previously with an Ecuadorean guesthouse owner called Salvador. I was knackered.

Luckily, everything around me was luxurious and splendid at the Casa Gangotena, a restored historic mansion overlooking Plaza San Francisco — Quito's old town. This five-star hotel is also located just twenty-five kilometres from the equator; thus far, I've never been so close. It's quite exciting. It's also really cold.

When I stepped out of the airport in Quito, the goosebumps had attacked my bare arms with a vengeance. Turns out that

1

while Ecuador's furthest reaches boast sticky, tropical jungles and beaches, its capital city, guarded by an army of snow-capped mountains, is currently freezing. And having spent the last eight months in Bali, I don't even own a coat. I think I may have to go shopping.

Anyway, there's lots to do and tons more to plan, because this is the very first leg of my South American journey, a trip that will hopefully take me to some of the most scenic, exciting and inspiring destinations on the planet. From Ecuador I'm flying down to Buenos Aires to do a Spanish course and then … well, honestly, I haven't got past that bit yet. I've downloaded a few guidebooks and reached out to friends for suggestions, so I'm kind of hoping things will fall into place.

It's funny how we can just do this nowadays, isn't it? I mean, planning a journey across several countries in which English isn't the primary language would have taken months, if not *years* of preparation, say, thirty years ago. Maps, a compass, a stack of paper and envelopes and a calendar with a set date on which to post a letter to your mum/gran/distant gypsy relative Rosie, who's expecting you at some point in the wilds of some Peruvian jungle destination, for which you need to book a boat ticket thirty-three days in advance from a tour operator that may or may not still exist on a certain shady street in La Paz … Jesus. No thanks. These days you just pop your smartphone in your pocket, pack some pants and get on the plane. Job done.

It's such a huge continent, obviously, and there are definitely things I'm itching to see: the salt flats in Bolivia, Machu Picchu, hammerhead sharks in the Galápagos, the homes of Malbec red and Eva Peron in Argentina, the hot Brazilian men in Rio's Copacabana, coffee plantations in Colombia, the strapping gauchos and glacial walls in the national parks of Patagonia. My friend Autumn, who's a photographer, is coming to join me for a while and we're already bouncing ideas around about a cruise through Tierra del Fuego, which is literally as close as you can get to Antarctica without going to Antarctica. Just thinking about it all makes me need to lie down.

Better just start with where I am now, in Ecuador with my good friend Farzana, who's just spent a month in Colombia and is all rosy cheeked with a freshly pumped ego, thanks to the flattering ways of its men. I added Medellín and the tropical Caribbean climes of Cartagena to my travel list as soon as she started talking.

While we're here in Quito however (must try not to rush ahead), we can actually take a trip to the centre of the world and stand on the line between both hemispheres — just for kicks. I'm interested to see if the water really does flush a different way down the toilet on each side. Farzana tells me we could Google it now and find out, but I want it to be a surprise.

Also, I'm told if we ride the TelefériQo, one of the world's highest aerial lifts, which isn't too far from here, we can see up to thirteen volcanoes if it's sunny. That's a lot of volcanoes. I've got to admit, it's a little unnerving being around so many. Stratovolcano Guagua Pichincha, just thirteen kilometres west of here, sent a whopping great mushroom cloud of ash up over Quito in 1999, covering the city.

I guess people thought it was safe, especially the ones who set off to climb it on that fateful day, because the last time it erupted before that was in 1660, which is so long ago that everyone was probably lulled into a false sense of security, thinking, 'Active, my arse — that thing's as dead as a dodo.' I'm keeping my eye on it. I don't trust it in the slightest.

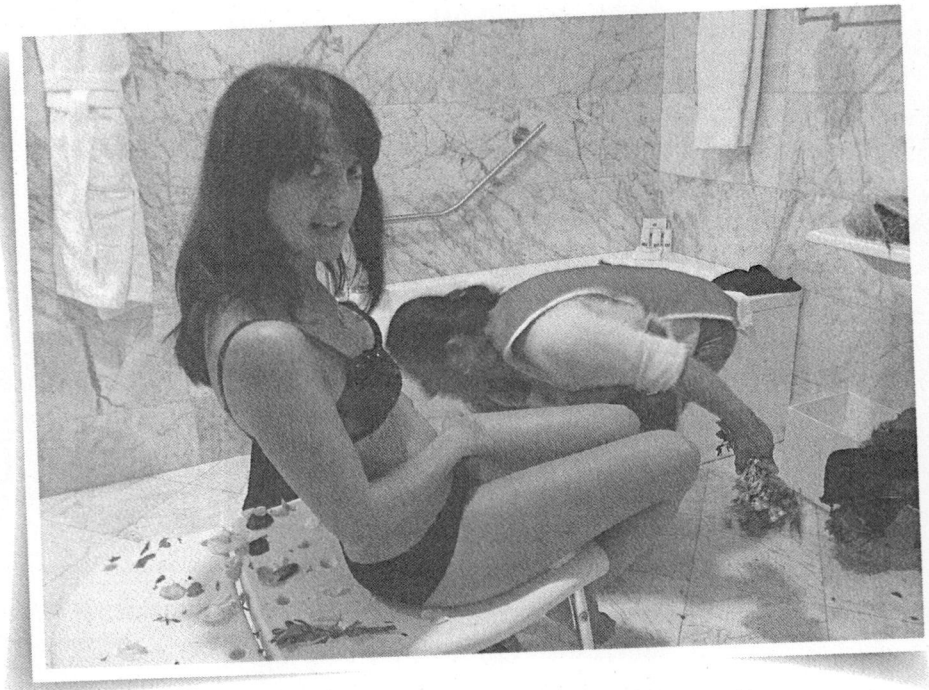

Those stinging nettles were still stinging the next day!

As Rosa fetched a fistful of stinging nettles from her arrangement of healing herbs in the sink, I felt another spark of excitement at being right at the start of a brand new adventure, with absolutely no idea of what will happen to me and around me over the next eight months. Then, as I smiled in sweet contentment, she whipped my entire body into one throbbing pulse with the nettles, causing welts to spring up on my thighs.

'Are they supposed to be causing this reaction?' I asked her in alarm, studying the rising bumps manifesting like alien spawn under my skin.

'Spanish Spanish Spanish Spanish *Spanish*,' she said, thrusting her arms out ebulliently and smacking me again on the neck with the nettles for good measure.

Of course, that's not what Rosa said exactly, but after just four days in South America I don't understand one word of Spanish so that's all I heard. In fact, I'm still not entirely sure if her nettle therapy worked to rid my body of evil, energy-zapping forces just now, or if the welts were just punishment for what she saw in my eyes as my mind drifted off, back to last night, with Salvador. Oh, Salvador.

If there's one thing I've garnered in the space of just four days, aside from the fact that no one understands me, and that I really should construct some sort of emergency volcano eruption survival kit, it's that the men here in South America are a different species entirely. Quite frankly, I'm shocked that I've never thought to come here before. I'm absolutely, one hundred per cent sure that South American men are what I've been missing in my life.

Why? Well, let me tell you why. They're animated, like cartoon characters bouncing about on a screen. They're made of sun and sex and spontaneity, and passion oozes out of every pore. I've never known anything like it. When I first met Salvador he greeted Farzana and me at the door and led us on a tour of his guesthouse, explaining in almost perfect English the intricacies of every restored seat cushion and the plumbing involved in turning a creaky house with two bathrooms into a hotel with seventeen. I was listening, but I wasn't. I was noticing how every movement was a dance, every step a sinewy act of seduction via toned arms, a broad chest and a sculpted arse in stonewashed jeans.

My hands started running through my hair. My lashes started batting, I straightened my outfit and moistened my lips, by which time he had lapsed into charismatic Spanish mode and was speaking to another guest regarding paying her bill. I noticed Jesus on a cross, on a chain around his neck. When he turned back to us he was probably only talking about the fact that we would need to hold our hands for five seconds on the toilet button if we were going to flush it properly without the risk of clogging, but my brain was already in his bedroom. My hands were already tearing off his clothes.

We went out that night. Farzana went home early. I never made it back to his guesthouse. Instead, Salvador and I danced flirtatiously in a club and went back to his friend's house, where we drank from a bottle of watermelon vodka and I told myself it didn't matter in the slightest if I never had another conversation in English, *ever* again. Verbal communication means nothing, I thought, as he danced around the kitchen. Who needs verbal banter, I thought, as he pulled me to my feet, took the bottle from my lips and pressed against me so hard I could feel every inch of him wedged against every inch of me.

I later learned Salvador had refused his friend's requests for a dirty 4 a.m. orgy. I never got a say in the matter. In my head, the whole evening was very romantic, but then again it's easy to hear what you want to hear when you're drunk and you don't know the Spanish word for threesome.

Anyway, Salvador was a perfect gentleman, letting me use his friend's toothbrush without telling him and getting me back to the guesthouse before 9.30 a.m., by which time Farzana was already halfway to a cloud forest with a man called Dante for some zip-lining. I spent the entire day in a state somewhere between sleep and feeling that a gecko with a pickaxe was removing my frontal lobe. Then I dragged myself to the Casa Gangotena and booked myself the Limpia. So yeah, now you know why I needed those reinvigorating nettles.

You should be able to bottle it, you know. A few drops of Latin American charm would make numerous countries I've visited infinitely more enjoyable. If you're the sort of person who revels in the delicious feeling of being under a spell, I can highly recommend a trip to Ecuador surrounded by this enchanting species ... but then I haven't been to Argentina yet. I've heard the men are even hotter there.

Musings from the middle of the world ...

The mammoth thirty-metre high monument marking the Mitad del Mundo (Middle of the World) outside Quito was built in the wrong place back in 1982. This means that while you can have a lovely time walking around the ethnographic museum inside, looking at headless figures in ancient llama wool shawls and photos of men with no teeth, all you're really doing when you get to the top is standing on a big lump of concrete in the middle of ... well, nowhere.

The actual line where Charles-Marie de La Condamine, a curly-haired, pointy-nosed French mathematician, made the measurements to prove the world wasn't flat in 1736, runs through Museo de Sitio Intiñan, which is about a five-minute drive up the road.

No one seems to mind going to both the monument and the museum, though, especially not the tour guides. Ours charged us AU$40 each to drive us to both spots, and then sat in her car smoking cigarettes while we guided ourselves.

Back to clever-clogs Charles. I can't actually believe he got the chance to prove the world wasn't round. Reading about him, he sounds like quite a guy, one who went on to do all sorts of cool stuff. At first, though, he really had to prove himself:

'Hello men-fellows, I do believe the world bulges in the middle.'

'Come now, Charles, last week you said earth wasn't the only planet in the sky.'

'It's not.'

'Come now!'

'Well, my friends, the King of France and the French Royal Academy of Sciences are sending me on an expedition to prove the world is not perfectly flat. I'm going to prove this as soon as I reach Ecuador. And after that I'm going to map the Amazon River based on astronomical observations. And after I've done all that, there will be a sixty-seven-kilometre-wide crater on the moon dedicated to me.'

'Oh Charles, dearest man. You are such a delightful dreamer. Have some mead before you go?'

While we're talking of impressive men, I think things are over with Salvador. Not that they ever really began, since he lives in a guesthouse with his mum, dad and brother, where the floorboards creak if you so much as look at them, so seeing him after the almost-orgy night was tricky. We did enjoy some fun textual relations as Farzana and I took part in some interesting experiments at the Museo de Sitio Intiñan, however.

These experiments included balancing a raw egg on a nail, which in other locations is impossible, apparently. I can't imagine why you'd ever want to balance an egg on a nail but there you go. Actually, I really do think that if you're going to make people do something this pointless it should at least be something fun, like slapping a stranger's face with a kipper on each hemisphere and videoing it for a special exhibit in the museum nearby ... perhaps in place of the llama wool shawl collection, which is a bit boring. But that's just me.

Another experiment was the toilet flushing one, which I was very excited about, although I left feeling rather underwhelmed by this, too. Don't get me wrong, it was interesting and everything but really, if you've gone all the way to the middle of the earth to answer a probing question about a toilet flush and someone whips out a *sink*, you're going to feel a little cheated.

Yes, they demonstrated what is scientifically known as the Coriolis effect with a sink, and some leaves that spun as the water was drained. Toilets and sinks are right next to each other in the showroom, too. How hard would it be to get a big loo and attach some wheels on it and do the experiment with that? Honestly.

Oh, but if you're wondering whether the water really does drain in different directions on different sides of the equator, I can tell you...

SPOILER ALERT

It does. It really does!!!

Back to Salvador. I told him I'd had fun from the Northern Hemisphere. He told me he'd had fun too as I stepped into the Southern Hemisphere.

As we followed our tour guide (not the driver, a different one because ours was still smoking in her car) around some of the original, hundred-year-old homes that belonged to the local indigenous people and gazed in awe at gruesome-looking shrunken heads, Salvador requested my friendship on Facebook. Eager to show Farzana some photos of his exposed six pack, I accepted.

And then I found out he has a girlfriend.

She'd written '*amore*' on his wall at precisely the same time as we'd been making out against another wall in his friend's kitchen and somehow he'd found a spare moment to 'like' her comment shortly afterwards. Hmm.

All is still well and good because Farzana and I are heading over to the Galápagos shortly anyway. We booked the return flights and a five-night cruise for just under AU$1800 each from a tour operator here in Quito. Sealing the last-minute deal involved a bit of a kerfuffle because here in Ecuador they don't like you using credit cards and generally whack on extortionate fees if you do. At the same time, you can only get roughly $600 out of the ATM in one day, so if you're booking a tour that costs more than that and have to pay it all in one go, like you do when you go last minute, you're buggered.

We wound up trying to get out of the credit card fee for about an hour. We even turned on the tears and told the operator we'd be poor for the rest of our trip if we paid any more. But it was kind of hard to cry poverty when we were booking time on a yacht.

When we couldn't get out of it, we were forced to pay half in cash and the rest on the card, with a ludicrous extra eighteen per cent on top. Ouch. Avoid a similar sting and take a lot of cash with you to Ecuador, or withdraw the maximum amount on three or four consecutive days *before* you book your Galápagos trip.

Oh, you can visit the Galápagos Islands for less than $1800, of course. But Farzana and I have decided to splash out as we splash about. While we don't mind budget accommodation on land, the last thing we need to experience is a rocking dorm room at sea with backpackers puking even more than usual over the side of their bunk beds. When Farzana leaves I've got a good eight months ahead of me, staying in hostels. Right now I'm enjoying every little luxury I can.

Boobies and other star attractions ...

Carrots. It's always the carrots. Even if you haven't eaten any carrots, they always seem to show up first when you're retching over the toilet bowl, wondering when the hell your stomach will settle and leave you free to roll into a self-pitying fetal ball on the floor. This is at least what Farzana told me after a night chucking her guts up out on the deck, and in the metre-wide closet that constitutes the bathroom in our five-star yacht.

Of course, it could have been papaya, I reasoned, the fruity orange Ecuadorean cousin that also chooses to surface first during terrible bouts of seasickness. But anyway, beginning our highly anticipated Galápagos cruise the other day, we sailed overnight from Cerro Dragon on Isla Santa Cruz, to Post Office Bay on Isla Floreana and realised that poor Farzana had left her sea legs somewhere on a pristine beach surrounded by sea lions. After a while I had no choice but to leave her lying in a crumpled heap on the five-star navy pinstriped sun lounge, while I prayed to the dimpled face of a seriously oversized moon for her recovery.

Ah, the moon! What a sight to behold here on the equator: the way it hangs in its Milky Way hammock between a squillion stars. You won't see as many stars as you will here anywhere else on this planet, trust me, not even if you go to every Oscars after-party ever thrown by Elton John.

The *Tip Top II* cruise ship (one of the Galápagos's original fleet vessels) swayed like Beyonce's hips in a concert arena as I studied the black pin-pricked blanket of the Galápagos sky, and I was left in no doubt whatsoever that we, as humans sailing though this life, are not alone. We simply can't be. Leaning over the railings that first night, I got lost in the majesty, the romantic possibility of galaxies stretching light years into infinity, until Farzana brought me back to earth by releasing another batch of vegetables.

The reason for such a spectacular display of stars above the Galápagos, according to our knowledgeable guide Andreas, is that on the equator you're looking at twice the number of constellations. The stars you can see from both the Southern and the Northern Hemisphere are all spread out before you in the centre of the world, crisscrossing in the night like lonesome gypsy travellers wandering at last into each other's paths. Some little stars are so bright and alive, they actually do twinkle.

Our guide Andreas loves nature like you wouldn't believe. He told me on our second night, as a group of us lay out on the sun lounges counting constellations, that when he drank ayahuasca in the Amazon rainforest he communicated with 'the spirit of the vine' herself. Ever since then, he's been able to communicate almost psychically with the animals.

You might laugh, but I swear, as we continue to walk together through some of the most insanely beautiful landscapes on our various island excursions, the animals we encounter don't bat an eyelid. Not just that, but Andreas can point out every single animal and bird he promises we'll see, usually within moments of promising it. It's almost like he calls them and they appear.

Fascinated, we wandered around huddled groups of charcoal-coloured marine iguanas on our first day, their red underbellies glowing like embers. We saw albatrosses with humongous yellow beaks eyeing us idly from their grassy nests as we passed, just inches away. Sally Lightfoot crabs scuttled in their scarlet droves over the rocks. Sea lions were everywhere. In fact, while most people who visit the Galápagos might ask 'will I definitely get to see the sea lions?' before they book their tickets (like we did), the truth is that you'll be hard-pressed *not* to see one here. You'll see thousands of sea lions and, yes, you can swim with them and, yes, they actually *want* you to swim with them, too!

They'll chase your boat through the blue. They'll waddle up to you on the beach and waddle back into the surf, and then turn around to see if you're following, like puppy dogs. If you're not, they'll do the same again until you step into the water. This experience alone made the cruise worthwhile, I think. You don't *have* to do a cruise in order to see the sea lions, though. You can go out to the islands on day tours from Santa Cruz if you buy a $400 (average) return flight from Quito.

It's worth remembering, however, that most of these day tours are overpriced and the guides — many of them locals with no qualifications — are known to be considerably less enthusiastic than actual naturalists, like Andreas, who are paid really well to work on the higher-end cruises and will tell you so many interesting facts as you go that your head will spin.

One field trip the other day saw us beaching our Zodiac (an inflatable dinghy for the uninformed) on sands so white I thought I'd be blinded. The whiteness sloped down into some of the clearest seawater on earth. It was as translucent as tap water. This was Gardner Bay, Isla Española — in the far southeast of the Galápagos archipelago and almost four million years old. Make sure your cruise includes a stop here and don't book it if it doesn't. This is without a doubt one of the most unspoiled … no, make that *the* most unspoiled part of the planet I have ever laid eyes on. It was actually surreal.

Lazing on this beach we were able to stand, sit or even lie within one metre of the sea lions, 'but no closer than one metre — that's the rule,' Andreas told us sternly. We all spent hours posing for the obligatory photos as these creatures, some

Surely a dream-come-true moment.

of them huge and menacing-looking, some just curious babies, eyed us in equal wonder. There is seriously nothing cuter than a baby sea lion. And there's nothing more impressive than spotting a cluster of a thousand or so marine iguanas, just lounging in the sun like dinosaurs who forgot to become extinct.

Andreas told us one story of a man who was caught at the airport with a marine iguana in his backpack. God knows how he thought he would get it to wherever he was going, but these creatures are so placid it's not hard to believe that you could scoop a few up and whisk away with them. They smell pretty bad, though. I'm not sure you'd want one, really.

None of the animals seem to have any fear of humans in the Galápagos, and Andreas explained that it's because none of them —

maybe with the exception of that poor iguana — have ever been harmed by humans. Every few months, they shut certain islands to cruise ship passengers and open different ones to encourage the continuation of each natural habitat without disturbance. The US$100 entrance fee, which everyone must pay in cash upon arrival at the Galápagos airport, is spent purely on maintaining this unique part of the world and its precious, rare ecosystems.

Charles Darwin first noted that the finches on each Galápagos island varied in the shape and size of their beaks, and thus, his theory of natural selection was born in 1839. It appeared that these finches had originally come from mainland South America, that they had colonised the islands at some point and had then over time evolved their distinct beaks according to their needs in each different island environment.

To this day, the Galápagos National Park Service and conservation teams are so concerned with keeping every island immaculate and individual that the cruise ship staff have been told to make all passengers wash their feet and shoes after each island visit to avoid cross-contamination. I've lost count of how many times I've been hosed down on this cruise. I'm actually surprised Farzana and I weren't put in quarantine before we were allowed to visit … but then, the authorities aren't aware of my filthy thoughts about Salvador (sigh).

Today we got to visit the Charles Darwin Research Station, but unfortunately we're just a few weeks too late to see its star, Lonesome George, the sole remaining Pinta Island tortoise. He refused to mate, apparently. He just wasn't a horny tortoise, so his entire subspecies fizzled out when he did, in June. Poor guy, though — all that pressure. Imagine if you and *only* you were responsible for the continuation of your entire race. It was all too much for George. He preferred eating cucumbers.

Before humans sailed up, the Galápagos Islands were home to literally tens of thousands of giant tortoises. The numbers fell to near extinction but there's now a recovery program run by the Charles Darwin Foundation, and it has been successful in bringing the numbers back up to over 20,000. You can walk around the research station and learn all about them, which, to be honest, isn't really the most exciting thing in the world. They don't do much, tortoises.

The blue-footed booby is perhaps the creature that most people look forward to encountering in the Galápagos. I won't bother with any puns now and, trust me, neither will you once you're here, because everyone does it for you, all over the place. You can't walk down the street in Santa Cruz without being accosted by a man displaying his rail of 'I heart Boobies' T-shirts.

These weird, long-winged seabirds look a bit like penguins crossed with seagulls and they really do have bright blue feet, as though they've waddled across a wet painting of the ocean.

Our group was lucky enough to witness the mating ritual, which is a strange dance-off between the male boobies, a bit like men vying for a girl's attention at a party. The female looks on from the perimeter, trying to decide which one she prefers as they flap and strut and lift each leg up in an effort to look masculine. The winner gets the girl and the privilege of building her a nest, and the loser goes off to try his luck with someone else.

It was during the enjoyment of this ritual that we also witnessed our first group of 'serious birdwatchers'. You won't see as many birdwatchers anywhere as you will in the Galápagos. As you can imagine, it is the holy grail for fans of things-with-wings and you can spot these people a mile off, usually because their telescopic lenses protrude into the corners of your humble iPhone snap shots, appearing way before you see the 'serious birdwatcher' in person.

What really sets a 'serious birdwatcher' apart from a regular birdwatcher, however, is the note-taking. Not content with photographing every single feather on the head of an Española mockingbird, or the butt-crack of a swallow-tailed gull, the 'serious' of the species must then whip out a clipboard and pen and busy themselves with noting why *these* feathers are so very different from the ones they shot yesterday, plus the date, time and exact location of each shot.

I know this because I stopped one man, part of a bird-watching tour group, and asked what they were all writing down. He was drooping under the weight of his equipment and his Canon lens was so long and so unconscionably wide, I'm pretty sure the Hubble Space Telescope would've had a tough job competing for close-ups.

'We have a competition, with prizes when we get home,' he said proudly. 'We have to make sure we all get shots of different birds.'

'But how do you tell the difference?' I queried. 'They all look the same to me!'

He frowned then, as though I was the most despicable racist ever to walk the face of the earth. 'Every single one is unique,' he said curtly, and lumbered on in his quest.

It seems I have a lot more to learn when it comes to discerning my feathers from my ... feathers ... and my carrots from my papayas, perhaps. But suffice to say that apart from the little problem of seasickness (which, by the way, was cured once Farzana took some special pills courtesy of a fellow shipmate) the Galápagos is turning out to be one of the most incredible experiences of my life. I should have booked more time here, really.

The volcano, the blizzard and the Kindle ...

We pulled to a stop at 5800 metres. The air was thinner than Miranda Kerr on a juice diet and the fact that the vehicle was still rocking even though the engine was off was rather worrying. Javier, our guide, hopped out and swung the door of the van open with an enthusiastic thrust. A gust of icy wind roared around my ears as he hollered something in Spanish above the noise.

I recoiled in horror in my seat, clutched my suede purse to my chest and turned my back to the door. Suede and wet weather do not mix well; this much I know.

The tour group jumped up excitedly and started pulling waterproof items from their backpacks. I felt a sinking feeling. It was obvious that my hot pink J.C. Penney zip-up cardy and patterned scarf from Bali weren't going to cut it in these climes. I huddled into them anyway and looked on in dismay as the smooching honeymooners who'd spent the whole journey from Quito making out in the seat in front of me produced items they'd hidden up to this point, and started zipping each other into them. I thought I'd been dressed appropriately for what the tour operator said would be 'a moderate to challenging adventure at the foot of the majestic snow-capped active volcano Cotopaxi', but it was starting to look like I should have brought an extra supply of synthetic zero degree high socks with me. And perhaps Shackleton's handbook.

Javier slid on a knitted balaclava and eyed me through the slits like a robber intent on stealing my snowshoes. I frowned and pulled out my Kindle to show him I would be passing up the possibility of turning into an ice-sculpture in front of strangers in favour of some light reading. Even without my embarrassingly slim Spanish vocabulary, my terrified expression as the sleet zoomed in and pummelled my naked cheeks must have conveyed the message that they would probably be hiking to the glacier without me.

When the tour operator in Quito took my $40 in cash for the fun day's exploration of Ecuador's Limpiopungo Lake and the national park, he never told me I might need to budget an extra $400 to stock up on winter clothing. Yesterday I bought some trainers from North Face, which are quite possibly the most expensive shoes I've ever bought, because I predict that I'll be doing a lot of walking on my upcoming travels and I'd prefer to be comfortable. But I'd figured I didn't need to go all out and buy the thermals, too — not when I had my J.C. Penney zip-up. I had considered myself fully prepared to 'soar with the condors and bike with the pumas in one of Ecuador's most stunning locations', but as the blizzard raged around the van now it struck me that the past year of lounging in tropical sun-soaked Bali has rendered me unable to even contemplate weather below seventy-five degrees Fahrenheit.

I was feeling more stupid by the second.

Still, the scenery was very pleasant when the group finally returned an hour and a half later and we took off back down the mountain, out of the snowstorm. Their waterproofs were dripping melting frost all over the floor of the van as they compared photos and chattered happily in Spanish. I saw a few of the pictures and, to be honest, I didn't feel too bad for having missed out … or at least, I told myself I didn't. It was cloudy at the top and it looked even colder. My mascara definitely would have run. Plus, I managed to read at least four more chapters of my book while they were gone and I could still feel my toes. Just.

The option to hop on a mountain bike once we'd crawled back down to a lower altitude was tempting, especially as I'd paid for a tour I hadn't actually taken part in yet. In truth, I was starting to feel like a wuss. Plus, I really wanted to bike with the pumas, as promised. But as the group strapped helmets on top of their huge woolly hats and it started to rain again, I decided that pumas would probably not be as active in wet weather and I was, by this point, really getting into Katniss's bow and arrow quest in *The Hunger Games* for the third time. In spite of everything, I felt as though I owed it to District Twelve to continue. Thanks to my Kindle I could live vicariously through *her* adventure and not have to worry about falling off a bike down a mountain or ruining my cardy.

Eventually the sun came out and blue skies served to highlight the majestic white peak of Cotopaxi, its snowcap spilling over like melting ice-cream in the sunshine. We stopped to take photos. The honeymooners loved it. They took at least a hundred snaps in various positions and even did those annoying 'trick shots' — you know, the ones you mostly feel obliged to do at famous landmarks, whereby you, say, pretend to tap the peak from a distance with your pointy finger? In this case they kissed either side of it at the same time. Disgusting. Even the snowcap puked … I swear I saw some ice fall off.

We went for a late lunch at a base camp, which was full of rosy-faced, eager English girls throwing tennis balls at each other, saying, 'Ra!' They'd set up tents in a field full of bored-looking llamas, so I can only assume they were part-way through some sort of intense hiking expedition and probably none of them had a Kindle.

What a day. I cursed the tour operator as I shivered alone, eating Ritz crackers in that rocking, wind-battered van, but it's not all his fault, of course. I think he did actually tell me how high we'd be above sea level on the tour. He did also mention the word glacier more than once, even if the posters on the walls of his office had showed smiling people beneath blue skies, hugging on a very unthreatening-looking block of ice.

Before today, if you had asked me if I was an outdoorsy sort of girl, I'd have waxed lyrical about the joys of strolling through Balinese rice paddies and lounging on catamarans in Dubai. But now I see that I've probably misunderstood the great outdoors in its true sense. I'm ashamed that I got on that tour bus. I could barely look at them all when we got off back in Quito. The honeymooners were very sweet and took a break from eating other's faces to peck me on both cheeks and wish me well. The whole group was planning dinner together, maybe some drinks and a photo swap. I just wanted to hide in my hostel dorm room and plan a much-needed bulky clothes shopping expedition.

24/07

Overly amorous guides and the urethra invasion …

'I don't usually wear underwear to bed', Kenny, the eleven-year-old, informed me as we swung side by side in our hammocks on the jungle lodge porch. 'I mean, sometimes I do, but I just find it uncomfortable, don't you?'

I looked up from my book, slightly shocked and not quite sure how to answer. However, as we moved on to discuss the surprise success of Justin Bieber — 'he hasn't even got very striking eyes' — and the sad demise of a man who'd died by licking a frog,

I realised I was actually quite enjoying my Amazon experience. I don't think I've had such a deep and meaningful conversation with an eleven-year-old since I was ... well, eleven.

For AU$200 I booked a three-night, four-day tour via one of the many operators in Quito's touristic-maze, La Mariscal, to experience the jungle with a bunch of randoms. I've come alone because Farzana had to fly home to London after our Galápagos adventures. And yes, I made sure I knew what I was letting myself in for with *this* trip.

Or so I thought.

To get to our lodge at the border of Ecuador, Colombia and Peru, I had to take an arduous overnight bus from Quito to Lago Agrio — an uninspiring town with a name that means 'sour lake'. This town was rainforest itself until oil was discovered in 1967 and the American oil-explorers built it up as a base. From this point my group and I were driven two hours to the river and put on a boat for another two hours. Getting to the Amazon is not easy. Still, here I am, deep in the green, currently under a blanket in my dorm room, with a family of stripy cockroaches scuttling all over the bathroom. A sleeping Taiwanese girl is snoring softly in the bunk above me and the door is bolted shut to my right, in spite of us being in the middle of nowhere. More on why in a minute.

The Cuyabeno Reserve has one of the most diverse ecosystems on the planet. This croaking rainforest is home to thousands of species of flora and fauna and hundreds of animals endemic to the area. Indigenous communities still practise shamanism and ancient medicinal rituals in villages dotted along the riverbanks.

When I arrived, I asked if we'd be seeing any tribes with their penises strapped to their waists — something they do to avoid the invasion of the candiru fish, which has a tendency to swim up the human urethra and parasitise it if you dare to pee in the river.

But allegedly the most exciting tribes, the ones who used to grunt and shrink heads in boiling cauldrons, live around the fringes of the Amazon, mostly in the border regions of Brazil. Shame.

'I do not want to see a tarantula,' I stated to our jungle guide, a strapping, black-haired man in his mid-thirties I'll call Mowgli, as soon as I stepped onto the boat.

'You and everyone else who comes here,' he replied, smirking.

Prior to signing up for the trip, I Googled what I was likely to encounter here and the Internet informed me there are approximately 3600 species of spiders inhabiting the Amazon basin. To not encounter one, I'd have to walk around blindfolded. To not encounter a tarantula, Mowgli told me, I'd have to keep my eyes off the ceiling in the jungle lodge dining room.

Our group consists of a family of Americans (including Kenny and his two brothers), two French friends, a cool Ecuadorean girl my age called Dani and her mum, and the girl from Taiwan, who doesn't speak English. Between our no-language-necessary appreciation of the jungle over the past few days, we all seem to have bonded. Except with Mowgli. He's the reason the door is currently bolted. Don't worry, I'm coming to it.

I estimate I'd been here roughly one hour and twenty minutes before I saw my first tarantula. Kenny actually spotted it, crawling out of the rafters about two metres above our heads. Mowgli hadn't been joking about the dining room ceiling. The rest of the group rushed in to see what all the noise was about and we all jumped around, making a fuss for about five minutes before we realised that in spite of its big, black, hairy presence, it was really quite boring, just sitting there like a pink-toed stuffed toy. They actually have *pink* toes, these ones. Not that it makes them any less scary-looking. It's like putting ballet shoes on the Grim Reaper.

Mowgli stood nonchalantly on the sidelines as we composed ourselves, before announcing we were heading out to see the sunset over the lake, to fish for piranhas and to look for the famed pink Amazonian river dolphins. These dolphins have no natural predators, so they can happily live and hunt alone, although Mowgli explained that they often choose to live in families. They're known to have a brain capacity that's forty per cent bigger than ours. Imagine that! It's hard to believe that dolphins haven't figured out a way of taking over the world. Or maybe they have but they've since decided it's all too much effort and they might as well stick to swimming around and eating fish, which is easier.

After a thrilling adventure involving sailing through sweeping branches, ducking on command and fishing for piranhas in the mangroves (I caught three — and while some guides will let you cook and eat them, we released all ours back into the water), we paddled around in our giant canoe in the cotton candy colours of the setting sun. The most the pink dolphins offered us, though, were a few bubbles and snorts, which broke the coffee-coloured surface of the water and proved to us their existence, at least.

'Did you know, the Amazon River itself releases more water into the sea in one day than the London Thames does in one whole year?' one of the guys in our group piped up.

We all shook our heads.

Not to be outdone with the facts, Mowgli sat up straighter. 'Did you know, a snake smells of earwax? That is how you know you are about to stand on one.'

Enlightened, we all shook our heads again and I realised, along with everyone else, probably, that I'd never even thought to smell my own earwax.

The smell of the rainforest is one of warm peat, like a greenhouse in a garden centre. It's absolutely bursting with life —

every time you turn your head there's a flicker of a butterfly's wing, a movement in a tree, the squawk of a bird taking flight. It's one living, breathing organism, the ineluctable circle of life and death. Every living thing plays a vital role here and every *dead* thing in due course becomes a life-giver, a buffet for the unborn, allowing in its passing something new to thrive. It's so mysterious and huge you cannot help but feel as though you're constantly on the verge of discovering a secret.

You rarely see any animals up close; it's always in the corner of your eye. But you can almost see Pachamama herself — Mother Nature — smiling through the canopy in a sunbeam, an unseen spirit of the wind swinging in a spider web between two ferns, big enough for a human to use as a hammock. It's so intense, so thick and in places so impenetrable that it threatens to swallow you if you go even slightly off course. The people who live here have a deep, deep respect for the rainforest.

'Last year, a biologist got lost in here,' Mowgli told us. 'She was found fourteen days later, eighty kilometres away in … how you say … in the door of death?'

'On death's doorstep?' I offered.

He ignored me.

'The worst thing you can do when you get lost in the jungle is keep moving,' he continued, looking at us seriously through dark, glinting eyes. 'If it ever happens to you, stay where you are. You'll be found. If you move, the jungle will consume you.'

Such words from such a man can make a woman moist, even without the clammy jungle climate. Rain pelted us occasionally from all angles through the tree tops, threatening to send us off course, and every time I followed Mowgli along the paths he'd cut with his machete I was consumed by the thought of the jungle consuming me.

After fishing, when we reached the lake at the end of the river, locals from nearby villages and tourists were competing in a canoe race and swimming. Call me daft, but I never expected to be able to swim in the Amazon.

'It's perfectly safe,' Mowgli informed us, 'as long as you save your toilet time for later.'

My urethra contracted just thinking about it but Kenny and his brothers jumped in and splashed about and they seemed just fine, so I lowered myself in to join them, keeping my eye out for piranhas and other evils. I don't have to be afraid of the candiru fish (it's not exactly an issue for girls), but as Kenny's uncle pointed out, they should introduce these to public swimming pools back home anyway — way too many people piss in those things without consequence.

Back in our motor-powered canoe, every now and then as we cruised the river, a dazzling blue *Morpho menelaus* butterfly the size of a sparrow would rise and fall like a buzzing electric current in the sky, and then hide itself from our lenses in a flowering bush. In the twilight, kingfishers swooped and as darkness threw the banks into shadow, our driver hurtled full-throttle towards the starting point of our night trek, using nothing but the stars and the familiar shapes of the treetops to guide him.

'He knows them like his hand,' Mowgli said from his place beside me at front of the boat, when I asked if we were likely to crash.

'You mean the *back* of his hand?' I corrected him.

He ignored me.

Our night trek was a forty-minute hike over flat land on what seemed to be a well-worn path. Mowgli seemed to spot things with some extrasensory power, because we'd all be admiring, say, a giant cricket, and suddenly he'd appear holding a frog, which he seemed to produce from nowhere. I half suspect he has a hundred props dotted about the place in case his visitors are disappointed, but I do admire the passion he has for the jungle and its critters, even the huge-pincered, multi-toothed beasts and bugs that make me want to scream bloody murder and vomit on my nice new trainers.

At one point, he whipped out his machete and cut down a branch to make a walking pole for Dani's mum, which made her gush her thanks in Spanish and the rest of us females gaze at him in wide-eyed wonder.

Mowgli, I've since discovered, is a man of the land, the kind who knows nothing of trivial things like Facebook, or Twitter, or clothes without camouflage printing on them. He has a mobile phone, he told me, but he rarely turns it on. Instead, he plugs into the jungle, where he's lived on and off for twenty-five years. He's seen anacondas two metres long. He's seen a thousand tourists scream at his spiders. He had a girlfriend once, but she didn't want to live in the Amazon, so he dumped her.

After the night trek, Mowgli asked if he could hold my hand on the way back to the lodge. I thought it was a bit weird, seeing as he'd ignored me for most of the day, but by the time I got round to replying, he'd already grabbed it and was pointing out the Southern Cross in an indigo sky speckled with stars.

Later on, Mowgli asked if I would accompany him in the canoe, just the two of us, so he could show me even more constellations. We'd just had dinner, during which he'd walked to the table, still in his camouflage combats and Action Man vest, carrying a live fruit bat by its wings. He'd just plucked it from the sky, in flight, it seemed. This simple act caused the eleven-year-old to shriek and every female in the room to swoon again.

Something inside warned me not to succumb to his charms, but … the way he'd wielded that machete and sliced it through the vines; the way he'd jumped up in the boat with his bare biceps glistening and gestured to every passing bird and butterfly; the way he doesn't even have a Facebook account … you just don't *get* men like this anywhere else. It all did something funny to my heart. I surrendered.

'You and me, we're twin souls,' Mowgli said, sitting next to me a little too closely after he'd rowed the wooden boat roughly three metres round the corner from the lodge and tied it to a tree, where we couldn't be seen.

'Really? Twin souls?' I said, furrowing my brow in the darkness and keeping my eye out for caimans along the riverbanks. Mowgli told us earlier that caimans don't tend to attack humans, but you never know when one of these mini-croc type things will be having an inquisitive day.

'Yes, I can tell.' He put his arm around me then, leaned in and sniffed my hair. I didn't ask why.

'How do you know we're twin souls?' I asked him. After all, we'd only met eight hours ago and we'd barely spoken.

He ignored me. 'I like you so much,' he said instead.

'Do you? Why?'

'When I saw you in your bikini I knew I liked you.'

'Oh, right.'

'Can I kiss you?'

'Um, well, we don't really know each other.'

'I want to kiss you so much.'

'Well. All right.' *Fuck it, why not? I'm in a canoe in the Amazon. This doesn't happen every day and I can't escape anyway. We're surrounded by caimans.*

After our kiss (which was decidedly unromantic, seeing as he merely shoved his tongue in my mouth and wriggled it about in a way that suggested he'd been studying lizards for too long), I made him row me back. But Mowgli decided to follow me to my room, meaning I had to run in order to shut and lock the door behind me. He proceeded to shadow me everywhere for the rest of the night, beckoning me from darkened doorways to get me to follow him into the jungle like a love-struck Tarzan unsure as to how to woo Jane. I started to get a bit creeped out.

For the whole of the next day he'd sidle up to me and touch me, whereupon I'd have to bat him off like a pesky horsefly. So yeah, this is exactly why I've been bolting the bedroom door shut at night. He's a little over-amorous, our jungle guide. I also found out he tried it on with Dani shortly after I'd run away to the dining room to play cards with Kenny and his brothers that first night. I think he knew he liked her when he saw her in a bikini, too.

Anyway, after another one of our treks, we made our way to a nearby village along the river, where we were immediately set upon by the community's pet woolly monkey, Nacho. I don't know if you've ever had the chance to play with a monkey but, seriously, it's one of the most fun things ever. I could have watched him all day. Nacho would swing about from tree to human shoulder to tree, and at one point, some German guys from another group who were drinking beers turned around to find him swigging the dregs from their discarded cans. Nacho actually thought he was human.

These two Germans, it emerged, had been taken to a Shaman's house the night before for an ayahuasca ceremony, which caused my ears to prick up. I had heard about this sacred, medicinal vine last year in Bali, and briefly from Andreas in the Galápagos. It grows in the Amazon, and people, most notably in Peru, have been using it for centuries to maintain contact with jungle and plant spirits. In case you want to go out and make it yourself, it's made specifically from the *Banisteriopsis caapi* vine, mixed with the leaves of a dimethyltryptamine-containing species of shrub, such as *Psychotria viridis.*

The effects of this powerful hallucinogenic brew are said to last up to eight hours and its traditional purpose is to open the door to your subconscious, reveal another dimension and put you back in touch with nature ... as if you could possibly fail to be so in a place like this. Mowgli's lodge may not have wi-fi, but I've never felt so connected in my whole life.

From what I've heard, ayahuasca calls you when you're ready, although, by the sounds of it, the German guys had done no research beforehand and simply thought it sounded like a great opportunity to get very, very high. Consequently, both vomited profusely, saw visions of hell and heaven and almost crapped their pants.

Mowgli said we could pay an extra ten dollars to try ayahuasca ourselves if we wanted, but I politely declined. I'm not so sure I can hear it calling me just yet. If it is, it's being muffled by the voice of reason. I don't really fancy losing my mind in the Amazon, miles away from anyone I know, with an overzealous Mowgli lingering in the shadows, intent on repeating our canoe kiss. And also, you just never know when a tribal head-shrinker might escape from Brazil and chop my brain out. I'd like to keep it clear for now, thanks.

29/07

Galápagossip ...

The Ecuadorean girl Dani and I bonded on our Amazon trip over the fact that we were both sought out for attempted sauciness by the creepy Mowgli. We bonded even further over Facebook chat the other day, after I informed her that Mowgli actually has a wife.

I know this because Kenny and his brothers invited me for a tour of their uncle's ice-cream factory (turns out he owns the second largest ice-cream company in Ecuador!) and then back to their house in Quito, where I was treated to the most delicious lunch in a home with an impressive floor-to-ceiling view of the city and its surrounding volcanoes.

As we dined on steaks and salads, followed by even more ice-cream, I suddenly remembered that I'd left my J.C. Penney zip-up in my room at the lodge, so Uncle Ice-Cream kindly called the tour company on my behalf to see if we could get it back. When he was on the phone, the lovely lady who'd helped to book their trip in the first place said that, yes, of course that was possible, and that her husband (aka Mowgli) would be sure to bring it to Quito when he next came back from the jungle.

What is it with these men?

Anyway, I told Dani of my vague plans to head back to the Galápagos for some scuba diving, seeing as I'd been thinking about those waters ever since I left them, and she invited me to her house on the island of Santa Cruz, where she happens to work as a teacher. So back I went. Before paying her a visit, however, I did another mini-cruise, this time a lot cheaper. I wanted to see some of the islands I never got to see with Farzana and, as it turned out, doing things a little less glamorously in the Galápagos was just as fun, especially because I met a cool travelling Aussie–Chinese couple who'd sold their house to travel the world, and a bored-looking French guy who, within seconds of hearing my voice, had stuck his nose in the air and informed us: 'English is such an *ugly* language.'

How fun! We all took great delight in tormenting him in proper British fashion after that, speaking very, very loudly next to him whenever he was trying to read.

The boat on the Gecko's Adventures cruise was a bit rickety but the roof deck was as good for drinking beers and cocktails on as the luxury *Tip Top II*'s had been for me and Farzana and, to be honest, the food was just as nice, if not slightly better. You always get buffet spreads on these things, no matter which class you travel. We explored the gorgeous Isla Lobos and Cerro Brujo, swam with even more sea lions, saw a lot more boobies and this time we even saw a blue whale near Kicker Rock. Its body was almost the length of our entire boat and even the French guy got excited when it spurted a watery greeting from its blowhole.

Back on land, I stayed one night at the beautiful Finch Bay Eco Hotel for a treat (for which you need to board a special boat to reach a special part of the island), looked for tortoises, watched ginormous pelicans swooping down over the swimming pool for the day and then decided it was time to stop being a travel snob and go budget. I booked myself into a shoddy hotel elsewhere with no window in the room — the cheapest I could find at $20 a night. You won't find any youth hostels here, at least not the sort you'll be used to on the Gringo Trail.

In the Galápagos you're spending the American dollar and, being one of the world's most expensive travel destinations, everything is extortionately priced, even the stuff in the supermarket. The cheapest place to eat, I discovered, thanks to Dani, is on Binford Avenue, where kiosks set up along the street serve locals set breakfasts ($3) and dinners ($4), which, while not cruise-ship standard, are actually pretty nice and will end up saving you a fortune. When it comes to booking scuba diving, however, you definitely don't want to cut corners.

Diving in the Galápagos is known for being some of the best in the world, but you're advised to have some experience because currents are very strong in places and it can be really dangerous. As I went around the various dive shops looking for one I felt comfortable with, I was stunned to find some who didn't even ask if I was qualified before trying to sell me a trip to the most dangerous dive site in the Galápagos — Gordon Rock.

Gordon Rock is the most popular dive site because it's where large schools of hammerhead sharks tend to congregate, but changing currents can turn it into a washing machine in an instant and, if you're not experienced, you could find yourself seriously out of your depth. Several people have died there in recent years — two so far in 2012. When I finally made it into the dive shop Academy Bay, I found an Aussie expat called Anne who told me several horror stories about these other operators, some of whom conduct trips even though they're not qualified divers themselves!

I was told that if I really wanted to see the sharks I should probably book a live-aboard cruise to Darwin and Wolf, two eroded volcanoes located very far north from the central islands and which can only be reached after two or three days of sailing. But on a trip like this I would almost be guaranteed sightings of great spotted whale sharks, whales, hammerheads, white tips, Galápagos sharks and more, thanks to the cold currents.

Well, obviously I thought, *fuck it, why not?* And then I thought, *well, because you can't afford it, silly. You're on a budget now, else you won't be able to do any other exciting thing later on.*

Eight-day live-aboard trips start at $4000, depending on the time of year. I could barely afford the day dive trips, really, after my two cruises (hmm), but having come all this way I decided to do at least one.

The cost of a two-dive trip with most companies from Santa Cruz is between $150 and $180 (in comparison, I was paying roughly $40 per dive in Indonesia). Doing your Open Water PADI (Professional Association of Diving Instructors) course in the Galápagos will cost, on average, $500 — *way* more than in many other parts of the world. Diving here will seriously blow your travel budget.

Grateful to have had all my questions answered in English by qualified dive instructors, I headed out with Academy Bay, who promised me a CD of photos on top of the adventure, so it was worth it. Sort of. Heading out to our first site was one of the bumpiest, most gut-wrenching boat journeys of my life. I nearly threw up my breakfast, and spent the majority of the voyage slamming into the guy next to me and apologising, even though I wasn't really sorry, because he was hot.

Daniel from Miami — a trainee medical doctor, tall, sandy-haired and on a day trip away from his family, with whom he'd come for a Galápagos holiday — was by far one of the sexiest specimens of man I've encountered so far on my trip. We swam hand-in-hand with the sea lions together, floated in the middle of a giant swirling ball of silver barracuda, glided alongside huge turtles and helped each other through the currents, which at one point were pretty strong. By the time we got back on the boat to Santa Cruz I don't think either of us minded slamming into each other so much.

After our dives, Daniel and I took a walk to beautiful Tortuga Beach and its vast stretch of white sand. It's just five minutes from Santa Cruz's main harbour in Puerto Ayora and then a forty-minute trek along a brick road, which I thought they should paint yellow, not just because I think all long and winding brick roads should be yellow but because it would make it easier to spot the lava lizards as they bake in camouflage. The entire walk makes you feel as though you're doing nothing but terrifying lizards, actually. They run away as you approach, although you do get the odd one who'll sit and look at you in wonder, like you're the most incredible and interesting creature on earth.

Daniel and I arranged to meet again that night, too, for a bit of karaoke, after I'd had dinner at Dani's, which was lovely. I got to hang out with all her friends and we cooked mini-pizzas and drank red wine around her garden table, talking about life in the Galápagos under another star-scattered sky. They spoke Spanish so fast it was like trying to keep up with a Grand Prix, but they all kindly took the time to translate, and so I got to learn who starts and spreads the Galápagossip.

Being such a small town, everyone knows who's new, who's sleeping with whom, which scuba divers are hooking up with which tourists and which naturalists are hooking up with which shop owners. It was like sitting in a real life soap opera.

Oli, a sweet girl who's lived on Santa Cruz for five years as a tour guide for children's groups (she also takes them all over Ecuador), loves it here because for her it's an example of how you don't need much to live a happy life. The Internet barely works and no one has a TV, so the only news from the outside world some of these people ever get is what comes in via the boats, or two-day-old newspapers.

'It's the simple life,' Oli told me, swinging her bare feet up onto an empty chair. 'I've never cared about politics or governments or knowing what people were wearing, and to me it's nice to live without feeling swayed by news or media.'

It made me wonder what it would be like to live in the Galápagos, actually. Rent here costs between $300 to $400 a month for a decent room in a house. For $700 a month you can pretty much have a whole house.

I also learned, however, that the water here in the Galápagos is dirty. Apparently, in spite of its pristine reputation and undeniable beauty from a boat, the water coming out of the taps here is so vile that it causes infections in your privates. So, Dani's friends told me, it's normal for girls living on Santa Cruz to wash themselves *down there* in pure water, which led to all sorts of 'princess' jokes around the garden table. It definitely made me hurry up in my shoddy hotel shower later on.

I'm not sure I will ever go back to the Galápagos, if only because it's so expensive to get to, even if you do it on a budget. But having been twice I can now tell you that you can't fail to be amazed by something, every single day ... even if it's just to find your monolingual self in a karaoke bar, surrounded by baffled Ecuadoreans, singing Shakira songs into a microphone in bad Spanish.

8/08

Argentinean first impressions ...

The smattering of bruises on my ribs is making me look more like I've been shacking up with a wife-beater than with a lovely Argentinean family here in Palermo, Buenos Aires. I don't know how to tell them my bed is causing me physical injury, because even though I'm paying to live here I don't want to upset them. My room in their house was arranged by my Spanish language school, Expanish, and having flown straight in from Quito knowing next to nothing about this city, I'm supposed to live with them for two weeks.

The springs responsible for the bruising are hidden inside what's allegedly a mattress, and because my host Julio is a man who once restored antique furniture for a living, I'm not entirely sure my bed hasn't already been restored. If it has, he might be offended that his new antique springs are affecting my sleep in a bad way and I wouldn't want that. Julio and his wife Sylvia have taken me into their home with as much love and kindness as Daddy Warbucks took in Annie.

I'm really hoping the sun'll come out tomorrow, though. Like Quito, Buenos Aires is cold. I've practically got my feet stuck in the bars of an electric heater as I type. I'm hoping it's not another restored antique, because I do worry from time to time about things like my bedroom burning down.

When I arrived at the house at 4 a.m. in the back of a taxi the other day, Julio was waiting up for me with a wide smile and a torrent of indecipherable Spanish (he speaks no English whatsoever), and although I was dazed and bewildered and exhausted, I noticed he looked a bit like Steve Martin and I warmed to him instantly. I did not, however, warm to the tiny three-metre squared box of a room he led me to, which was so mind-numbingly freezing that I woke up an hour later with snot running down over my top lip. I was too tired and out of it to notice the heater in the corner. I actually thought it was a fan.

My body is in shock, I can feel a cold coming on and, while there are no blizzards like there were on my ill-fated minivan tour to Cotopaxi, my Bali wardrobe still isn't gonna cut it. At least I can justify finally doing my bulky clothes shop and this neighborhood seems the perfect place for it. Palermo feels a bit Bohemian, like London's Camden, mixed with New York's East Village.

I've not seen much else of Buenos Aires yet, to be honest, because my time here so far has consisted of heading to Expanish, where I'm taking my intense Spanish course every day from 9 a.m.

to 1 p.m., and then trying to navigate my way back home again. This traffic-clogged journey, that seems to take up four hours of my day, would usually only take me thirty minutes each way, so says Carmen, the cute Swiss girl who's also living with my new family and studying at Expanish. But Buenos Aires is currently suffering a subway (*subte*) strike.

This strike has been going on since I arrived and, from what I can gather, it's not looking like it's going to stop any time soon. Workers are asking for a twenty-eight per cent pay increase and better working conditions, and while everyone argues and refuses to take responsibility for the subway in general, some 900,000 of the city's commuters who use the *subte* each day (including me now) are having to cram onto alternative transport.

I'm too new to know much about the politics here yet, but I do know that one third of Argentineans still live in poverty and, while they have a reputation globally for being quite stuck-up and egotistical, as well as undergoing more psychotherapy and cosmetic surgery than any other nation, the country is struggling with a sputtering economy, which is hitting everyone hard. As a result, the slightest upset in any political sense can cause an uproar.

It seems that the root cause of the *subte* strike is a power struggle between the president and the mayor, a man called Mauricio Macri, who isn't very popular. In fact, the subway workers' union secretary-general, Roberto Pianelli, tells the *Buenos Aires Herald*: 'We never took into consideration that we were negotiating with an animal like Macri, who doesn't give a dime for the people. The City Mayor is way more dangerous than a monkey with a knife, he's like a monkey with an automatic gun.'

I can't say I've ever heard such public mockery as I'm hearing here. Things must be tense if they're assigning their leaders imaginary weapons and calling them monkeys.

Anyway, it's super annoying not being able to get around very easily, not least because of the weather. I can't go shopping very easily in the rain and even though I've since discovered the heater in my room, which offers a warm night at least, I never got my J.C. Penney zip-up back from Mowgli. Thanks to a lack of decent shopping in Quito, I had to buy the only other warm item available — a terrible, unflattering, grey round-neck sweater with the word 'Quito' on it. It makes me look like a pet shop worker. I feel like I'm supposed to have a mullet when I wear it. And maybe live somewhere like Idaho. I'm not sure why it invokes these feelings … perhaps I saw something similar on telly.

I did think perhaps if I buy a bulky coat I could also sleep on top of it, lessen the digging of the mattress springs into my rib cage and solve both problems at once. But meanwhile, as I've been shivering my way around in pain, here's what I've noticed about Buenos Aires:

Everyone kisses everyone else

It's a sexy mix here, thanks to nineteenth-century Spanish and Italian immigrants bringing their tall, dark, brooding looks into things. In fact, unlike in Ecuador, Bolivia and Peru, only one per cent of Argentina's population is indigenous. A prime example of the passion of Latin Americans, which was perhaps introduced with those thankful immigrants, is the kissing thing, which happens all the time. And I'm not just talking between the overly-amorous *novios* (boyfriends and girlfriends), either.

Last night I went to the laundromat with a girl called Michelle, who I met at Expanish. As she went to leave with her bag of freshly washed undergarments, the rotund man behind the counter leaned over and planted a kiss on her cheek.

Michelle told me that last weekend she was also kissed by the lady who'd just done her nails. I see this happening all around me and I don't know if it's because I'm British but seriously … although it's nice to witness such abundant affection, I'm not sure I want people kissing me when I don't know them. Especially not men who've just washed my knickers.

There is dog shit absolutely everywhere

We're talking major turdage here. You can't take five steps along the pavement without seeing a pile of *mierda* heaped in front of you like a serving of bad Mr Whippy. Walking about has you weaving your way through the streets like an army cadet on some sort of specialty shit-dodging assault course. They're big shits, too. I mean, we're not talking the crap of a chihuahua here, I don't think. From the size of these piles, you'd think most people in Buenos Aires owned elephants.

At dinner with Michelle the other night, her friend Tom told me that the dog-walkers of Buenos Aires aren't allowed by law to walk more than eight dogs. They regularly do so anyway and many of them don't clean up after their pooches, either. Tom told me that because you can earn up to ten pesos per dog, per day, lots of people walk ten at a time and earn up to 4000 pesos a month. Almost US$1000 per month isn't bad when all you're doing is walking around for a couple of hours a day, texting your mates and pretending not see that mountain of shit your K9 clients are dropping in their wake.

Everyone smokes

If not everyone, then definitely more people smoke in Buenos Aires than anywhere else in the world. Julio smokes not at the dinner table, but just to the right of it, about a metre away, as though there's a designated pocket of air he's allowed to pollute in the corner that won't curl its way anywhere else.

I could, of course, be noticing the smokers more here because people still seem to smoke in bars and restaurants as and when they please, and also because I've just come from Bali: a place of health, fresh air and wellbeing. But I swear the cigarette smoke is contributing to my new cough and sore throat. You can't walk anywhere without getting a lungful of it here.

There's sweet temptation on every corner

There are windows full of cakes and pastries everywhere you turn in this city; every other store is a bakery of some kind and every other businessman in the city centre is tucking into a plate of empanadas on his lunch break. I've also noticed the Porteños (Buenos Aires locals) have an obsession with Milka, which is a great chocolate by all accounts, but on a stroll along most streets in Buenos Aires, especially in the CBD, your eyeballs are accosted constantly by the purple ocean of it. There's no escaping it. In fact, to avoid the ultimate thigh expansion that will occur if I keep allowing it to lure me in, it's probably best I keep my eyes down on the dog shit.

People queue for buses

They actually stand in a polite line on the street and queue in an orderly fashion to get on the bus. How fantastic is that? At first I wondered why everyone was standing around in lines on the side of the road, but then I realised that they were actually being courteous. I felt a warm rush of appreciation towards the people of Buenos Aires. In other cities it's a given that you'll either elbow someone's rib cage or have your own face squished into the back of someone else before you can board the bus or the Metro. This orderly queue-forming thing is quite refreshing … unless you find yourself standing in dog shit.

No one has any money

When I say money, I mean actual bank notes. Perhaps due to the ever fluctuating economy, there's been no newly printed money in Argentina for what seems like a century and every note you find yourself pulling out of your purse is so withered and filthy you feel as though you've just rooted through a skip for it. Buy some hand sanitizer.

Several times now I've been out to make a purchase with only the one large note a cash machine has given me, and the shopkeeper has stared at my outstretched hand in alarm and disdain, before asking if I have anything smaller. When I shake my head, often they will snatch the proffered note and storm off in a huff … and come back having made a journey through three more shops, an outdoor market and their own mum's house just to locate some change.

They show dead bodies on the telly

I was eating a breakfast of tiny, dried, cold toast pieces from a packet and a coffee (which seems to be the norm where I'm staying, and indeed in Buenos Aires) when I looked up at the telly to see a man who'd just been shot. His bloody arm was dangling out from beneath a tarp as police and a dog wandered nonchalantly around him like he wasn't even there. At first I thought perhaps it was a police drama, but then I realised it was just the morning news.

Everyone goes out after I've gone to bed

I still can't get my head around the fact that everyone seems to go out for the night at around 1 a.m. here, sometimes later. If you want dinner first, prime time for eating in restaurants in Buenos Aires is between 11 p.m. and midnight.

On my first morning at Julio and Sylvia's, I dragged myself out of bed by 9 a.m., not wanting to appear rude by sleeping in, but I was alone downstairs all morning with their huge, scary dog Tito. Eventually I went out to explore Palermo, but everything was dead. Literally nothing was open. I couldn't even get a coffee. I thought perhaps the apocalypse had occurred overnight and I'd been left all alone in the world with Tito, like Will Smith in *I Am Legend*, but after a few more hours things started to come to life again. When I went back to the house Carmen told me no one goes to bed till 7 a.m., so no one gets up before 2 p.m. on a weekend. It's quite a weird lifestyle to get used to.

Buenos Aires is definitely keeping me on my toes so far and it's only just started to get interesting, I'm sure. I just wish spring would spring as quickly as my mattress seems to be doing.

13/08

Conjugation deliberation ...

I've been studying at Expanish in the city for almost a week now and at lunchtime every day I walk around the block looking for the nicest thing to eat. A normal lunchtime mission, you might think. Well, here in central Buenos Aires, where everyone's in a rush and no one's got time for you even if you *do* speak Spanish,

I'll admit I'm not just looking for the nicest thing to eat. I'm looking for the easiest food item in a window that I might point to, in order to save myself and everybody else the uncomfortable moment in which my needs are lost in translation and everyone in a queue turns to stare at me.

I know this is ridiculous. I should be relishing the chance to learn Spanish in a Spanish-speaking country. I should be out there wedging myself into cafe queues on purpose, just to get old ladies to scream at me, just to get hot guys to notice me … interaction is the key, right?

But the more I try to learn, the harder it seems. The more I sit in that classroom surrounded by sheets of paper and images of apples, chairs and cutlery being held up in front of me like I'm a nuclear war survivor with half a brain in rehab, the more I think, *Is this really necessary?* The same as I never saw the point of maths in school when my calculator did everything for me, no matter how interested I might be in Spanish, there's always a little voice in my head that says, *Google Translate is pretty accurate, why don't you stop all this nonsense and go and have another empanada?*

But *then* I think, shit, I can't do that, because I can't ask for an empanada without whipping out my phone and bringing up Google Translate, which wouldn't work in a bakery here anyway because I still have an Ecuadorean SIM in my phone, which means I don't have mobile Internet in Argentina, and bakeries don't tend to have wi-fi. And I can't ask anyone how or where to find wi-fi, either. Arrrgh! It's just all too complicated. I can't do anything but endure the classroom learning process, really. Eventually, I figure, some things will start to sink in.

I wish there was some kind of button we could press in our brains that switched on different languages. If they can put it in a phone, can't they put it into me? I'd give anything to have an inbuilt Google Translate app right now because … I'm going to come right out and say it: I don't like feeling silenced, squashed under the weight of my own incompetence. I don't like not being understood. I don't enjoy not understanding other people. I'm a nosey person who likes to know *everything* and I don't like feeling left out and stupid. And when you're learning a new language in an unfamiliar place, you feel all of the above, to the point of doubting everything you thought you knew. I need a little old Argentinean man to follow me around playing a violin, so sad is my situation. But even he would play songs I didn't know and then I'd feel shit for having invited him.

I'm being defeatist here, I know.

'My first week was *muy difficil*,' said the studious Carmen as I sat forlornly at the kitchen table the other morning, trying to make sense of a pot of lard by the name of *dulce de leche* (another national dish that blows my mind).

'It took me three weeks to learn anything!' she continued, before taking the pot and smearing some of the caramel-coloured substance onto her cold mini toast bits. She then turned around and emitted a stream of fluent Spanish at Sylvia, making our hostess laugh in a charmed fashion, as only those with a knack for picking up languages at the drop of a hat can do.

I hate to say this, but I am experiencing a level of culture shock here in Argentina that is somewhat unprecedented in me. At least, I think it's culture shock. Thinking back, I'm pretty sure I've never had it before, so I really have nothing to compare it to.

There were a few times I was shocked by the culture when I lived in Dubai, I guess … well, OK, there were many times. But there, most people spoke English. In Bali last year, the Balinese seemed only too happy to try to explain in English why they sacrifice chickens and why they ask semi-naked old men to pull their teeth out on their wedding day, or even why they steam their vaginas from time to time. Here in Argentina, it's Spanish or nothing at all in most situations. If you don't understand, well, that's your fault, you ignoramus. The family dog, Tito, knows more about what's going on at dinner time than me. I've started to cock my head when he does to show I'm listening. Eventually, though, I'm going to have to talk.

The verbs and their conjugation are the hardest. To be honest, I had to remind myself all over again what a verb is, what a noun is and what the hell conjugation is when it's at home. You're probably thinking, *You're a writer, how can you possibly not know this?* But I'm telling you, I forgot. I use words like we all do. I don't think about what they *are*, or *why* they are, or *where* they are or *when* they occur; they're just words, aren't they?

'The truth is,' said our teacher Lio on the first day, as my three classmates — a German guy, a Dutchman and a Brazilian girl — and I sat gawping at the verb *'ser'* on his whiteboard, 'you use verb conjugation in English whenever you speak, but you might not even know you're doing it because the English verb changes are a lot simpler than they are in Spanish.'

You're not kidding!

There are also a lot of Spanish words that you think are the same as English words, but aren't. For example, *'estoy embarazada'* said flirtatiously, as in, 'Oh my, I am so embarrassed, I messed up my Spanish in front of you!' is actually letting on that you're pregnant, which isn't an ideal way to win a date.

My teacher Lio is great. My classmates are all lovely. The school is excellent and everyone there appears to go out of their way to make sure everyone else is having fun and enjoying themselves. It's definitely not them; it's me. I learned a bit of Indonesian last year but that was only for a couple of hours every week. This is full-on, full-time study with mountains of homework. It's draining, it's daunting and it's hard. I hate to say this too, but I've a feeling I'll learn more if I change to private lessons, preferably with a hot local twenty-something male who wants to practise in a series of exciting locations, to help it all sink in.

I hate to be a quitter, though.

Being here makes me wonder how the hell I ever learned English. Having called my mum and asked, she confirmed that yes, I picked it up quite quickly when I was two. I'm not sure why it is then, thirty years later, when I'm more advanced, more willing to learn and less distracted by things like shiny spoons and Elmo, that I can't even remember how to say, 'Is that dog shit on your shoes, Julio, or Milka?'

I've had to email my friend Autumn, who's flying out to join me soon for some Patagonian adventures, and let her know that she should get onto all the Spanish apps and learning programs she possibly can in advance. Meanwhile, I'll just have to keep at it.

At least I can ask for *wine* now I suppose, which is as good a place to start as any. *'Uno mas vino tinto, por favor!'*

23/08

Bed-wetting, bad dates and The Lion King in Hebrew ...

The other night I had a blind date with a local guy called Eduardo. He's a friend of a friend from Sydney and he kindly offered to show me the nightlife in the Buenos Aires *barrio* of San Telmo. I've been practising my Spanish with Eduardo on Facebook chat and, although I declined his online invitation to join him and his mates for an *asado* first, we arranged to meet afterwards in a bar, at 9.30 p.m.

The Argentineans love *asados*, by the way. These are basically BBQs, usually in people's back yards, that would make your average Aussie griller weep into his perfectly marinated prime ribs. During my first week, I attended one at the home of a very hospitable man I met via some other students at Expanish and found the whole thing quite thrilling, if a little scary.

An *asado* can last all day and all night and the main aim is to consume as much meat as is humanly possible. The catch is that you really never know what it is you're eating. Every single part of the animal is consumed and absolutely nothing is spared in this act of *carne* carnage. You could be tucking into a bull's testicle and thinking it's beef cheek, or a pig's brain, thinking it's a deep-fried cheese ball. It's just another situation where the lack of a Spanish vocabulary puts a girl in seriously dangerous waters.

After an *asado* it's expected that you'll sit around smacking your lips, burping and drinking red wine, before heading out to a nightclub. At least, that's what I experienced at my first one. While *asados* are sociable and delicious affairs, the bulk indigestion and resulting strings of meat wrapped around your back teeth aren't exactly ideal precursors for hitting a dance floor, but this is how the Porteños roll so I rolled with it ... and felt a bit sick.

Anyway, 9.30 p.m. swung around. I ordered myself a drink at the bar and waited. 9.45 came and went. 10 p.m. I sat there checking my phone for updates, but Eduardo was silent. 10.30 ticked along, as did 11. By then I was chatting in Spanglish to some very nice guys, both of whom had bought me a couple more drinks. I imagined Eduardo must have passed out in a meat coma and forgotten me, but much to my amazement midnight rolled around and in he walked. We recognised each other from our Facebook photos.

He pottered over to the bar, doused in a special Argentinean cologne of Marlboro and meat sauce and dressed in a made-to-fit designer shirt that seems typical of proud, fashion-conscious Porteño men. I was surprised to see him, as you would be. I know by now that people don't go out here until midnight, maybe even later, but showing up almost three hours late for a date is kind of the same as not showing up at all, isn't it?

I expected Eduardo to apologise profusely, to wrack his hands in guilt and offer to buy me copious amounts of drinks to make up for his unacceptable tardiness, but instead he ran his fingers through his hair, sighed, patted his stomach in rather a bored fashion and said, 'Shall we go?'

Waving goodbye to my new friends, I was marched out of the bar and bundled into a taxi, where I assumed I was about to be taken to a tango hall, or a salsa bar, or something culturally splendid that would make having been left in a bar for almost three hours worthwhile.

Alas. I was delivered instead to a nightclub so vast and pounding and full of smoke I felt as though I'd been dragged into the very pits of hell. To his credit, Eduardo did pay the entrance fee for me, which was some extortionate price I'd never have paid on my own. He then ordered some drinks (an entire bottle of vodka in an ice-bucket) and ushered us over to his mates, where we proceeded to scream at each other for two hours in an effort to be heard. I didn't get to see any of San Telmo. I just got even more of a sore throat. By the time I got back to my hostel, and Eduardo had tried his best to snog me in the back of a taxi, I was actually quite relieved the night had ended.

Ah yes, I've moved out of Julio and Sylvia's. My time was up. I can't say Julio's enthusiasm and mildly chastising rants about the Falklands around the dinner table weren't interesting, my Spanish is finally improving, too, and everyone including Carmen was lovely, but the bed was starting to cripple me. Plus, Julio kept turning lights off after me throughout the house. It's not that I was forgetting to turn them off myself, but he seemed to leap for the switches before I could ever flip them. This made me feel as though he assumed I wouldn't remember, which made me feel a bit awkward. It also made me wonder if he thought I'd also forgotten how I started the problems in the Falklands.

I've moved into the Milhouse Avenue hostel, which is closer to the train line. Now that the *subte* is finally working again it makes getting to class much easier. It's also much cheaper to stay in a hostel.

I'm discovering that staying in Buenos Aires is eating away at my bank balance like you wouldn't believe. It's not just the food. The *choripans* (chorizo in a giant crusty baguette — my God!), Milka bars, *alfajors* (caramel biscuit sandwiches) and *jamon y queso medialunas* (ham and cheese croissants) are irresistible and not doing my figure any favours. But everything's more expensive here than in Ecuador. Hostel living is a means of survival now, and for an entire week I've been sleeping ... or catching sleep where possible in a bottom bunk, witnessing a non-stop stream of twenty-somethings from all walks of life walk in and walk about ridiculously wasted. I may have joined in, on occasion ...

Milhouse is renowned as being *the* party hostel in Buenos Aires. The staff are all absolutely awesome. They'll book any bus ticket or tour you like and there are tons of activities to keep you occupied (do the free salsa class!), but be warned: sleeping here is a game of chance. You never know who is going to show up, or when they'll leave. You can shut your eyes in the bunk next to a delightful nineteen-year-old trainee vet from Cairns, and open them to the beer-farting arse end of a vile boy from Wigan who wears a T-shirt listing all the ways to dump a girlfriend he's probably never had (this really happened).

This boy in particular took great joy in shouting absolutely every word at great volume in the dorm, mostly between the hours of 4 and 5 a.m., right next to my face, and drooling in his sleep. I'm not entirely sure, but he may have been on the retarded spectrum.

In the space of a week I have gained a special insight into the behaviour patterns of young travellers from different countries. The *first* time I woke up on my first night in the hostel was when Marcus, a chubby Frenchman, stumbled in drunk and started snoring like a warthog. The second was when the English guy, who's been fighting with his girlfriend at high decibel constantly since they both moved in, woke us all up by falling off his top bunk. It wasn't the worst thing he did, mind you.

Vini, my lovely Brazilian room mate who looks a bit like Robert Pattinson in Twilight without the white make-up (hot, but a bit too young for me, sadly), thought it was raining when the sound of water woke him up. But then he realised, to all of our dismay, that the English guy was pissing on the floor. The sound of this urinary waterfall failed to penetrate my earplugs (an absolute travel essential: do pack many), but his actual piss did not fail to penetrate his mattress when he climbed back into bed and went to the toilet again in his dreams.

I can tell you, it's only the English who piss on their bunk beds. It's only the English who piss on their bunk beds, don't remember it, start a riot and then get kicked out. He and his girlfriend were promptly evicted the next morning and the mattress was carried out and disposed of — hopefully. I never smelled it burning, so the jury's still out on whether they simply let it dry and moved it into another dorm.

Aside from the English, the second naughtiest, I think, are probably the Aussie guys, who travel in packs and are always the last up drinking in the common area. They vomit a lot. The Israelis are the ones chatting everyone up around the bar and the French and German men appear to be the first to bed and the first to start snoring. There's also almost always a sleeping man— just one solo snoozer under a crumpled sheet — no matter what time of day you enter the dorm. Of course, this is all based on my observations *so far*. Things could change. I still have many, many nights in hostels ahead of me, so my findings are certain to become more concrete.

Can I just say now, though, that people who snore should not be allowed in hostels. It's probably one of the most selfish things you can do. If you know you're a snorer and you book yourself into a shared dorm room, you are knowingly inflicting a night of discomfort onto innocent strangers.

Someone needs to set up a hostel in each city just for snorers, in my opinion. Or at least hostels need to ask people if they're inclined to snore when they check in and lead them to a special 'snorers' dorm' (or a 'snorm' as it will eventually come to be called), so that everyone can sleep in their allocated places in peace. Snorers never wake each other up, I've noticed. They only wake the rest of us up ... well, those of us who haven't already been woken up by the English guys pissing on the floor.

As the stripy boxer-short covered bulging ball sack lowered itself from the top bunk into my direct line of vision this morning, I thought, *man, I'm getting too old for this youth hostel thing*. So when my friend Autumn comes to join me soon, we're going to have a few nights of luxury time in some nice hotels before heading on over to Chile. She's glad about this. When I told her that her photographic equipment would be very safe at Milhouse because everyone gets their own big metal cage in the dorm, she said: 'A cage? I don't want a *cage*! I want a room with a lock on it!'

I'm not entirely sure she knows what's ahead of her on the backpackers' circuit. The other night I went across the street to dinner with an Israeli guy called Dror, who was wearing his pajama bottoms. Over our pizzas he started singing songs from *The Lion King* in Hebrew, so I joined in with the English lyrics until we made a peculiar duet, taking on the *Circle of Life* in sleepwear with a ketchup bottle for a microphone. A transvestite diner in a terribly ill-fitting wig just wouldn't stop staring at us.

To keep myself out of trouble, and perhaps from going out in my pajamas, I've booked myself up for a host of evening activities. My new friend Tom, an American I met through my Expanish friend Michelle, works in Palermo and, as well as sampling all the new treats his restaurant orders in (sssh), we've been touring various restaurants together, getting fatter.

My diet, as well as all those other snacks, now consists of some of the best steak I've ever consumed in my life and oodles of cheese. I've probably gained at least five kilos but, to be honest, I don't really mind because I've been told that once I get to Bolivia and Peru I'll lose tons of weight. I've met a lot of people who've had terrible food poisoning in these countries. It might be worth remembering to do these countries last, so you can eat what you want and then shed the excess weight before you go home. Yes! Go ahead. Eat all the steaks and cheese you bloody well want. Go to every *asado* you possibly can and arrange all your dates after midnight. Whatever you do you'll be able to redeem yourself sooner or later. That's something the *Lonely Planet* won't tell you.

27/08

A couple of humbling encounters ...

I know I've already mentioned this, but I swear I have never encountered this many snorers in my entire life. It's getting ridiculous now. Last night I was kept awake by the insufferable attempts made by a man called Juan to suck the very ceiling from our dorm room in his sleep. In and out he breathed, every intake an industrial vacuum. Had Juan been outside and not enclosed in a four-bed dormitory in an imaginatively titled hostel/inn called Hostel Inn, I firmly believe he could have sucked a jet plane from its flight path and brought it to land on his face.

As I type, I'm on an overnight *cama* (sleep) class bus back from Iguazu Falls. My seat is an actual bed. I am practically horizontal under my blanket with my head on my soft pillow, trying not to punch the balding head of the man in front. He is also snoring. I've had two mini bottles of bad 2010 Malbec courtesy of some mild begging in bad Spanish and I still can't blur the edges of my discomfort. I'm considering buckling up because, at the rate he's going, unless I strap myself in tight I'm gonna be sucked into the vortex that is his huge gaping mouth by the time we've even come close to getting back to Buenos Aires.

Anyway, because I clearly won't be able to sleep now, in spite of paying almost $100 for a higher class bus seat in order to do so, I will tell you instead about Iguazu Falls — the reason I boarded this bus full of air-thieves in the first place.

This place where lands collide with water, between Argentina and Brazil, humbled me into silence when I first saw it. It's a jaw-dropping natural masterpiece, a moving oil painting running off its canvas onto a gallery floor of the lushest green. It was well worth a seventeen-hour bus ride from Buenos Aires just to witness, and *maybe* even worth enduring these bouts of snoring (I said maybe).

The space in the earth into which Iguazu Falls gushes its eternal flow is one you get the feeling each country may have tried to claim, had the sheer magnitude of this chasm not humbled them into sharing. Standing on the right bank you're in Brazilian territory, which is home to twenty per cent of the falls; on the left bank, Argentina hosts the other eighty; and across it all there exist a number of waterfalls between sixty to eighty-two metres in height.

The first sight of them from the Argentinean side, as I rounded a corner with my new Milhouse friend Ash, left me reeling — not unlike the time I first saw Niagara Falls, when I was twenty-one. I shed a tear back then, which I blamed on the spray smashing into my face as I leaned over the railings in New York State.

That was back when all we had to do in the here and now was stare and feel the force and embrace the wonder — before the urge to video or 'check in' on Foursquare or send a tweet started distracting us from actually living these magical moments for ourselves.

With Niagara Falls, it might also have been the sheer magnitude of it, the way the world slid into perspective as my tiny insignificant self floundered in the shadow of its fury, or it might have been the fact that I was deluded, having driven eight hours from New York City in a minivan with eight girls eating Cheez Doodles and listening to Britney Spears, but either way, I'll never forget that feeling of nature overwhelming me completely.

Iguazu Falls is even more impressive.

Upon first glimpse, these falls pin you to the spot like an ant under a giant shoe. The spray grazes your face with cold,

Iguazu Falls is so powerful it can take your
hairstyle away, as well as your breath.

tiny bullets that sting and make you crave getting closer, the
way you would to a guru or some other magnificent wise man
with a secret to share. It's like witnessing the world's end from
a distance: that moment so often depicted in movies, where
stars collide and tectonic plates shift and the planet splits in
two, right in the middle of the ocean, taking everything and
everyone with it right down into the depths of the Earth's core.
A beautiful disaster.

Ash and I stood there on various viewing points, beholding the gurgling froth of it, particularly in a narrow chasm named Garganta del Diablo — the Devil's Throat. Round and round and round the water swirled, as though being stirred by an invisible witch with a giant spoon, as a mist between thirty and 150 metres tall threatened to hide us and soak our hair.

This relentless disgorging and gushing and rushing of the river made me wonder at the meaning of it all. When you think about it, Iguazu Falls both exists and doesn't at the same time. In that moment of existence, when it's in your face and screaming and you can feel the watery fists from it pounding, breaking rocks and the occasional tourist's camera, it is also something else, somewhere else. The water is constantly moving. You think, where does it all go, in the end? Where does it all go? And you know the answer. It goes right back to where it started from — into the ocean, where it evaporates up into the clouds, and falls back down onto the land as rain, to eventually find itself here again. There is no end.

It's a long ride from Buenos Aires and back. Ash and I took advantage of a package arranged by Milhouse, which included two nights in the Hostel Inn (that boasts a swimming pool, which we didn't use because it was too cold). The two main towns on either side, Puerto Iguazu in Argentina and Foz do Iguacu in Brazil, offer a host of reasonably priced accommodation, although food everywhere is expensive. In the national park (where the Falls are), we paid over the odds for a couple of empanadas and some coffee, and it costs foreigners three times as much as it costs Argentineans to get into the park in the first place. But suck it up because Iguazu Falls is definitely worth it.

It's also worth taking the boat ride under the falls. You'll get soaked but this is when you really feel Iguazu's ineffable power.

The other tour on offer, a so-called eco-tour along the river, is a bit rubbish, to be honest. You're basically just being rowed in a canoe as a bored-sounding man points out a few flowers. He pointed to a caiman but I couldn't see it. Hmm. Skip that (which makes for a cheaper ticket) and spend more time walking around, and get to the park early to avoid being squished like a sardine and getting an Asian V-sign in all your photos. There really is nothing worse. Of course, you can see Iguazu Falls if you're heading to Brazil too (though you'll pay even more for that!), but at the moment my plans to get there for the Rio Carnival in February are only vague and I didn't want to miss out on seeing the falls altogether. No one should miss this.

No matter what happens in your life, big or small, good or bad, Iguazu Falls will still be there, tumbling into infinity, and nothing we can ever do will stop it. There are some things in this world more powerful than all of us can ever hope to be, you know? Unfortunately, snorers on buses are one of them.

02/09

House-sitting for the rich and famous ...

My friend Autumn arrived from Sydney the other day with a suitcase and a disproportionately large plastic bag. When I asked what was inside the bag she said, 'Koala bears!'

Autumn has brought with her to Buenos Aires thirty large, stuffed koala bears, which we are to distribute throughout our travels over these next couple of months together. As she's a photographer, we're to document the giving of these bears in a series of photos on our blogs to mark our journey. It's a lovely thought. I'm not yet quite sure how we're supposed to get them all onto buses, though.

We have a lot of ground to cover, including much of Patagonia and a cruise through Tierra del Fuego — a wildlife-riddled archipelago off the southernmost tip of South America, which few people ever get to see. We are literally travelling to the end of planet earth. With a bag of stuffed toys. It's a true test of friendship, if ever there was one.

The first challenge was getting the koala bears from one end of Palermo to the other. We stayed for two nights at a ridiculously chic hotel called Home, which was a well-deserved treat after Milhouse (although hanging with Dror and the transvestites *was* fun) and saw us staying up all night gossiping over bottles of Malbec and playing the *Evita* soundtrack on loop.

The Evita Peron Museum, which we felt obliged to visit, turned out to be one of the most entertaining, yet most baffling museums I've ever been to, thanks to an audio guide that insisted we run about the place in no particular order, looking for exhibits that weren't where they were supposed to be. Make sure you've got nothing else on your agenda for the day, if you're planning to do it — it's going to take you some time.

Anyway, Home was the kind of hotel we could have stayed in for a week, with its amazingly presented food items, such as scrambled eggs in tiny jars, and a whirlpool tub in the bedroom. It's the kind of Home I'll clearly never have, actually, but it's good to dream. After that, we had an invitation to join some friends I'd met out and about at a place called Jardin Escondido, which happens to be the summer home of the esteemed movie director, Francis Ford Coppola (ooh-er!). He rents it out, apparently, to those looking for a quiet hideaway in Buenos Aires.

Knocking on the door with our cases and bag of koala bears, we were welcomed inside by our friends and a couple of super friendly Argentineans called Fernando and Germán, who showed us to our rooms.

I let Autumn have the room Francis Ford Coppola sleeps in because I'm nice like that and also because I was slightly wary of finding a horse's head in the bed (well, you never know when he might slip a little movie prop in a random place, just for kicks), but the whole house was sinfully sexy, with absolutely no severed heads anywhere. I particularly liked the stash of Francis Ford Coppola movies by the giant TV and Francis Ford Coppola books on the coffee table ... just in case he forgets what he's achieved when he stays.

Think oak bookshelves, leather couches, the sweet smell of incense and expensive candles, cow-skin carpets and vases brimming over with pretty blooms. It's a gorgeous place, one that made me realise why the man has made so many good movies ... if all his homes are like this, he must be permanently inspired, although it must have been a momentary urge for something more obtuse than a scented candle in his room that led to the horse's head thing.

Fernando and Germán informed us that we'd all be having an *asado* on our first night, so after an afternoon spent visiting the zoo (which turned out to be shut — error), the beautiful old La Recoleta Cemetery, then the brightly coloured, slightly dodgy tourist trap that is La Boca (one of the poorest *barrios* in Buenos Aires built by Italian immigrants along the old port), we headed back to Coppola's toting bottles of red wine. Oh, by the way, do not buy any *choripans* in La Boca: we practically vomited ours back up again as we struggled to eat the cheap meat while watching overzealous performers dance the tango.

It's definitely more a photographic opportunity than a dining destination.

Germán cooked everything on a huge grill in the garden as we all drank vodka cocktails. His brother arrived, too, and I seized the opportunity to practise my Spanish on both of them. It's getting a little better now, I think, thanks to my classes. And when the meat offerings were ready, we all sat around the dining room table for a ridiculously long time, tucking into ribs, steaks and chicken.

After that, bellies full and burping, we went to a tango hall. Naturally.

La Catedral was filled with locals stepping and swirling to sexy beats and the *milonga* (the event itself) was basically held in a dark, cavernous room with old bicycles and stuff hanging from the ceiling. It was one of those nights you only have when you're least expecting it. You know the sort that takes you by surprise and makes you wish you'd shaved your legs and washed your hair and put on something other than a tatty bra and unwashed skirt?

I have to say, Germán's brother turned out to be incredibly nice. I got the chance to learn the tango with him and Autumn got the chance to take some documentary photos of the scene, which probably won't make it onto any blogs with the koalas. Neither will the drunken videos we made back at Francis's house, displaying my new tango skills, or lack thereof, on his immaculate cow-skin carpet.

After such a great time in Buenos Aires, and thanks to suffering a formidable hangover, the last thing Autumn and I feel like doing now is taking an overnight bus to Mendoza. But there's more wine to drink up there when we're finally over the wine we drank last night and we're meeting a fun-sounding girl called Kendra who's set to show us the sights.

Of course, as we left Jardin Escondido we handed out a few koalas to the lovely people who helped make Buenos Aires so special, so we only have to take twenty-seven across the country now.

How not to act in a vineyard ...

We were about fifteen minutes into our tour of the beautiful Hacienda del Plata in the wine district Luján de Cuyo. A handsome sixty-two-year-old winemaker called Pablo Gonzalez, with skin like the sun and an outfit consisting entirely of denim, was explaining how he and his team tenderly tie the vines with natural twine to the trellis wires.

It was a glorious, sunny day, with the icy white Andes standing tall against a clear blue sky. Autumn was running around taking photos. It was just us, our wonderful host Kendra and this radiant winemaker standing in the midst of rows and rows and rows of beautiful, budding Malbec grapes. So really, the last thing I needed to do was purge the entire contents of my stomach on the ground.

I held my breath, thinking maybe it would help. Maybe if I didn't breathe, my body would be tricked into thinking I was dead and the vomit I knew was building up inside me would never be evicted.

As Pablo crouched before his precious vines and explained how his family has been running this winery in some form or another at the base of the mountains since the eighteenth century, I couldn't help but wonder if anyone had ever been sick all over the harvest and ruined it. From the way he was talking, I was pretty sure that even the slightest bit of puke could potentially sour the irresistible mysticism of the Andes, which Pablo explained is captured in his wines.

Eventually I could take it no more. I made my exit as fast as a vampire newborn, through the vines and across the gravel path with my hand pressed firmly over my mouth. I made it to the toilet only milliseconds after Pablo's son, Juan Pablo, poked his head out of a nearby door. I dread to think what he heard coming from the bathroom as my breakfast, as well as last night's dinner, made its grand reappearance.

I didn't make it back to the vines. Instead, I was driven shame-faced back to Club Tapiz, the homely haven and ex-winery we're staying at, where I'm now sitting huddled by the fire, feeling sorry for myself and trying not to be sick again.

As I type, Autumn is still out with Kendra enjoying the first day of our planned four-day tour of everything that's awesome about Mendoza. As I sit here half buried in cushions, miserably wondering why a stomach bug is attacking me now when there's precious Malbec to drink and men-of-the-land to talk to me about vines (Juan Pablo was hot, well ... what I saw of his confused face as I dashed past him on my way to vomit), Autumn is off meeting more denim-clad ex-gauchos at wineries with fancy names and even fancier wines. Carmelo Patti, Renacer, Monte Quieto, Terrazas de los Andes ... the exotic list goes on without me.

We first met Kendra last night at a bar and restaurant called The Vines of Mendoza. She works for a company called Uncorking Argentina, which basically provides wine-dummies like us with a personal guide for the city. This means we're getting taken to all the best places while we're here and hopefully won't be left floundering in rubbish tourist traps. It was a no-brainer for Autumn and me because we're on a pretty tight schedule, seeing as we have to make it all the way down to Punta Arenas in Chile to board our Patagonian cruise ship in less than three weeks.

Having taken the overnight super *cama* class Andesmar bus from Buenos Aires (which included individual flat screen televisions with movie selection, wi-fi, flat beds and unlimited champagne all for 590 pesos one-way), we were both pretty knackered. Note: just because you're lying on a flat bed doesn't mean the bus doesn't bump up and down all night, keeping you awake. It doesn't mean men won't snore, either.

But Kendra had organised a tasting and a classy dinner with a renowned Argentinean head chef named Pablo Ranea at the restaurant Azafrán, and the second we met her bubbly American self, tiredness was banished, wine slurping commenced and we knew we were in for a fun few days. Autumn and I requested wine, wine, wine, wine, food and some horse riding, and a bit more wine for our tour, which is what has been arranged. I did not specify a stomach bug, but perhaps this is just karma paying me back for when Farzana was sick over the side of the boat in the Galápagos and I just drank beer and read my Kindle and edited photos of myself lying with sea lions.

Kendra moved to Mendoza from the US after college and, quite simply, fell in love with wine. She's been here for the past three years and seems to know everyone — from famous winemakers, to photographers, to restaurant owners, chefs and — *everyone*. As we chatted and our host from The Vines of Mendoza prepared our very first wine tasting, Kendra impressed us by switching with enviable ease from English to fluent Spanish. We learned a lot as we swigged and didn't spit (perhaps the first in a few errors that led to my tummy troubles today).

I've always been fascinated with wine, but the Argentinean girl pouring our drinks around the tasting table explained how she, too, became so fascinated with it that she quit her college studies in law and switched to a winemaking course instead. She's working in the bar while she studies, like many of the students who've moved to the area out of a passion for learning more about … their passion.

'Winemaking is really a simple process that anyone can learn,' she told us as she swirled and then sniffed her own glass. 'But good winemaking is an art. You need to learn as you go by tasting other people's success stories, as well as their mistakes.'

She invited us to taste a late-harvest white wine with a strong blue cheese, which was incredible. I always thought red wine was best with strong cheese, but apparently not. Apparently, red wine is best with chocolate, and white wine is the bevvy of choice for cheese.

'You don't need a moment to drink good wine because the wine is making the moment!' our knowledgeable host informed us as we sipped more of the wine and the cheese came to life on our tongues.

I thought this was exceptionally well demonstrated, and well said, especially as her English was by no means perfect, but the fact that even non-English speakers can speak so eloquently about wine and be understood by all is a testament to the passion of the people of Mendoza in general. As I'm learning here in South America, passion can be understood in any language. The girls I've met in Mendoza speak about wine in the same way that the boys of Ecuador speak about girls.

Kendra explained how she feels the passion of winemaking in Mendoza far more than she's felt it anywhere in her home country. 'In Argentina, drinking wine is an event to be cherished and shared,' she told us as we swirled and sniffed and swigged yet another fine Malbec Reserve from the highly regarded winemaker

Michel Rolland, who's so famous that a bottle with his signature on it immediately doubles in value. 'It's the same as eating here. Eating is a time when people come together to engage, not a means to an end like it is in a lot of other places.'

I like that eating isn't just seen as a means to an end here. Thinking about it, whereas McDonald's, Burger King and Subway are still everywhere you look in these parts, you don't really see the abundance of fast food spin-offs here like you do in other countries. Cafes and local restaurants that have been in business for years are still drawing huge crowds. Argentineans are creatures of habit, but those habits seem to involve visiting their much-loved regular haunts in the name of comfort, familiarity and sharing as much with the staff as they do with their own friends and family.

At the restaurant Azafrán, which is known as one of Argentina's best restaurants, Pablo Ranea, who's been whipping up his creations here since 2006, came out to personally say hi, because, like I said, Kendra knows everyone in Mendoza and Mendocinians are immensely proud of their food.

Pablo proceeded to serve us some of the most incredible empanadas — make that *the* most incredible empanadas — I have ever had, all filled with chunky steak meat and oozing gravy, encased in perfect pastry half-moons. Oh my God. If one of these empanadas was a man, I would marry it. The restaurant is pretty pricey but trust me, even if you just order the empanadas, you will die a happy bunny.

Anyway, Autumn, Kendra and I sat there for a while making noises like 'mmmm' and 'ohmygodthisissooogood', and were then joined by a fascinating American man called Jon Staenberg, a venture capital expert from Seattle who has a fifty-acre vineyard here in Mendoza called Hand of God. As we chatted over yet more wine, which was paired by the sommelier to a range of dishes such as cheese-crusted *bife de lomo*, or the most amazing fillet steak, if you're no meat expert, Jon told us all about how his intriguingly named business came to be.

I naturally assumed he and his college friend-turned-business partner ran this winery from a religious ranch somewhere with crucifixes on every wall, the fruits of their labour being a rich, blood-red wine they then bottle with love and spiritual wellbeing. But no. Hand of God, he told me, was named after the controversial World Cup goal scored by Argentinean soccer hero Diego Maradona in 1986. There's a lot I have to learn about soccer. And wine, for that matter.

Did you know there are companies that specialise entirely in fixing wine-tasting rooms with different lights? I had no idea how much thought goes into these things until Kendra and these equally passionate wine aficionados started telling us. Lights in tasting rooms are supposed to be of a particular colour and brightness, and all walls should ideally be white, because different colours can trigger different emotions and stop you thinking about the wine.

Green, for example, is supposed to make you think of meat. I'm still not entirely sure why — the only thing I can think of is that animals eat grass. Blue apparently makes you think of citrus and can magically conjure notes in your mind that aren't even in your wine.

When Autumn and I had our tour of Club Tapiz, we were shown a darkroom that's pitch black. It reminded me of a time I went speed-dating in the dark (not a wise move on anyone's part for a number of reasons), but that aside, this particular room works in a similar way to the bright lights and white walls: when you taste your wine in complete darkness, you're unaffected by anything else, allowing your senses to work out more about the nose, body and flavours of the wine. How clever is that?

I think Autumn has just returned, and judging from her message on my Facebook wall, I did indeed miss a wonderful day of fun among the wineries. Hmph. The fire is dying down and thankfully so are my stomach cramps, and as I haven't puked in a few hours, maybe the bug has vacated my system. I hope so. There's so much more to learn and digest in this city, it's almost criminal not to be able to keep it down.

10/09

Gaucho girls and the perfect climax ...

I don't know about you but I've always had a truly romantic image of what it must be like to be a gaucho. Or *with* a gaucho. I imagined a brooding group of sun-kissed men, with taut muscles and horse whispering qualities and a penchant for romps in hay, all set to reduce any woman in range to a quivering puddle.

As it turns out, not all of them are like that.

When Kendra, our wine guru and fast-becoming friend, collected us for another day of alcohol-infused exploits, it wasn't long before we were speeding off to the highest altitude vineyard in Mendoza, the rather funkily named Zorzal. Contrary to my imaginings, Zorzal was not a wine-filled space pod elevated above the ground, although they did have some rather space-agey looking eggs on the forecourt. I maintain that these really would make excellent rocket ships if only they weren't being used to ferment wine.

Sitting in the tasting room around a large table surrounded by barrels, the guys at Zorzal poured us the bottled fruits of their harvest, which proved a delicious testament to how well this young winery has been doing since it opened in 2008. I particularly loved the Climax Owners Blend 2010. It's probably the nicest wine I've had in Mendoza so far — or ever. Look it up. It's soft, sensual and soothing like the tango singer it's named after (though in Russia it's seen as even cheekier, as climax means menopause over there).

I'm liking all this new wine knowledge, you know? It makes me feel learned. Last week I thought a good wine was anything without a screw cap.

And so it was that, fuelled by a sufficient amount of booze, Autumn, Kendra and I headed up into the mountains for some horse riding with the sexy, chiselled cowboys of our imaginations. Here at La Quebrada del Cóndor, amid the snowy slopes of the Cordón del Plata range, scintillating views and yet another *asado* were waiting for us, along with some significantly porkier gauchos than the ones we'd envisioned.

It's not that I was disappointed when the smiley-faced, grey-haired, rotund gaucho opened the door of his humble hut in the middle of a field. The house was the house of my romantic dreams, what with its smoking chimney and grilled meat fumes, and bottles of red wine being poured generously into glasses as if we hadn't had enough already. I think I was just surprised. No one was exhibiting any horse whispering, or sun-kissed naked torsos. I couldn't see any hay bales anywhere, either. Or anyone under fifty.

No matter, we enjoyed a spectacular feast of chorizo and beef rumps and glazed onions grilled to perfection, as we asked our hosts about the numerous black and white photos on the brick walls depicting gauchos from generations past. Some of those were bare-chested and even appeared to be whispering to horses, which made me think perhaps a slew of straight *Brokeback Mountain*-style hotties were waiting for us around the corner, once we'd finished lunch.

They weren't.

But by then we were quite tipsy and over it anyway. Our older, knowledgeable gauchos were gallant men of the land and were pretty darn impressive on horseback, even in their flowing, gargantuan ponchos which, when filled with wind, served to make them look even bigger than their horses.

They galloped around the green and mustard plains and *we* trotted, as carefully as we could, being full of red wine and *asado*. Autumn somehow managed to carry her camera throughout the whole ride, which made for a lot of wonky photos of horses' hooves and a great one of Kendra falling off as her saddle slipped sideways. Luckily her horse was walking at the time and not attempting to jump over an icy stream.

The jagged, white and brown painted backdrop of the Andes made for a memorable afternoon riding around, although it was freezing cold. I know I've mentioned how these winter climes are taking some getting used to. Shopping was all just too expensive in Buenos Aires and as a traveller I'm starting to think I should have as little to carry as possible (learnt that from trying to shove the koala bears onto a bus more than anything else). My Quito jumper is getting a lot more wear than it should right now, because it's easy to forget when you're in a mild city that a few kilometres out in the mountains can be a totally different temperature.

I had to borrow a gaucho's gloves and another's huge puffy jacket just to brave the ride. Even if the gauchos had been young and hot and up for a romp in a hay bale, it would have been way too cold and I would have spent the best part of an hour getting all my clothes off. Not very romantic, really.

Autumn and I are starting to think we could happily live forever in Mendoza. We're not the only ones, either. An earthquake in 1861 destroyed the city and another in 1985 did some serious damage, but a Taste of Mendoza tour (as recommended by the *Lonely Planet*) with a lovely local lady called Magdalena provided even more proof as to why potential earthquakes will never put people off coming here, or staying.

We discovered things like how Mendoza actually means Cold Mountain, how the little squares around the city have been built to offer safe open-air spaces to run to in the event of an earthquake, and how the drainage system is infinitely superior to others throughout the world (drainage systems are fascinating, I'll have you know).

Magdalena also offered us copious amounts of the drink *mate* (pronounced mah-tay) as we wandered around the city. This is a favourite drink here in Argentina and I'm growing quite fond of it. *Mate* is made by steeping the ground leaves and stems of the yerba mate plant. You sip it through a metal straw with a filter in it, so you don't end up with unflattering bits of plant stuff in your teeth. Everywhere you go, you'll see people drinking it from special flasks. I think it's a slight upper. We felt pretty good after sipping it as we sat on our wooden bench by the river in the gorgeous Parque General San Martín, learning the stories surrounding a nearby haunted house.

All in all, Mendoza is a tantalising land of sun, culture and wine, and in spite of its gauchos not being exactly as anticipated, the scenery is some of the most photogenic around. And there's still time to find a sexy gaucho, I suppose; there's plenty more of South America to see. We shall prevail.

Before packing our bags once more, we deposited another koala with the lovely Magdalena, and one with Kendra, too, which took us down to twenty-five — an acceptable number, we felt, to carry with us over the border to Santiago.

Whistle stop Santiago and a lesson in history ...

As we took a juddering bus from Mendoza through the Andes, the views of snow-capped peaks gave a hungover Autumn and me an everlasting first impression of Chile. Then, at the border, Autumn's case was randomly selected to be opened and searched, so she had the pleasure of unloading onto a table piles of laundry, both clean and dirty, together with camera and laptop cables and one or two stray koalas, as an entire busload of people looked on in amusement.

For some time we were held up by her giant family-sized barrels of calcium-magnesium tablets and protein powder, which she'd packed in the hopes that maybe we would eat them instead of vast amounts of cheese and Malbec. Obviously we haven't touched them since she arrived; nor have we used the skipping rope with weights in the handles that she also packed in anticipation of a daily workout. It's the thought that counts, though. And at least the sniffer dog had something to do.

Our final night with Kendra had seen us making the most of a wine-tasting event at the Intercontinental Hotel, and by 'making the most' I mean we sampled maybe eighty top varietals from Mendoza's exceptional array of vineyards before hooking up with some of Kendra's friends in a nightclub. By the end of it, we weren't exactly feeling on top form.

We made it back to our room at a cute B&B called Casa Lila at 7 a.m. and slept straight through the alarm at nine, so that owners Pablo and Mariela and possibly their dog Olivia all had to take it in turns to try and wake us up.

After a panicked flurry of shoving things into suitcases and sitting on them, Pablo drove our still-tipsy selves at full speed to the bus station, where we promptly missed the bus for which we'd paid almost $50 each.

Luckily the views and two cans of Red Bull took our minds off the misery as we waited for the next bus, surrounded by a pile of booze-absorbing empanadas. Unfortunately they didn't wipe the recurring flashbacks of dancing barefoot in a stranger's kitchen somewhere in Mendoza only hours before, singing *Call Me Maybe* while eating pizza.

With only two days in Santiago before heading south to Chile's volcanic action capital of Pucón, Autumn and I arrived with our bags in a disgruntled heap at The Aubrey in Santiago's hipster hub, Bellavista. We're still glam-packing it a bit because Autumn has photos to take for a book of hotels she's working on, but after this we have a whole heap more hostels to stay in.

The Aubrey didn't judge us. Well, not out loud anyway. The Aubrey is the kind of place that scolds your hangover with its pure, visual splendour.

'How dare you look so rubbish within these walls!' it challenges, with its heated terrace swimming pool, outdoor tables in the shape of snuffling pigs and mansion-house interior complete with authentically squeaking staircases.

'Sort your life out!' it cries as you struggle up the stairs with your pathetic backpacker's rucksack and Winnie the Pooh suitcase, passing immaculately dressed businesswomen in suits and men in expensive shoes.

Over complimentary pisco sours (a must-have cocktail in Chile, although, to be honest, I think pisco — a grape brandy — tastes a bit like Dettol), we narrowed down the most important things to do and see in the city. These were: eat seafood, eat more seafood and visit the Museo de la Memoria y los Derechos Humanos — the Museum of Memory and Human Rights. Then we failed to do anything with our day except eat some *choclo con lomo* (which is some sort of sweet corn concoction served with delicious, tender beef), at a corner restaurant called Galindo (amazing!), complain about the excessive number of smokers in the place (why must people still do this next to others who are eating?), and fall asleep.

The next morning, shopping called. We headed to Calle Bandera, a street of vintage and second-hand shops a block away from Plaza de Armas in the heart of Santiago, which can entertain you for hours with some absolute bargains. We bought nothing but a second-hand winter jacket each, however, because we're told it's going to be very cold down south, especially when we get on the cruise from Punta Arenas to Ushuaia, the capital of Tierra del Fuego. I've made the mistake of not being prepared for these trips before, of course, so I wanted to make sure we were both well equipped this time. I still shudder when I think of my minivan day in Ecuador.

The jackets we bought are disgusting. They're so bad they would have been horrible even when they were made and first worn with love in the 90s. Autumn's is big, puffy and white, and mine is bulky, fat and black. Walking down the street wearing them, we caught a look at our sad shapes in a shop window and renamed ourselves Marshmallow and Tyre Man.

In our new apparel, we ate some lovely seafood in Mercado Central — a busy, noisy, stinky place with a circus atmosphere and amazing live music provided by guys walking around with violins and guitars — and then it was time for our Chilean history lesson.

As soon as you exit the Metro station Quinta Normal, the giant green box of a building that contains the Museo de la Memoria looms over you, casting an instant shadow on your mood. I don't think we were quite prepared for it. Exiting this museum after what must have been almost four hours, we felt like we'd been strapped into a rollercoaster ride and slapped about the face by reality. Wow. The mountains that guard this city in their soldier's coats of smog have seen some very, very dark times.

As we walked around the nearby Parque Quinta Normal, clutching styrofoam cups of steaming Nescafé and dodging kids speeding across the gravel paths on tricycles, a voice on a loudspeaker, sounding eerily like that of one of the armed soldiers we'd just been listening to, boomed from a stand near the boating lake and made us both jump. If there's one thing to put you on edge, it's watching televised images of death, chaos and destruction in pretty much the same space as it happened, not even forty years ago.

If you do one thing in Santiago, or Santiarsehole as it's often labelled most unfairly thanks to the smog that arches over it all like a filthy rainbow, skip the seafood, don't even bother with the vintage clothes, but do not, I repeat, do *not* miss this museum. If you're on a budget, go anyway because it's free.

This three-storey space is dedicated to raising awareness of the shocking human rights violations committed by the State of Chile between 1973 and 1990. Via a series of documents, installations, television and radio broadcasts, plus the audio guide, if you pay an extra thousand pesos like we did, you're swept through the military coup, the subsequent oppression endured by Chileans, the forced exile of thousands, the horrendous torture imposed on prisoners, and then the resistance, finally leading to the disbandment of the ruling junta, which had by 1990 brought the country to its knees. Take some tissues.

I wasn't even born when all the trouble started and I was just a kid when stories of this dictatorship broke across the world. I vaguely remember the celebrations on the news when at last there was a return to democracy, but I knew very little of the junta and General Pinochet's control ... and not just because I was too busy dancing around to Wham in my Doc Martens.

In those days, there was no social media to enlighten us where official media lied, no Facebook updates sharing photos and posts depicting torture and heartbreak, no mobile phones or Twitter feeds to enable cries for help or news of loved ones to be heard.

When the Chilean military overthrew Salvador Allende's Marxist government; when Allende himself committed suicide in despair; when the junta suspended the constitution and Congress, imposed a curfew and censorship and halted all political activity; when artists, film-makers and journalists were murdered for trying to show the truth, I, like many others my age at the time carried on regardless, going to school, dressing up pretty, never knowing how lucky I was to be safe and sheltered.

I think the museum's images of the men lining up in their 70s flares with their hands in the air and guns at their backs are the ones that stick with me most. Back when the rest of the world was getting into disco, bad sideburns and glitter balls, many of these handsome young men in their prime were in exile, forced to leave everything and everyone they knew. The only Saturday Night Fever experienced by others was via electrocution, as they were strapped to metal beds in detention centres (many in secret locations), covered in water and zapped by military officers in the name of extracting information about those opposing the regime.

Women were often sexually abused, prisoners of both sexes were shackled naked and blindfolded, exposed to extreme temperatures, crammed into tiny cells or placed in solitary confinement and tortured in hideous games of Russian roulette.

Anyone who's free to express themselves as easily as we do today might have a hard time believing how the press itself played an important role during the regime, distorting the truth, and supporting or covering up heinous crimes. In a world full of people who now know far too much about each other, keeping secrets on such a massive scale is unthinkable. But it happened in Chile.

I think sometimes we travel without really knowing very much about the places we go. I know I do. Perhaps we have a vague idea … perhaps we read a few pages in a guidebook, do a bit of Googling. To those who were sheltered from understanding the severity of Pinochet's rule like I was, Chile is probably still more an adventure capital full of volcanoes, zip lines and hot springs, than it is a living shrine to lost hope and lost citizens, or a shining example of what *can* be achieved by the power of the people. The Chileans moved mountains in their fight for a return to democracy, but not before more than 3000 innocent people died or 'disappeared' at the hands of state agents.

As Autumn and I make our way down south through this country's impressive national parks, scoffing empanadas, soaking in hot springs and bundling up against the cold on the way to Patagonia dressed as Marshmallow and Tyre Man, there will always be an extra chill in the air, thanks to this Santiago history lesson. And a deeper appreciation, I think, of the Chilean spirit of resilience.

Sex soup, the hubby-hunt and the house of the devil ...

Sometimes I dream that I'm a lumberjack's wife, living in a little house my husband built. Every night he comes back from a hard day's work in the snowy forests with a sack full of logs, dumps them by the fire, takes off his checkered coat, his checkered shirt, his checkered neckerchief, pats the dog and seduces me on a sheepskin rug. It's a simple existence, but we like it.

When Autumn and I rolled into the tiny mountain town of Pucón the other day in our hellish bus (never, ever ride overnight through Chile with the company Condor — their vehicles do not glide through the journey like a bird), I felt all my lumberjack dreams coming true.

'I want to move here,' I announced, wheeling Winnie up the pavement and zipping myself into my Tyre Man costume.

'Me too,' Autumn said, donning her Marshmallow coat and pointing into the distance with her tripod case. 'Look!'

And there it was. Villarrica. Chile's most active volcano and the one that most people come to Pucón just to climb. It shone magnificently and icing-sugar-white, all 2847 metres of it, against the blue of the morning sky and my jaw dropped. My eyes bulged. I forgot the way the bus had bumped my arse into numbness on the ten-hour sleepless journey from Santiago and saw instead the joyous future I would have living in one of the little wooden houses that are absolutely everywhere in town, petting German Shepherds, stoking the fire, learning to ski.

Of course I would excel at skiing and bag a hot ski instructor/ lumberjack boyfriend and we'd marry in a snow-covered cabin by a lake. My dress would be as white as the perfectly triangular volcano. Our bridesmaids would arrive on llamas.

'I'm here now,' I thought. 'I'm home.'

Gazing at the clouds rolling lazily across the distant hills, I even saw beyond the death of my heroic husband, who'd meet his end saving tourists in a dramatic avalanche/landslide sometime in the 2030s, before he had the chance to get all shrivelled and unsexy. I saw myself growing old here, baking beef pies and growing fat and rosy-cheeked and knowing all my neighbours, wearing a knitted poncho, probably with tassels. Perhaps I'd even start a women's club or a cooking group.

'I'm here now,' I thought. 'I'm definitely home.'

Perhaps part of the charm here in Pucón is that it's winter now and the hordes of tourists who flock here in the summer months are nowhere to be seen. It's mostly locals now, and bad travel-planners, like us.

'Aay, it's not really peak season, eh,' said Dave, the Kiwi manager at our hostel of choice, the tiny Paradise Pucón. The housekeeper nodded as she put Adele's album on repeat for about the ninth time (does anyone on this planet not have this album?) and continued to sweep the ashes from the floor around the open fire.

An ex-snowboarding instructor, Dave's been in Chile for almost six years and his cozy little hostel is yet another Walton-esque wooden cabin, sporting a porch with a barbecue grill and a small garden with a hammock stretching between two trees. He also has a collection of bikes, which he hires out to guests, and he's planning to start his own cycling tour company soon.

We dumped our bags in our room and noticed there was no heating anywhere, apart from the fire. If you're looking for rustic, this is it. The place is so cold you literally have to sit a metre from the flames to warm your bones before legging it to your room and burying yourself for the night under at least seven blankets and the thickest duvet known to man. I could barely move in bed, such was the weight on top of me. And it still took an hour for my teeth to stop chattering.

'Aah, rug up and get over it, eh,' Dave said, when I mentioned for about the tenth time that I was permanently freezing. This is why I like Kiwis. They're very down to earth. They're also very outdoorsy. Kiwi Dave has a whiteboard on the dining room wall listing every single type of activity you can do in Pucón and its surroundings. In the mornings he dances into the kitchen shouting the same mantra: 'Come on, team Paradise! What are we gonna do today, eh?'

What are we gonna do today? I looked at Dave with slightly less enthusiasm as I smeared Vegemite on my toast and yawned. Well, for a start, I thought, I am not climbing the volcano. Sorry, but no.

Villarrica's original name is Rucapillán, which in the Mapuche tongue translates ominously as 'house of the devil'. As though the devil must constantly remind people of his presence, he's lit several firework displays in his house over the last few decades, the most recent of which occurred in 1984. Prior to that, he held quite a party in 1971, when an eruption caused 200 casualties and a ten-metre-thick and 200-metre-wide torrent of lava to gush towards Lake Calafquén, destroying everything in its path.

My fear of scaling the thing has a bit to do with not being a mountaineer and a lot to do with the fact that we read a review of one person's experience with a Villarrica climbing tour on TripAdvisor a few days back. The girl wrote that two Swiss boys died in front of her on the tour by falling off the volcano. Apparently the weather was just too bad and the paths were slippery. How awful is that? It's the wrong season now, apparently.

Still, Autumn and I don't really mind being here in winter. Having the place free from *turistas* gives her more room to take photos without all those giant backpacks backing up in her lens, and me more freedom to imagine I'm a Walton. There's also more space for us both in the hot springs — one of the very best things about being in a land so volcanic.

On our first night, at Dave's suggestion, we headed to Loz Pozones, which is probably the most popular *termas* to visit if you're staying in Pucón. There are six thermal pools altogether, which start really hot and get progressively cooler as you move along. There's nothing quite like the rush that comes with stripping down to your bikini when it's six degrees outside and running barefoot — across mud so cold it makes your feet hurt — to a steaming natural stone pool. Lowering ourselves into the waters, we realised the sky was also star-splattered, chock full of twinkling constellations. It was like being in a steamy little winter wonderland. Or a sexy planetarium.

Technically you should be able to relax here; quiet your mind with the sound of the gushing Liucura River close by. On our evening visit, however, we couldn't relax completely. The pools may have been relatively empty compared to how they are in summer, but it seems the extra space in winter attracts the more amorous of Chile's lovers, looking to rub their bodies against each other where no one they know will see them.

Autumn and I had to sit there, trying our best not to stare, as the pool filled up with more bumpers and grinders than a Playboy mansion hot tub. We could hardly look away, though, when a lady with a boob job stood on a rock and started posing for her boyfriend's camera in a neon yellow bikini comprising two thin strips covering her nipples, and a g-string. At one point, I think we were the only two females not straddling a man. As we busied ourselves searching for the Big Dipper, I'm pretty sure about nine couples had quiet, steamy sex in this body of water we shared..

'What are we doing today, eh, team Paradise!' Dave exclaimed again the next morning as we smeared even more Vegemite on our toast, much to the disgust of our new Chilean friends. 'Horse riding? Cycling? Skiing? Ah yeeeeah, you girls should totes go skiing. Powder's great up there. If you want, you can climb up Villarrica and ski down! Wa-hey!'

We shook our heads politely again. The volcano story scared me and it still seemed a bit risky. We opted for some rafting on the Trancura River instead, which was pretty hair-raising in itself, and then we went vintage shopping. That's right.

What most people don't realise when they arrive in Chile's adventure capital of Pucón is that this little town, populated largely by poncho-wearing gauchos (also of the older, wide and greying variety), is a vintage clothes shopper's heaven. Here we found spectacular dresses from the 80s and 90s that would cost a fortune in other places. We stocked up on some truly gorgeous knee-length floral skirts, which will look lovely when we finally come to strolling through a park that isn't covered in icicles.

At another recommendation, we borrowed Dave's bikes and cycled to the Hotel Antumalal, which involved a heart-hammering puff uphill. It's the place where Queen Elizabeth stayed when she visited, and Neil Armstrong, too, at one point. You can see their photos in the lobby.

Even more open fires welcomed us into this posh hotel, along with floor-to-ceiling windows overlooking an azure lake, pretty lawns and gardens buzzing with bumblebees, pink shrubs and lilac flowers. Bushy trees nuzzled the earth like furry green sheep on the distant and almost perpendicularly steep hillsides. Autumn and I paid to use their super-posh spa for the afternoon (highly recommended for a treat) and finally took advantage of a hot tub with no people having sex in it.

That afternoon, we took another bike ride round the outskirts of Pucón with Dave and a few others. We rode out to see Villarrica from a rickety old bridge, which looked as though cars probably shouldn't be driving across it, even though they were, and along the way we stopped by rivers of the sort you might expect to see bears catching salmon in, in a *National Geographic* photo spread. It made me want to see the volcano up close.

So, the next morning, when Dave announced, 'What are we doing today, eh, team Paradise!' I looked up from my Vegemite and told him I'd like to get inside the 'house of the devil'. He rubbed his hands together and told me he would drive me himself.

Dave, a guy from Brazil, Pecos (Dave's equally enthusiastic dog) and I spent the morning stopping to throw (or chase) snowballs as the sun sizzled in a blue sky above a road that quickly turned to thick, thick snow the further we climbed. Walking up to the volcano felt like we'd stumbled onto the set of a Christmas movie and getting inside it was pretty cool, albeit with a Spanish-speaking guide I couldn't understand at all. I know it wouldn't exactly be authentic but someone would make a fortune giving English tours in some parts of South America. My Spanish is improving every day, of course, but it doesn't help much with seismic monitors and geothermal energy tracking.

I did manage to learn that, while no one can really know when Villarrica will erupt again, judging by its 'pattern', it's probably going to happen quite soon, which wasn't exactly comforting to hear as I was standing inside it.

I should say that Autumn had had every intention of joining us on this volcanic jaunt, but something strange had happened.

Just as she went to get in the car with us, she said she felt like she was seeing two of me. Funnily enough, a guy in the hostel had spent the night before experimenting with some local acid he'd bought from an old lady dressed as a teenager, which we think he may have laid on the kitchen's chopping board ... just a few hours before we sliced some bread on it for breakfast. Suspicious.

Whereas I think it would have added to the experience, Autumn didn't much fancy heading to the 'house of the devil' on acid, so she went to sit down in a quiet place while we sped off to inspect the devil's homemade geomorphological miracles. Underground ceilings dripping with brown minerals made the caves in Villarica's belly look like they were composed of melting, brown chocolate.

When our guide turned the lights out to show us what total darkness looks like, I couldn't help imagining what those Chilean miners from Copiapó must have gone through not so long ago, when they were trapped for over sixty days in the blackness; the sound of dripping and heartbeats and shoes shuffling on grit the only noises they could hear when voices fell silent. It's amazing to think of their first three weeks after the collapse, when everyone presumed they were dead — until a drill hole was made and the drill came back up with a note on it.

It's enough to give anyone sleepless nights and I was glad at that point that Autumn hadn't come. It wasn't the right place to be tripping at all.

It turned out she was fine, of course. I found her in a cozy cafe drinking coffee, and after I ordered my *vino tinto*, we went back to scouring the town's slim-pickings for potential hot ski instructor/ lumberjack husbands from our place by the fire. Bliss.

'What are we doing today, eh, team Paradise!' Dave called out the next day.

'We're leaving now, so we're giving you a koala bear,' Autumn replied. 'Would you like one, or two?'

26/09

Shrines and miscalculated travel times ...

One thing you can't fail to miss as you drive the incomprehensible distances across these South American countries are the shrines erected every few kilometres in the wilderness. Every now and then you'll be admiring the vast landscapes, the way the pampas grass sways and how its colours merge one into the other through your window, when you'll see one, sticking out like a sore thumb: a tiny house with a little pitched roof that looks as though it might be home to a family of religious elves. Oh, there are shrines along some roads in Australia too, but they're nowhere near as elaborate as these.

Often at night these miniature houses will be lit, shining like beacons thanks to an abundance of flickering candles. In the daylight, as you whizz past in a bus or car, you'll notice the Virgin Mary smiling serenely as the wind slaps her face like a savage.

On the drive from Punta Arenas (a rather dismal, cold city in which we did nothing, really, except visit a cemetery and eat some nice seafood before bunking down in our hostel) to the EcoCamp Patagonia in Torres del Paine, we saw a fair few of these houses by the roadside. Our friendly driver José explained in Spanglish their significance.

'They are called *animita*,' he said, 'and each one is a memory of the dead.'

A lot of people die on these open roads in unpredictable weather conditions, and when fatalities occur, the families of the deceased maintain a roadside shrine, keeping the memory of their loved one alive by visiting often with gifts and prayers and, quite obviously, lighters and matches. We stopped to take photos of a particularly impressive one built of brick, like a pizza oven featuring three glass cases inside it. Smashed up tail lights and fake flowers decorated the base of one case. In another was a white marble statue of the Virgin Mary, two framed photographs of smiling, dark-haired men with crossed arms and a container brimming over with cigarettes. José explained that it was built to remember an accident between a bus and a truck in which a father and son, the men in the photographs, both died.

These shrines are beautiful and must cost a fortune to both build and maintain. That's not even taking into consideration the distances these families have to travel in order to pay their respects on a regular basis. Until you've been driven overnight from big city to big city on a bumpy bus, or felt hour after hour after hour pass with the same unchanging views, it's hard to imagine the vast expanse of wilderness that must often be covered before you reach your destination. Of course, many Aussies will know the meaning of a 'long drive'. But Chile in particular is huge.

In Southern Chile, there are small towns like anywhere but these aren't places you'd want to stop overnight with a backpack and a can of tuna, speaking in broken Spanish about locating a plug for your hairdryer. Often you'll see solo homes at the foot of rocky mountains or on flat windswept plains, with no electricity cables connected anywhere. Not only is there no satellite TV, no wi-fi and no nightly happy hour to appease the spoilt glam-packer, here the land is wild and so too are the people, I'm sure.

It all looks very romantic, watching strong men on horseback rounding up herds of nervous sheep in the late afternoon sun with the help of four glossy-coated dogs, but that's from a car window. Get up close and your much-admired gaucho has skin like leather, breath that smells of burnt beef and no interest whatsoever in discussing anything that isn't related to his flock of domestic alpacas.

Autumn and I totally underestimated how long it would take to reach each place in this country. Distances are deceiving on maps, especially small maps, like the ones on our iPhones (ahem). We had no idea it would be a twenty-three hour journey from Pucón down to Punta Arenas via a night bus, two taxis and a plane; nor that it would *then* take almost another full day of travelling from the atmospherically challenged Punta Arenas to get to the EcoCamp Patagonia in Torres del Paine.

Usually this particular journey takes four to five hours, but José had to stop to let us take photos, let us get lunch, let us get lost on the way back to the van from the toilet, etc. At one point, we saw no less than three ginormous eagles in the space of ten minutes. We pulled to the roadside each time to try and capture them on camera and, each time, watched them soar away over the scraggly trees before we could take a picture.

Long rides have their highs and lows, but if you're planning to travel Chile, I would definitely advise you to book your transport as much in advance as possible, especially plane rides and *especially* around public holidays, else you'll be backtracking like we had to do from Pucón back up to Santiago in order to fly back down south. Error.

Anyway, I suppose most journeys, although long, offer the chance to reflect on what's happened so far and also to think about the people who make these lonely trips on a regular basis, either for work, leisure or to pay homage to a loved one who never got to make it to their final destination at all.

28/09

Home sweet dome ...

I jolted upright in the middle of the night, thinking my duvet was on fire. Sweat was pouring down my neck, my hair was damp, and I looked up to see the open jaws of hell at the end of my bed. After maybe three seconds of fearing for my life and waiting for Satan himself to crawl under the covers, I realised it was just the log fire reaching its peak in our little dome-shaped home and that flaming hell was actually safely confined behind a glass door.

Having woken Autumn with my shrieks, she said it was my fault I was hot because I piled on the logs before falling asleep, in case we froze.

Reflections in Torres del Paine.

There's just no controlling the temperature in Patagonia's Torres del Paine, no matter how hard we try. As with the majority of places we've visited so far, we've come here at what people are calling 'the wrong time'. The EcoCamp Patagonia, nestled in what looks like a patch of Hobbit real estate at the base of the three jagged, pink granite mountains which puncture the sky above this 2422-square-kilometre national park, seemed a far better option for 'the wrong time of year' than pitching a windproof tent by an icy lake.

To be fair, for the last two days the weather has been surprisingly sunny and dry, proving once again there's no wrong time to be anywhere, really. There's a 'not as popular' time, but these are so far turning out to be quieter, less crowded by tourists, with random bursts of amazing weather that we get all to ourselves.

Perhaps the total opposite of waking in a sweaty mess in front of a fire was the teeth-chattering chill that came with holding a glass of ice-cold whisky yesterday, as the wind whipped relentlessly around our ears on the deck of a moving boat. The ice in my glass had just been chiselled off an iceberg, one of many floating like sculptures carved by the hand of God on Lago Grey, a glacial lake. It's fair to say neither Autumn nor I had ever drunk an iceberg before yesterday, but the thrill of doing so made up for the fact that we were forced to huddle deep into our unattractive Marshmallow and Tyre Man outfits while we did it.

A group of Brazilian ladies on holiday to escape their husbands batted their eyelashes at their perplexed tour guide and managed to obtain and consume several bottles of complimentary whisky as we floated around the jutting, glacial blue masses. Within half an hour of sipping their first drinks they were drunk and had started a little karaoke session inside the boat, using the captain's microphone.

We watched them with amusement through the windows from our place on the deck as it was explained to us why the more compact and towering glaciers are all a Smurf-skin shade of blue. It turns out that this is because whereas the red/long wavelengths in white light are absorbed by the ice, the blue/short wavelengths are transmitted and scattered across it. The further light travels in ice, the bluer it appears. Or something like that. I was finding the facts a little hard to grasp, being more than a little buzzed on whisky.

We went inside to sing with the Brazilians and our guides took photos to embarrass us with later. I joined in with a song that's been following me all over South America, called 'Quiero Casarme Contigo' by the Colombian singing sensation, Carlos Vives. It's a song that appears to get more airplay here than, say, Queen's 'Bohemian Rhapsody' or John Lennon's 'Imagine' have *ever* had since they were written. I don't think I've gone a day without hearing it somewhere. I defy you to Google it and not get it stuck in your head.

Right now I am listening to a rather sexy, long-haired EcoCamp guide called Diego playing it on his guitar. I can see his ponytail blowing in the soft breeze as he sits on a sun-soaked bench overlooking what must be a hundred kilometres of green open space stretching beneath Torres del Paine's line of ragged peaks that rise like spiky serpents out of a cottony ocean of clouds. This Chilean part of Patagonia is unbelievably bewitching.

It's also easy to see why Chileans refer to their country in general as *el ultimo rincon del mundo* — the last corner of the world. Out here in Patagonia, you really do feel as though you're a million miles away from everything else. If you're planning to see it with your boyfriend or girlfriend, I envy you, as it's probably one of the most romantic locations I've ever visited.

Autumn and I walked from the EcoCamp out to the milky blue Lago Nordenskjold today, with two girls from Melbourne and our two Chilean guides, Claudio and the guitar-playing Diego. As soon as we left the EcoCamp and caught our first glimpse of the craggy slopes and grassy plains resplendent with spouting signs that winter's almost over, we forgot how unfit we are thanks to never using that skipping rope with weights in the handles that Autumn packed. We concentrated instead on spotting the wildlife around the lake. We saw tiny frogs, beetles, lizards, scorpions and a fair few guanaco (part of the camel family) carcasses to prove that pumas are out here too, somewhere.

In Torres del Paine, the precipitous peaks are encircled by condors. Bleating lambs scurry after flocculent sheep, hares hop across vast, windswept steppes, and nandus, which look like small ostriches, waddle away from you faster than you can focus your camera on them.

We passed a bunch of prickly shrubs called mother-in-law's seat and learned that all berries growing in Torres del Paine are edible. There's no way you'll go out like the guy in *Into the Wild*, if you go wild here. Also, the park was given UNESCO status in 1978, so you can embark on numerous trails safe in the knowledge that you won't be shot accidentally by a deer hunter, either.

The most popular trail in the park is the W Circuit — a three to four day hike, during which you can camp or stay at designated *refugios* along the way. This would be a cheaper, much more rustic way to see Torres del Paine, and several people doing this have come in to share dinner and drinks with us around the communal table at EcoCamp, just for a touch of heat and comfort. It sounds like quite an adventure — one I wouldn't mind doing myself one day. But having seen their wind-slapped cheeks and stoplight red noses at this time of year, I think Autumn and I would both prefer to be woken up by a demon fire every night, than by the jabbing hands of Jack Frost beside an icy lake.

It was during our hike to Lago Nordenskjold that I met Mirador, the special stick. Don't you love it when you find a good stick? It adds an element of adventure to any outing, I say. With nothing but the great outdoors around you, you're free to be a kid again and even give your stick a name and magical powers, like you used to. I called mine Mirador, because that's what was written on the signpost next to where I found it.

Claudio later told me *mirador* means 'lookout point' in Spanish, but it was too late by then. Mirador and I were inseparable and plus, when you say it really slowly in a deep, low voice, it sounds like the name of a warlock. Go on, say it. Say 'Mirador' in a low voice, slowly.

See? Warlock. You can't abandon a warlock once you've found one.

Mirador also came with me on our hikes to Lago Azul and Laguna Amarga, the latter of which means 'bitter', as this ancient pool of milky water is very high in minerals, very salty and has a PH content of eleven. No life can survive in it, so the surroundings are eerily silent, devoid of all the birds and wildlife we've been spotting elsewhere.

Our guides from EcoCamp all love birds. They're very knowledgeable about everything, really, and speak great English, so I'm finally learning something firsthand without having to Google it all afterwards, but I would say their specialty is definitely birds. Every now and then on our drives to various hiking trails, the van will come to a halt, we'll all jolt forward and Claudio and Diego will jump out, dark hair flying out behind them, stubbled chins pointing skyward along with their cameras.

'Look! An Andean condor!' they'll cry. 'Look, a long-tailed meadowlark! A southern crested cara cara! And is that … no it can't be! Is that a black-chested buzzard eagle with a red-gartered coot?'

After the Galápagos, I thought I was destined to view birdwatchers a bit like I view hikers: old men with rucksacks on their backs and binoculars round their necks, sporting hats to stop the bird shit getting in their hair and cameras with ginormous lenses compensating for everything else they're lacking in life as they hide behind trees and bushes. But I've been wrong. Birdwatchers are sexy. At least, they are in Chile.

Anyway, my own hunt for the elusive puma was unsuccessful, in spite of Mirador's magic puma-attracting spell, because pumas are terrified of humans and it's extremely rare to spot them here. In fact, you're more likely to spot a UFO, according to Jose our driver, who's actually seen them — the UFOs, that is. Apparently, UFO sightings are quite common in Chile and Argentina, especially in a town in northern Argentina called Capilla del Monte, which is home to a sacred mountain called Uritorco and the hundreds of spiritual pilgrims who flock there at any one time. I think I'm going to have to go there.

As well as pointing out the shrines on the way to Torres del Paine, Jose pointed to dips and cracks in the towering peaks, which have on his various drives been known to shimmer with inexplicable lights. A chemical reaction, you might think. A low flying aircraft? Maybe so.

But you know what? Out here in the last corner of the world, a frozen Narnia where icebergs can chill your whisky, pumas can pounce as soon as you become complacent, and a magical stick can be as powerful as your imagination will let it, an alien nation existing in the shadows doesn't actually seem so ridiculous at all.

Tierra del Fuego and some wild OATs ...

Deep in the fjord, the ice on the banks to one side of our ship was frozen into the shapes of tidal waves that looked as though a surfer in snow-gear might appear on a crest and freeze like an icicle halfway down the mountainside. I sat with Autumn and three koalas on one bed, drinking red wine as she captured these blue-white, otherworldly scenes with a wide-angle lens through the window.

The good ship *Stella Australis*, with its ever-changing views, is proving an exceptional home on our cruise from Punta Arenas over to Argentina's Ushuaia, not least because we paid a bit more for a suite, and because all food *and* drinks are included. It's an expensive addition to our trip at almost US$2500 each for the four-night voyage, but there's really no other way to see Tierra del Fuego, or reach Cape Horn — the end of the world. We figured, if we're travelling this far, we may as well go as far as possible.

Of course, as far south as possible would have meant going to Antarctica, which is only 650 kilometres from Cape Horn. But as usual it's 'not the right time' to visit, the season for Antarctica being from November through March.

Contrary to popular belief, visiting Antarctica on your trip through South America doesn't have to break the bank. We're told that in season, a last minute cruise from Ushuaia into the frothing wrath of the Drake Passage and beyond to walk in Shackleton's footsteps can cost as little as $4000 if you're willing to share a triple cabin and aren't too fussy about your food. We're also told it pays to stock up on sea-sickness pills, tour a number of agencies to compare prices when you arrive, and rent your expedition clothing in Ushuaia to save lugging your own about. Also, be flexible. Apparently it's not uncommon for people to have to wait one or two weeks in Ushuaia before finally securing a sacred place on a ship.

Cruising to Cape Horn on the *Stella Australis*, a boat with just a hundred cabins and a gourmet nightly buffet that would put any hotel in Vegas to shame (mini king crab hot pot, anyone?), is exciting enough for us. Plus, our shipmates are a group of retired passengers from California. The place cards on their allocated tables in the dining room read OAT, and I, Autumn, and our new friends Stephanie (Australian), Rachel (Swiss) and Mariela (German), the only other solo female travellers on board under thirty-five, have been trying to figure out what that OAT stands for. We can only imagine it's Old Age Travellers.

Now, you might be thinking you'd prefer a sexy oceanic fiesta with a wet T-shirt competition every night at nine in the hot tub, instead of bingo at six before bed time, but cruising with old people is like having access to a hundred grandmas all wanting to tell you about something wonderful. And you're at sea, so there's no way they can get distracted by *The Antiques Roadshow*, abandon you mid-sentence and then forget what they were saying. Also, they go to bed early, leaving you with full reign over the song book during the scheduled karaoke night on the top deck; or, as is the case for Autumn and me, they allow you to be the stars of the cruise ship fashion show.

Tierra del Fuego (meaning Land of Fire) is separated from mainland Argentina by the Strait of Magellan, with a total area of roughly 48,000 km². It's one of the most untouched and unspoilt places on the earth and therefore one of the most extraordinary. There are no park rangers. Only the *Stella Australis* and, I think, one other ship ever visit some of the sites on this voyage, which means that we as passengers are responsible for the landscape. Our expedition leader explained how the guides and other staff on the ships sometimes have to pitch in to help build bridges through the park, to enable the relatively few visitors to explore in safety.

On our first disembarkation in Ainsworth Bay — a coastal inlet fed by the meltwater of the retreating Marinelli Glacier — my feet sank up to my knees in fluffy snow. I looked about at the enchanted forest surrounding us as I struggled to walk behind my shipmates and honestly felt more magic in the air than could ever have been conjured up by Mirador.

Here is a true ethereal wonderland, where bursts of colour in the form of hardy shrubs rise triumphantly like splayed fingers on buried hands. As Autumn and I and our new friends posed in our mismatching winter warmers on washed up chunks of glacier ice, I thought about the fact that hardly anyone gets to walk paths like this. Hardly anyone gets to make-believe they're the Snow Queen reigning over such a magical forest. And in this sub-polar Magellan forest, few people get to see these trees, gnawed to the size of small stools by beavers in the quest to build their dams. I felt exceptionally grateful.

As our guide explained the whys and hows of the environment and my feet grew numb in my trainers, I watched a four-year-old kid trip and fall in the snow over and over again, each time almost being buried by the sheer volume of it. But each time her grin was wider and her laughter louder and it was heartwarming to think of how she'll store these memories. Being from Sydney, she'd never seen or stood in snow before.

Heading back to the Zodiacs for some hot chocolate and whisky (they give you whisky after each departure on this ship

I always wanted to be an ice queen in Narnia ...

of dreams), my hands were numb with the cold, but while I was waiting for my turn to go back to the ship I met three guys from different parts of Chile who are actually living for three months in Ainsworth Bay. They're researching elephant seals and rely on the cruise ships to bring them supplies.

I had a chat with them. They were all quite good looking, so naturally I started imagining what we'd do at night if the ship sailed off without me and I had to share their tent. They showed me their waterproof clipboard, which they write on in waterproof pencil, and which had a lot of notes on it about elephant seals. I'm still not entirely sure if elephant seals *really* exist in Ainsworth Bay or if these guys are just so cold and starved between deliveries that they see things on the horizon, but I nodded encouragingly and promptly fetched them some warming whisky in polystyrene cups.

I left hoping they find what they're looking for. We'd seen an empty beaver's dam, two geese, a forest and some snow in Ainsworth Bay and that was about it. It's beautiful and everything, probably one of the most incredible patches of the earth I've ever had the good fortune to set foot upon, but there's a reason people visit for a couple of hours and then go back to king crab hot pots and unlimited wine.

After lunch, we headed back out to see some waddling Magellan penguins (endemic to the Southern Hemisphere) and a flock of what must have been at least 5000 cormorants all dropping their white loads like dangerous missiles onto a giant black rock … and, occasionally, us. We all threw our hands over our heads, pulled our hoods up, but couldn't stop looking anyway. It's almost impossible to describe the light in people's eyes when they see things like this, things they've travelled far and wide to see that go beyond all expectation. You catch it now and again and it almost makes you want to cry.

Whether you're an OAT, or a child, or something in-between, there's a binding power that banishes age, I think, when you're standing together in awe like this. It's these shared moments, in my opinion, that make travelling so enriching, so addictive — like all these little jolts of happiness you're sending out and receiving might in some way keep a person young. It's got to be good for the soul.

Tonight's fashion show in the Sky Lounge is calling, so it's time to pack this laptop away and attempt to do my hair. I'm not entirely sure how much fashion exists on board this ship, to be honest. Marshmallow and Tyre Man won't be making an appearance, that's for sure, and the most appealing items in the ship's shop seem to be waterproof trousers in various colours and a *Stella Australis* windproof jacket. Still, I'm sure the entertainment officer's got something fun up his thermal sleeve to pass the time before we raise the flag at Cape Horn tomorrow.

We've since found out that OAT stands for Overseas Adventure Travel, by the way; not what we originally thought. So in a way, I'm an OAT, too. And so is everyone we're meeting on our journey.

03/10

The end of the world ...

No sooner had we checked into the somewhat deceivingly named Antarctica Hostel in Ushuaia, than Autumn and I learned of the kidnapping of two girls, one Australian and one Brit, abducted as they floated in a canoe in the Cuyabeno Nature Reserve the other day. This happened at the Colombian border with Ecuador, exactly where I stayed with the amorous Mowgli not so long ago.

Thankfully the girls were freed not long afterwards, but it's horrifying to think of how much worse it could have been for them, or how they must have felt out there as captives in the sweaty jungle. It happened, too, as the FARC, Colombia's armed communist guerrilla group, entered a peace process with the government following almost fifty years of war. I guess it goes to show that you can never be too careful when you're travelling in these countries, no matter how safe you think you'll be.

Thanks to things like Facebook and Foursquare, it's very rare that people don't know where we are when we're moving around the world these days, but it's mad to think that these silly habits of 'checking in' or tagging fellow travellers in photos might turn out to be actual lifelines … not that there's an Internet connection in the Amazon.

Anyway, back to Ushuaia. For all intents and purposes, this town is expensive. It's the gateway to Antarctica and isn't a place you're expected to want to linger, and thanks to everything having to be transported long distances to get here — usually by container ship — even in the supermarkets, prices for food and drinks are extortionate. It reminds me a bit of the Galápagos, as far as stretching the budget is concerned. Our hostel is costing us almost $20 a night for a dorm bed, too, as opposed to the usual $10.

I suppose we can't really complain, though, seeing as we spent a small fortune on getting here in style!

Sadly, Autumn has decided that instead of travelling back up north through Argentina and on into Bolivia with me, she is going to take the seven last remaining koala bears back to Buenos Aires and then into Uruguay. There, she'll head for the beach at the glamorous Punta del Este, which is home to Uruguay's elite sun-seekers. I guess I can understand that after all this cold she wants some sun and sand, and to stay in one place for a while. And we *have* been a little extravagant in our glam-packing so far.

I've decided I'll be flying via Buenos Aires up to Córdoba, where I plan to visit the sacred hill of Uritorco and look for aliens in nearby Capilla del Monte. Ever since Jose mentioned it, I've been intrigued. It'll be weird, travelling alone again after all this time, but Autumn and I have had some incredible experiences together since we first sang along to Madonna and Antonio Banderas in the fancy Home hotel back in Palermo. Just the other day, having sailed through the Murray Channel and Nassau Bay, we reached the rocky promontory of Cape Horn National Park at dawn's light on our final cruising day. Discovered in 1616 and declared a World Biosphere Reserve in 2005, for years Cape Horn was an important navigation route for sailing ships between the Pacific and Atlantic oceans. It was at the nearby Wulaia Bay that Charles Darwin, during his voyage on the HMS *Beagle*, landed in 1833.

The cold was a living thing in Cape Horn, pressing down on us and slowing our progress as we struggled to walk in our fluorescent lifejackets. Standing on a grassy verge behind the Albatross statue — a monument constructed at the highest point for the countless sailors who've lost their lives in the area — maintaining any body heat was futile. But with our arms wrapped around our own chests, Autumn and I grinned at each other, and then at the thrashing waves — the only things separating us from Antarctica. And then we jumped up and down on the spot to stop our toes falling off.

We met a family who live out here in the remote and bleak beyond — a place so windswept that the trees grow at an angle and where the ghosts of almost 800 nearby shipwrecks are free to roam the land. Their ten-year-old son ran around us with his dog, seemingly glad of the company.

Apparently there's huge competition for the privilege of living here on Cape Horn and the chosen family gets tax-free benefits, as well as the chance to operate the lighthouse. It would take a special kind of person to be able to handle it, though. I could barely feel my face, hands or feet by the time I got back onto the boat. I even refused my regular whisky, for fear that the glass might fall from my fingers and shatter.

As a result of spending far too much time on the ship's decks trying to take photos, I now have another stinking cold.

The silence of Ushuaia's creepy penitentiary-turned-museum was rudely broken by the sound of my nose-blowing as we walked around it yesterday, attempting to make sense of the iffy translations and baffling over the bad spelling.

In spite of this, it's an interesting place to learn a bit about the history of the prison, as well as everything you've ever wanted to know about Shackleton, or the navigation by others of the South Pacific and South Atlantic. We wouldn't have got to discover all this if we'd gone dog-sledding as originally planned. Much to our disappointment, we arrived in Ushuaia just *one* day after the end of dog sledding season.

'It's the wrong time of year for that now,' said the guy, predictably, at the reception desk when we checked into the Antarctica Hostel. Interestingly, we're also too *early* for beaver season. It's a weird kind of animal-free limbo here at the moment but, at the right time of year, you can go on a tour at night to watch the beavers build their dams. I find this interesting because I can't help but imagine a smartly dressed family of beavers travelling into the city in turn, just to watch a construction team build a house.

At another museum, the Museo Maritimo y del Presidio, we also learned a lot about the Yamana people, the natives of Tierra del Fuego, who didn't actually wear clothes until the Europeans reached them. To fight the cold, they smothered themselves in sea lion blubber. That's something to remember if you're thinking you've got nothing to wear, isn't it? They also lit fires in their little canoes and huddled around them, and it was these fires, eventually spotted by European explorers as they passed by in their ships, that gave the place its name — Land of Fire.

Someone told us we'd be able to eat beaver in Ushuaia (oh, stop it), but we haven't been able find it anywhere so far. Someone told me it tastes like a fishy kind of chicken, which is intriguing. I like to think I'd try it if I came across it, but you never know. I thought the same thing about tarantulas in Cambodia last year, but when faced with their spindly barbecued legs, I screamed the market down, caused a nearby baby to cry and ran back to the tour bus, quivering.

On our first night out on dry land, Autumn and I went for a decidedly non-beavery dinner with a guy called Chris from the hostel, who spent the majority of the evening bringing the conversation around to the girlfriend he'd just broken up with.

'This is nice wine, isn't it?' I'd say.

'Yes it is, my girlfriend used to love this wine,' he'd reply.

'I can't wait to get to the beach in Uruguay,' Autumn would enthuse.

'My girlfriend knows someone in Uruguay,' he'd say, morosely.

'What's the square root of 9,904,567?' I'd ask.

'My girlfriend was the better one at maths,' he'd tell us.

Or words to that effect.

Eventually Chris went home in a melancholy funk of his own creation and Autumn and I hooked up with two Argentinean guys who entertained us with bad dance moves in a local bar and took great delight in posing for photos wearing Marshmallow and Tyre Man. They were way more fun. I especially liked the handsome Pedro when he told me between kisses to my fingers, 'You have a beautiful sound in your mouth when you speak,' although, having literally travelled to the end of the world and looked in vague hope for an eligible man, I still have a feeling I'll be travelling onwards unattached.

At least I don't have to worry about carrying those koala bears anymore, I suppose.

Smurfing it at Oktoberfest ...

I clambered down from yet another top bunk this morning in the Mate Hostel, Córdoba, to find one of the Brazilians who'd been partying hard the night before in the common room was fast asleep in the bunk below. Because he'd kept me awake way past my bedtime, I thought his hostel karma was about due, so I applied a firm, quick foot to his backside, which was half poking out of his duvet like a waning moon. Then I smiled faux-apologetically when his eyes flashed open.

Much to my surprise, Alberto sprung out of bed with the urgency of someone who was late to catch a plane and announced that he was so glad I'd woken him up because: 'We have to get to Oktoberfest!'

Seeing as though my only other plan for the day was to wander round the Che Guevara museum in Alta Garcia feeling sorry for myself while making spontaneous, irregular hacking sounds (my cold has now turned into a brutal chest cough), I thought that, actually, checking out an Argentinean Oktoberfest and drinking some soothing beer might be a better option. Besides, it was way too rainy to go condor-spotting in the national park, which is what a lot of people come to Córdoba to do ... as well as paragliding.

And so it was that I, Alberto and his friend Vini, who'd last night had to be scraped off the common room floor after he'd fallen asleep on it mid-party, set off for the bus terminal to buy our tickets to a place called Villa General Belgrano. A return journey cost us about 70 pesos each and after our two-hour bus ride, during which I learned a lot about Brazil from Alberto while

Vini fell asleep again and drooled on the window curtain, we disembarked ... into a cartoon.

The small town of Villa General Belgrano is surrounded by splendiferous green hills and the houses are much like those in Pucón, all constructed of wooden panelling, only more European looking. Apparently hardly anyone visits Villa General Belgrano outside of its annual Oktoberfest because there's really not much else going on, but I for one can definitely see myself living permanently in a town that looks as though it should be popping out of a cinema screen in animated 3D graphics. Driving in, I truly felt as though Papa Smurf might just spring out from behind a giant flower and point the way to the Mushroom Ball.

In Villa General Belgrano, humongous signposts on either side of the road look as though they've been carved straight out of giant, gnarly Disney trees. The wood-panelled pub and restaurant walls appear to bend as though they might disentangle themselves from their respective floors and ceilings and make off with the trees once more. Arrows swirl with a tease before they point in the right direction and all words are in written in a font and colour so cheerful you can practically hear a children's TV presenter squealing them with enthusiasm as you read. For example, the word *lavanderia*, instead of just meaning laundry as it does everywhere else, means, 'Fabulous clothing party in fun world! Yay! Let's all go NOW!' in Villa General Belgrano.

It's just all so delightfully joyful. Even my cough forgot to bother me for a while as I took in the sights with amusement.

The town plays host to an annual beer party during the first two weeks of October because it actually models itself on Germany. This is because, after the Battle of the River Plate in

1939 (I hadn't heard of it either, don't worry), a German ship was sunk and 130 of the surviving sailors settled in the village, bringing with them the compulsory pastry, beer and chocolate recipes, probably. Honestly, it's so far removed from every other place you would ever see in Argentina that you really do feel as though you've been swept away from the country of steaks and tango and placed in the German countryside.

The only hint that Alberto, a barely conscious Vini and I were still in Argentina as we took the five-minute walk from the bus station towards the main street was the sound and smell of those alluring *choripans* served sizzling in bread rolls — with sauerkraut. Locals and tourists in teutonically kitsch felt hats and shops featuring grinning oversized gnomes on their doorsteps further assured me I was day-tripping in a cartoon mad land.

Phil Collins was playing in all the *todo artesanal* (craft) stores as I snapped photos of the fairytale atmosphere and bought some German inspired *alfajores* – those yummy chocolate covered biscuits I discovered in Buenos Aires. Both Vini and Alberto bought barrel-esque souvenir beer mugs with 'Oktoberfest 2012, Villa General Belgrano' written in Gothic script across them. Vini dropped his shortly afterwards when he tripped on a pile of discarded beer bottles underneath a lamppost and chipped the handle. But he said that it merely added to the charm and went about filling it with yet more *'Mak Bier — Brautradition seit 1959'*.

Seeing as though my cough was still lingering on the sidelines, I decided I probably shouldn't enjoy more than one beer, but the one I tried was decent enough and Vini and Alberto seemed to enjoy all of theirs. In fact, after we ate more sausages, sipped some hot wine from a steaming street-side barrel and danced to a live German band in the main square with our arms crossed and the mud splattering all over our jeans, the Brazilians decided they liked it so much in German World that they were going to stay. I'm not sure they quite got the message that the bus I was catching back to Córdoba really *was* the last one, and that they really *would* have to find somewhere else to stay without any of their belongings, but I was too tired to worry. I left them jumping up and down with their giant mugs like inebriated leprechauns and headed back to the bus station alone, eating an *alfajore* and taking a few more photos of gnomes along the way for good measure.

If you're from Europe and you're travelling through Córdoba and have had your fill of national parks, you really have to go to Villa General Belgrano and stay the night, if you can, especially if you're feeling homesick. Grab yourself a strudel and Skype your mum and, trust me, it'll be like you never left.

Oh, and if you happen to spot some dark-haired boys mooning the passersby through a window from a bunk bed, you'll know Alberto and Vini never left, either.

10/10

Maestros Ascendidos and the quartz factor...

'So why are you here?' I asked Francisco as he scraped a wooden chair across the hostel common room floor and pulled up beside me.

'I'm here for the awakening,' he told me matter-of-factly, sitting down and running his fingers through his tousled hair. I couldn't help but feel momentarily mesmerised. Ever since Jose the driver at the EcoCamp Patagonia told me about Capilla del Monte and its regular UFO sightings, I've been dying to get here and check things out myself, but nowhere in my wildest alien-hunting dreams did a hotter, younger version of David Duchovny ever feature. Here he was anyway, sitting beside me in a bulky weatherproof jacket, piercing me sporadically with dancing Argentinean eyes *and* talking about extraterrestrials. I thought I'd died and gone to heaven.

'We're going through a transition phase now. The energies are shifting,' Francisco told me as I snapped the lid of my laptop shut and gave him my full attention. 'On December ... how you say ... twenty-one, there will be an awakening. I am here to learn as much as I can from them before that happens.'

'Them?' My head was spinning. 'Who are *they*?'

He smiled, as though in on a secret I could never possibly fully understand, and leant forward on his chair. 'The *Maestros Ascendidos*,' was his soft reply.

I shivered in anticipation.

The small town of Capilla del Monte is often bypassed by backpackers heading through Argentina. It's a three-hour bus ride from Córdoba's centre, so I guess you could visit on a day trip if you wanted, but I've chosen to stay in this town for a few days. While it's a pretty nondescript place in the midst of the Sierras Chicas mountain range, its biggest hill, Cerro Uritorco, has long been Argentina's centre of paranormal phenomena.

On any given day, long-haired hippies in floaty fisherman pants gather at the base of Uritorco to chant or worship unseen forces. Many take the long hike to climb it in the hope of actually seeing 'them' and they quite often do, because inside this regular looking mountain is an ancient underground city called Erks, which is ... wait for it ...

The gateway to another dimension.

The collective curiosity of soul searchers has now turned this unremarkable little town into a spiritual hotspot. Shops are filled with rainbow crystals and dangling fairy and troll ornaments. A stroll around the streets, after I ditched my bags at the Los Tres Gomez hostel, revealed giant alien figures lingering ominously in doorways.

Posters promoting yoga and reiki sessions and lectures by various spiritual leaders are stuck to shop windows with stickers in the shape of pointy, extraterrestrial faces. It's like Roswell in Argentina, and like all good hippy towns it also smells vaguely of incense, the smoky coils of which linger enchantingly in your nostrils as you breathe in all the hype.

'The *Maestros Ascendidos* are showing us the light, we just have to listen,' Francisco continued as I leaned forward to match his body language and wished I'd worn make-up to the common room table. He really was being as mysterious as Mulder by this point. As he chattered on I couldn't fight the fantasy of us both running hand in hand towards the entrance to Erks, me in a red wig, him shouting, 'Scully! If we don't return from the fifth dimension, I want you to know, I've loved you since episode one!'

You just never know who you're going to meet when you stay in hostels, which is why I keep doing it, I suppose. It's like a drug. The next hit always has the potential to be even more fun than the last.

Francisco's staying in this hostel in Capilla del Monte while repairs are being made to his house around the corner. Looking at him, I decided he couldn't be more than thirty years old. He moved here from Buenos Aires two years ago, after a series of visions spanning seven years showed him various images of himself in a past life as a priest — a priest who was secretly unhappy with the cards life had dealt him.

'I would see myself giving orders to people, but wanting to break them, too. I wanted things that a priest shouldn't have,' he said, looking sad. He actually looked at one point as though he might cry. 'In my current life, I was in training as a yoga instructor, but when my visions got too … how you say … big, no, strong, no, emotionfull … I quit my yoga training.'

'You quit yoga training because you were a priest in your past life?' I asked.

'Yes, because the visions showed me I was just echoing my past life. If I became a yoga instructor, I would still be standing in a room telling people what to do.'

Francisco also told me that, a few weeks ago, he got the feeling he had to talk to a particular tourist he saw at the base of Uritorco, and when he did, the tourist immediately pulled up two photographs on his camera showing a sky full of lights he called UFOs (*OVNIs* in Spanish), taken the night before. The tourist claimed he hadn't seen the lights when he looked through the lens, which Francisco explained was probably because his camera was more advanced than his heart.

'You have to see things with your heart, and not your mind,' he told me, his weatherproof jacket scrunching as he folded his arms. 'We are coming into a stage of the planet's life where we'll soon be unable to deny the … how you say … forces, that are trying to show us the way to a better existence. We're all in transition. This is why there are so many wars and everyone is so angry and confused,' he told me earnestly. 'We are all tools for the energies to use. But sometimes, Becky, we need tools to become tools.'

I nodded, and was just trying to get my head around the

potential consequences of becoming a self-proclaimed tool at the gateway to another dimension in Argentina ... in a red wig ... when he pulled out the neck of his baggy jumper and produced the biggest quartz crystal I have ever seen. This six-sided prism, resplendent with six-sided pyramids at each end, was tied around his neck with a pink ribbon. It was so huge and light-absorbing I half expected the entire hostel to short-circuit and plug sockets to sizzle as he waved it about.

Clutching his tool in his fist, Francisco told me I have to be careful if I want to climb Uritorco myself. 'If the mountain doesn't want you on it, you'll soon know. It will push you off,' he said, ominously.

The whole of Capilla del Monte, including the mountain, is built on quartz, which is a highly powerful crystal known for its deep metaphysical and healing properties. It's also, apparently, a well-known tool for aiding spiritual growth, so by wearing a giant chunk of it around his neck, Francisco is channelling the energies of the *Maestros Ascendidos* directly into his body and receiving their messages. It's really quite clever. He sees their lights all the time because he's so advanced and has been through training ... training which involved sitting on a chair in his house in Buenos Aires, studying the visions of himself as a priest some 200 years ago.

Francisco has to remain fully open at all times, he says, something that's difficult to do in a chaotic city like Buenos Aires. In Capilla del Monte he has room to focus and let in the love. He learns more about the real meaning of his life every day and he'll definitely be ready for the awakening when it happens in December. In spite of this, however, he never knows when a message from the *Maestros Ascendidos* might strike and change things completely.

'It must be like getting a text message, only having it go directly to your heart instead of your phone,' I commented. Could it be that I was beginning to understand?

'That's exactly what it is,' he replied, his face a picture of tranquility as he tucked the quartz crystal safely back inside his jumper. 'As long as you're a listener, you will eventually be a receiver. Let's hug.'

'Sorry?'

'Hug me.'

He stood up, pulled me to my feet and wrapped his arms around me. 'We hug heart to heart,' he said. 'Can you feel it?'

I nodded, only marginally romanced now. Mulder never hugged Scully heart to heart until at least the fourth season. If this were an *X-Files* episode, he'd be ruining the sexual tension before it had even started to mount.

'Can you feel it?' he asked again, tightening his arms so that my face was properly squashed in his jacket. I told him I could, although, to be honest, the only thing I could feel at this point was his humongous quartz crystal digging into my boobs. Strangely, though, as I pulled away, I found I was shaking ... physically shaking all over. My hands were trembling so much I could barely grip the seat to sit back down. Weird.

'So who are the *Maestros Ascendidos*?' I ventured when I could speak again. I fully expected him to describe the pointy-faced aliens I'd seen around town. 'Have you seen them in any spaceships?'

Francisco shook his head and appeared to be struggling for words. I thought for a second that he'd been thrown, like me, by our intense physical connection, and I felt quite good about that. But then I realised his English was just not as advanced as his spiritual connection to the divine, because he pointed at my computer and started jabbering really fast in Spanish. He grabbed the Mac, lifted the lid and with furious fingers typed a URL into the search bar.

'This website will tell you everything,' he said, clicking the helpful Google Translate button so I could read it in English. 'Everything,' he repeated, in a meaningful tone.

Then, as I turned to the screen and started reading, he exhaled long and hard, like he'd just scaled Uritorco in his mind and said, 'I must go now. I am tired. I do not normally talk to people. Perhaps I will walk the mountain with you tomorrow, but I will have to see what my heart tells me to do after breakfast.'

'OK,' I whispered. And off he went, squeaking in his weatherproof jacket, surprisingly straight-backed under the weight of his quartz, leaving me to peruse a garish purple website full of articles with headers like, '"Solving Negativity: Nuances of individual and mass relations", by Archangel Metatron.'

A further image search on *Maestros Ascendidos* — or the Ascended Masters — reveals pages of what look like bearded guardian angels looking very wise in the midst of their own multi-coloured auras. Not a grey oval face or basketball sized eyeball in sight. And as for the photos Francisco says he's seen of mysterious lights around Uritorco, I still can't find too many online. Are more people really seeing things with their hearts than with their eyes these days in Capilla del Monte?

If what Francisco says is to be believed, perhaps these so-called aliens are just the concentrated positive energies we must focus on in order to be visited by the truth. And if these energies are real, is 'the truth' not so much *out there*, as it is already living inside us?

My X-heroes would investigate further. It could be time to dig out that red wig.

Tumbleweeds and the OVNI disappointment...

I made my way back to the kitchen bright and early the next morning, keen for Francisco and me to spend the day climbing Uritorco together in the sunshine.

During the night, my fantasies had spun us both through a world of tunnels and bright lights and falling in love throughout the saga of our dramatic rescue, having both been kidnapped by an evil ET. On and on went our quest, our eternal bickering on the topic of 'orbs' versus 'dust particles catching the sun', our lovemaking in different dimensions, right through to the movie version that would eventually be made about our life together, living in a house made of quartz, on a mountain.

But alas, Francisco's chair was now empty. And so were the rest, except for one, filled by a girl reading a *Lonely Planet*. Perhaps Francisco's heart had told him that my head was full of ridiculous notions and he'd gone back to hang out with the *Maestros Ascendidos*, or to receive more messages from his past self on his own.

I ate my bread (a loaf of which was the only thing on offer on the breakfast table — typical here in South America), drank my obligatory bitter, hostel coffee and pondered what to do. Perhaps he'd show up in a little bit … but then, he had told me that the energies on Uritorco were more powerful in the early morning and, if we were going to go, it would have to be at this time.

I buttered some more bread and started idle chit chat with the *Lonely Planet* reader, an Israeli girl, who told me she'd seen Francisco driving away earlier with a dog poking out of his car window and a bag of sandwiches. *Dammit.*

Still, resolving to do what Mulder or Scully would do without the other, I decided to make my way to Uritorco and go alien hunting alone. The Israeli girl had climbed some of the mountain the day before and said it was difficult and that I should probably change my shoes. Granted, black knee-high boots (albeit waterproof flat ones bought during a rain storm in Buenos Aires) probably aren't ideal footwear in these situations, even if Dana Scully endured all manner of tricky situations wearing heels.

So, I headed back to the dorm to put my muddy North Face trainers on, and this was when a robust woman in her mid-fifties emerged from the bathroom with her toothbrush hanging out of her mouth and told me that if I was planning to climb the mountain I was welcome to go with her.

Sylvia from Salta (where I'll be going next), chattered happily in broken English about her reason for being in Capilla del Monte as we walked the three kilometres to the base of Uritorco. She's here with a group of people from all over Argentina who worship the deceased spiritual healer Graciela Busto, and regularly make pilgrimages in his name.

Graciela Busto wrote a series of books while he was alive, one of which was called *Conversations with God* (not the similarly titled *Conversations With God: An Uncommon Dialogue* by Neale Walsch, which is a true inspiration, by the way — you must read it), and he was a legend for thousands of people. Sylvia pulled out a photo of him in his prime, standing at a podium in an orange smock, sporting a huge, black frizzy hairstyle. After she kissed it, she told me that she and a bunch of Graciela Busto worshippers she had only ever spoken to online were planning to gather at the base of the mountain and chant some special prayers in accordance with his teachings. Later in the afternoon they were also going to sit in a temple and hold hands for a while.

'I love him, I love him, I love him,' she kept on saying, gesturing to the sky. Judging by what I could save from being lost in translation, Sylvia also believes in the healing energies that are concentrated around this mountain. She, too, mentioned quartz and its power to enhance the feeling of love, an emotion she appears to feel especially strongly when she's in this town … unless it's normal for Sylvia to walk around kissing photos and telling the sky she loves it.

I'd like to say the four-hour walk up the mountain with Sylvia was one of intellectual conversation, of sharing conspiracy theories mixed with the odd sighting of a UFO, but in all honesty it was a rather boring, rather sweaty, rather uncomfortable trek up a brown hill that Scully definitely could have done in heels, and that I could only just about manage in my trainers. No one talked to me, either, probably because, in spite of my continuous efforts and definite improvement, my Spanish is in no way up to conversing with people about extraterrestrial visitations and the metaphysical healing properties of mountainous terrain.

When we got to the top, we looked at the view for a bit, which was quite nice, I suppose, but really nothing compared to what Autumn and I had seen in Torres del Paine and Tierra del Fuego. And then we walked back down again.

When Sylvia and her new friends headed off to their temple, I decided to go back into town and find the Centro de Informes OVNI (UFO Information Centre). I had some questions, mainly involving why I hadn't seen any. I turned up in a dusty side street to find the 'centre' was actually someone's house, complete with a huge billboard outside featuring a hovering spacecraft. It looked normal enough, not at all like you might expect a house of extraterrestrial purpose to look, which of course made me even more intrigued.

I rang the bell beside a locked gate, fully expecting a geek in round-rimmed glasses with unwashed hair to emerge in an 'I Want To Believe' T-shirt, but there was nothing and no one. I peered across the railings and saw a giant green inflatable alien staring at the garden from the porch. Pretty flowers danced in the wind. A tumbleweed in the form of a discarded plastic bag floated past in the breeze, but there were still no humans in sight. I rang again. Still no answer. I can't say I was really surprised, though.

I've noticed since arriving in this town that Capilla del Monte is the kind of place in which the afternoon siesta seems to last all day. Shops and restaurants seem to be open from 10 a.m. till noon and then again after roughly 8 p.m. During the day, packs of street dogs roam around in large numbers and, as you're generally the only person outside during daylight, they tend to all gather round you and follow you wherever you go, causing you to feel like some sort of powerful Pied Piper, with an iPod instead of a flute. It's kind of cool. I led my K9 crew round the block twice and into a park, and did a little bit of a dance, which made them jump and wag their tails. Then I realised I probably looked weird and stopped. *Then* I realised that this is probably what happens to people who stay in Capilla del Monte too long.

Defeated and resigned to the fact that I was not going to find out any more information regarding UFOs or the *Maestros Ascendidos*, I wandered back (followed by a silky-haired spaniel cross, and later, a friend of hers) to one of only a few places I knew would be open, the Valpisa Rock and Pizza. This gargantuan restaurant spanning half a block appears to model itself on the Hard Rock Cafe, but as I sank into a booth with red plastic seats and ordered a *vino tinto* with yet more Adele blasting into my ears from a speaker, it felt more like dining in an empty stadium. It was one of those lonely travelling moments when everything's just a bit shit, to be honest.

On the way to the bus station, bound for Córdoba once more with my worldly belongings in the back of a taxi, I told the driver of my disappointment at not seeing any *Maestros Ascendidos*, or OVNIs. When I mentioned how I didn't even get to look inside the Centro de Informes OVNI, he shot me a sympathetic look and promptly pulled the car over to the curb. Before I even had a chance to ask him what he was doing, he'd whipped out a photo from the glove box showing Uritorco in the grainy moonlight. Beside it, to the right, almost too far away to tell but not too far away for it not to be possible, was a metallic-looking hovering disc.

'OVNI!' he proclaimed proudly. 'I have see *quatro* time!'

I haven't seen anything out of the ordinary myself in Capilla del Monte, except Francisco's unfathomably large quartz adornment and, now, the taxi driver's photo, which could of course be showing nothing more than a reflection from a llama farmer's flashlight. But I learned in Bali that 'there are more things in heaven and earth, Horatio, than are dreamt of in your philosophy', and there are clearly more things in Argentina than I thought possible, too. And if anyone's looking for their answer to Fox Mulder now that the *X-Files* is off-air, his sexy, disheveled, truth-seeking counterpart is very much alive and well here ... somewhere. He doesn't have a job at the moment, I don't think. But he used to be a priest.

An escape to the English countryside ...

When I was at school, my best friend Claire had a pony. I've forgotten his name but I used to call him Poo Bum, because he always had a constant trickle of shit running out of his behind. Apparently it was a medical condition that no amount of drugs from the vet would fix, but Claire loved that shitty-bummed pony like I loved my first Kylie album and first edition Game Boy.

Every Saturday morning I would accompany Claire to the field where Poo Bum lived and watch as she lovingly brushed his mane and tail, and then tacked him up and went riding. I was fascinated. As they trotted off over the hill leaving me swinging on the gate, a beacon in pink humming 'Especially For You', I would watch them in admiration and envy, and wonder when I would become a horsewoman myself. I waited a long time. Until now.

When my car pulled into Estancia Los Potreros — an impressive, sprawling Argentinean expanse of green fields and grazing horses that gives guests the chance to ride and get involved in *estancia* life — the vision before me was fresh from the pages of a Jane Austen novel. The sun was shining, the sky was blue and I instantly felt re-energised. Handsome, *young* gauchos (finally!) in neckerchiefs and flat caps leaned on fences, parakeets squawked in the trees, guides in jodhpurs carried tack, dogs barked and wagged their tails, horses whinnied, chickens pecked at the grass, and Kevin and Louisa Begg, the *estancia*'s king and queen, greeted me in matching berets (or *boinas*, as is the correct name) carrying a glass of lemonade on a silver tray. It was paradise after a few too many Quilmes beers the night before ...

I'd walked into the Mate Hostel in Córdoba, having returned late from Capilla del Monte, to the roar of a group of roughly twenty Brazilian men singing some sort of soccer chant in front of a giant projector screen. In the dorm I found Mike, a bald-headed, tattoo-splattered man from Scotland, travelling alone till 2015 for reasons he did not divulge. Mike was lounging on a beanbag, swigging from a bottle of Quilmes, streaming a movie on the impossibly slow Internet connection and cursing every time it paused and churned.

On noticing that I wasn't about to get any sleep any time soon, I did what any other normal, solo travelling female would do. I invited Mike out for dinner.

Over plates of fried chicken and chips in a street-side cafe off Plaza San Martin, Mike told me all about his two marriages, his stint in the army and the following years he spent packing boxes in cold food factories. Swigging yet more Quilmes, he talked at length about his lesbian daughter's six-year marriage and the fact that he was stopped at customs in Bolivia for having the cremated remains of his two dead bulldogs in a vitamin jar in his suitcase. It was an interesting night. I was a little bit afraid of going to sleep in the dorm with Mike in there too once we got back, so eventually I did what I'd been trying to avoid in the first place: sat up in the lounge with the Brazilians and drank some Quilmes. And then I drank some more Quilmes.

So, justifiably I was knackered when I arrived at Estancia Los Potreros, but thankfully I was in good hands and just ten minutes after Winnie had been hauled into the gloriously maintained, 300-year-old farmhouse, I was sitting at the dining room table with the other guests, tucking into bacon and eggs. Shortly after *that*, I was saddled up on a horse, playing polo for the first time in my life.

Estancia Los Potreros, a 6500-acre organic working cattle farm with roughly 120 horses and 600 adult Aberdeen Angus cows, dates back to 1574, when mules were bred in the hills around Córdoba for the silver mining work in Peru. In the last century, the mules have been replaced by cattle, and four generations of Kevin's Argentinean family have been running it for just under 100 years. The snow white buildings with their red corrugated roofs, surrounded by immaculate green lawns that by all rights should be hosting bowling championships between large-skirted ladies and men in top hats, reminded me of an England that hasn't been seen in a very long time. English accents sounded out at every turn. Kevin Begg, as it happens, while Argentinean, was educated in England, and Louisa is proud to be a Hampshire girl.

I love a good love story, so I was intrigued to learn how the two met. An article from *National Geographic Traveller*, handed to me proudly over the table by Louisa (much to Kevin's chagrin), details how sparks flew between them after Louisa came for a holiday at the *estancia* in 2005. She was supposed to go back home and start a job at a services company, but after meeting Kevin, fate had other ideas. A series of emails followed, a holiday to Ireland came next, and within days, Kevin proposed. Six weeks later, Louisa had packed her bags and moved to Argentina, where they've run the *estancia* together ever since. Aww.

They were married in 2007. Kevin told me that, afterwards, he wanted to use the bridal gown fabric for horse ankle wrappings so they could get even more wear out of the expensive dress, but apparently Louisa said no. I'm still not sure if he was joking.

Anyway, I should tell you here, owning a fake Ted Baker polo shirt is the closest I've ever come to involving myself in polo. Louisa is a champion, though — one of the few female players in Argentina and the proud owner of numerous awards.

I was terrified of hitting my poor horse about the head with an overzealous swing as I trotted across the field aiming for the ball, but surprisingly I did manage to strike the ball a good few times without injuring anyone. It was one of the most fun things I've ever done!

It didn't take long to realise that the way people ride in Argentina is very different from how they do at home. There's none of that fannying about trying to hold the reins correctly with both hands, none of that struggling to sit up as straight as possible while obeying an uptight instructor barking on about posture. Basically, in Argentina you just climb on, hold the reins in one hand straight out in front of you, kick, and you're off. You ride like the gauchos do, which is to say you do what you want, as long as you don't fall off. The saddles are huge and covered in comfy sheepskin, too. It's all about comfort, seeing as gauchos have to spend so long on horseback.

At Estancia Los Potreros we rode out twice every day on huge treks. I cantered, too, for the first time ever. Bursts of wild mint, sage and rosemary assaulted our nostrils as we made our way through thick, yellow grass, past lush blooms of purple and red spring flowers. We kept our eyes open for wild boar, foxes, hares, condors and the elusive puma while we were at it, although, as in Torres del Paine, it's really rare to spot a puma here. Before long the Quilmes hangover (and Mike's cremated bulldogs) seemed like a distant dream.

We rode mostly Criollos and Paso Peruanos, which are different from any other horse, so I'm told, because they can walk at the speed at which most other horses canter, in a funny sort of hurried step that feels smoother than trotting. I felt so safe on my horse that I even helped to round up some horses grazing in the distant fields on my last night. Me — a real live gaucho girl —

and the other guests cantered across the plains, driving the other horses through gate after gate and finally into the paddock behind the farmhouse. I never felt so confident around Poo Bum ... so maybe I always just needed to come to Argentina!

During meal times we sat around the communal dining table for hours on end and heard all about Kevin and Louisa's most interesting past guests, like the eccentric man they discovered hadn't slept in his bed for three nights. On asking if there was a problem with his bed, he replied that he'd been sleeping on the floor to keep the resident cat, Rosita, company. Bizarre. You'd better be good when you visit, otherwise you'll be talked about over dinner, too. And you'd be wise to get along with cats as well.

I learned a lot about the gauchos. They're put on horses when they're just babies, so they grow up fearless. Louisa told me about one kid, no older than seven, she saw riding bareback at a show recently. I can vouch for the fact that these gauchos are like no species of man you'll find anywhere else. They're absolutely amazing to watch in action.

On my first day I was riding a twenty-year-old horse that plodded along with me on it like a camel the entire time — no doubt chosen to keep me safe. But as soon as the resident gaucho Daniel got on, it turned into a wild, youthful stallion again, bucking and galloping across the grass at lightning speed as he competed in the weekly gaucho games. These were fun, by the way — try hooking a stick through a dangling loop from the back of a moving horse. I couldn't, obviously, but the gauchos can do it pretty much blindfolded, with their feet not even in the stirrups. It's enough to make you drool on your chin strap.

When Deb and Chris, a lovely couple from the UK, had to leave on my second day, we all waved them off at the gate like they were family members, and Deb cried as she was driven

Gauchos in action at Estancia Los Potreros.

away, waving her hanky out of the window and promising to be back soon as she had started her own polo club back at home. I was surprised I didn't wail when I had to leave myself — there's definitely something magical about this place. Estancia Los Potreros is in the guidebooks but, being a bit expensive, it's listed as a treat. You'll also visit the *estancia* as part of an overland tour through Argentina if you go with the company Dragoman, but with that group, while you'll get to ride, you won't get to stay in the farmhouse. You'll pitch tents around Kevin and Louisa's house, taste fine wines in their dining room and do things a more rustic way, which, to be honest, would probably be just as great. It's such a beautiful place that however you work it into your trip, it's going to be amazing.

As I myself was driven away, I thanked Kevin and Louisa profusely. I might not ever be a proper horsewoman, wandering around the house in jodhpurs with a whip, smelling of fresh hay and saying things like 'tally ho!', but I think I've come as close as I ever will to living the hot gaucho-riddled *estancia* life that most women can only ever dream of.

18/10

Travelling economy minus …

It's kind of hit and miss getting the buses here in South America, although I'm hesitant to complain out loud because people I meet keep telling me that no matter how shit you might think your bus is, it's nothing compared to the kind of ride you're going to get in Bolivia, or Peru.

'Just you wait,' they say, with an ominous glint in their eyes, which makes me shudder, because sometimes, short of putting a herd of pigs on the top deck and having them flick their filthy tails in my face all night while crapping in the aisle, I don't see how travelling by bus can get much worse.

Let's talk about buses.

I just paid the equivalent of AU$50 for my Córdoba to Salta journey and, seeing as I took the same class bus with the exact same company from Buenos Aires to Iguazu Falls (Andesmar) not long ago, I was expecting some modicum of comfort and safety. However, before I got on at the bus station, I was patted down behind a man who, having had the same thing done to him, had had a gun taken away and retained.

I saw another man boarding the bus with a machete, which apparently was allowed, unlike the gun, and he sat there holding it, eyes darting, as though at any moment he might be forced to use it.

You can go one class up, if you want, which I did with Autumn from Buenos Aires to Mendoza. It's a lot more expensive (I think almost $100 for that one), but it's worth it at least once for the experience. The best bus, the premium kind, allows for soft, padded, leather seats that mould to your bum cheeks and recline all the way back. Literally *all* the way back, so you're basically in bed on a bus.

These premium buses also feature personal TV screens on the seat-backs with a host of movies in different languages, wi-fi (which admittedly doesn't always work) and smiley men who can't do enough for you, coming around every thirty minutes or so with a drinks trolley starring wine and champagne. Your food arrives in large steaming portions with those exciting peel-back lids, so dinner is always a fun surprise. It's generally chicken and rice of some sort, followed by an unfathomably sweet dessert, usually topped with a dollop of *dulce de leche* and served with a shot of whisky, or more wine to ensure you beat that sugar buzz and pass out, comfortably numb.

On our premium-class ride from Santiago to Pucón, Autumn and I even got a game of bingo. A short guy with a fashionable mullet (I guess you could call him the entertainment coordinator) had stood at the front in his shiny waistcoat, grinning maniacally, enthusing into a mic and generally trying his hardest to make people excited about the twisty-turny ten- to twelve-hour journey that lay ahead. We couldn't really play because our Spanish numbers weren't embedded in our brains deep enough to follow as fast as we needed to, but it lightened the mood and, one would hope, made any secret machete-carriers feel a little less angry about being on board.

When I boarded this time, weary from my stay at the aforementioned Mate Hostel, with my head full of *Maestros Ascendidos* and still aching from the horse riding, I was disappointed to find my seat was not only *not* made of leather, but that it resembled a filthy seat on the London underground — one of the ones that are still covered in fabric and therefore hiding twenty kinds of human piss, sperm and rat's feces (this has been proven with tests, I read it in the *Metro*). I sat down cautiously, wondering if the little bingo man in the waistcoat would hurry by and tell me I was in the wrong seat and that my comfy leather one was on another level. Then, when he didn't show up I tried to recline the seat I was in, only to find it was stuck.

I should have known it wasn't going to be a classy journey when the bus pulled up at the terminal in Córdoba, actually. The windows looked like they hadn't been washed for a month. When I got on, two children in the seats opposite mine were prodding at a goldfish in water, inside a plastic drink bottle. While watching the poor fish slowly lose its will to live, I struggled to find the most comfortable position in my dirty seat, just as a large, buxom woman in her fifties, with shimmering blue eye-shadow and red lipstick, settled herself next to me, and gently reclined. Grrr.

I noticed from her profile as she played with her phone that, thanks to all her make-up, she looked a bit like a clown. I was afraid of her, not least because when someone you don't know takes an aisle seat of any kind next to you, you're going to have to ask to climb over them at some point, and there's nothing more awkward than climbing over a stranger at very close range in a moving vehicle, never mind one who looks like a scary clown.

Shortly after we set off, the TV screen flickered into life and I found myself quite excited at the prospect of a movie. When they start the movies on these buses, they usually serve the drinks and food. I readjusted my travel pillow and waited, looking all around me for the fold-down tray but failing to locate it.

A movie called *Ricky* came on. It was French with Spanish subtitles. Worse than that, it appeared to be a serious drama about a baby boy with chicken wings sprouting out of his shoulders. I sat there, pondering the highs and lows of birthing a flying baby, listening to French accents mingle with Spanish as the people on board, most of whom were clearly too far away from a screen to be able to read the subtitles, started calling their friends on their phones. The drinks trolley still hadn't come. Perhaps they're just waiting till a bit later, I thought.

It got to 11 p.m. My stomach was growling, I really needed a wee, my mouth was parched, *Ricky* had long finished but I could no longer ask the clown if I could climb over her, because she was asleep. I switched on my Kindle and started reading *The Gringo Trail* to take my mind off things. The guys in this book (an hilarious account of travelling South America) always get themselves into sillier situations, so I thought perhaps the words would soothe me to sleep. I was just getting into another tale when I noticed a strange noise coming from the clown. She wasn't snoring. Rather, as she slept, her red-painted lips were pressing together and releasing as though she was blowing up an invisible balloon and I watched for a moment, baffled. This blowing motion then grew faster and started to incorporate her tongue, resulting in a half lip-smacking, half hissing sort of sound —like Anthony Hopkins in *Silence of the Lambs*.

Was she making out with some sexy guy in her own mind? Was she alone in her tasty little dream world, eating a chocolate ice-cream? Either way, her night-time soliloquy was deeply unsettling, so I put *The Gringo Trail* away and fished out my iPod. Luckily I had all of this to hand because people always tell you never to put your bags in the overhead shelves on buses, no matter what class of journey you've paid for. On a bright note, you can always reach your gadgets when you need them. On a not so bright note, due to the lack of room beneath the seats, this usually means you're trying to sleep with your legs scrunched up on top of your rucksack.

At some point, with my head crumpled into the travel pillow and my knees up around my chest, I managed to drift off. When I woke up, my iPod shuffle had decided to play Disney's *Tangled* soundtrack, which I thought was quite appropriate, seeing as I was now so contorted I could have, once disentangled, run away with the clown to the circus. She was awake now, tapping into her phone again, her red-lipstick cracked and dry and fading. I wanted to ask her what she'd been dreaming about but decided it would be way too much effort, plus I didn't want to hurt her feelings with the suggestion she sleeps like Hannibal Lecter.

The food and drink never came. I've never taken a bus ride in Argentina or Chile where at least *some* kind of sustenance hasn't been shoved at my sleeping body, but we got no snacks, no water and definitely no bingo. I'm not entirely sure why this particular Andesmar bus ride was so different, but when I finally stepped off in Salta, tired, angry, hungry, thirsty and even more afraid of clowns than ever, it was not a moment too soon.

Getting buses here is part of the adventure, I should add. And it's inevitable that you're going to have to take a lot, as the continent is just too great (and expensive) to fly everywhere. I shouldn't moan, really. But just you try and stay perky after your fifteenth, long-haul overland journey in a row.

I should tell you, too, leave the goldfish, guns and machetes at home, but do bring a whole lot of patience, a good book, some snacks, a travel pillow, a sense of humour and quite possibly your own secret stash of tequila.

19/10

Inca kids, frogs with shells and a Dangerous Bitch ...

I've never really been into mummies. Seeking out the withering remains of some ancient human wrapped in cloth is not my idea of a good time. But a guy I met in Córdoba told me that if I was coming to Salta I should visit the Museo de Arqueología de Alta Montaña (MAAM), which houses three perfectly mummified Inca kids. He said that one look at these Llullaillaco children would change my mind and I'd start to look at mummies with new eyes.

I doubted it. In fact, I wondered if he was the sort of person who works in an old people's home and practises weird things with bandages in the middle of the night. But still, knackered from my bus ride, I decided a trip any further than the town centre was out of the question, so I headed down there to the museum yesterday to check these mummies out.

Salta itself seems a fairly sizeable city. I'm here because it's on my route north towards Bolivia. It has a nice colonial centre with a pink cathedral in a square surrounded by cafes, plenty of ice-cream eating opportunities and free wi-fi. You can buy un-toasted tostadas in perfect triangles absolutely everywhere, and a lot of bad neon clothing, too, but that's about it, by the looks of things.

At the museum, I paid my 40 pesos and was led to a dark room in which several very informative boards in English, surrounded by various artifacts, detailed old Inca rituals. They explained how the three kids were discovered in 1999 when a group of scientists stumbled upon a hidden temple at the summit of the Llullaillaco volcano. The children had been preserved perfectly by the freezing temperatures up there.

The museum has in its care a fifteen-year-old 'maiden', a six-year-old girl who's since been damaged Harry Potter style by a rogue lightning bolt, and a seven-year-old boy. You can see photos of their hunched and twisted bodies, revealing eerily perfect skin, before you even arrive at the glass case.

Apparently these poor kids were all fed some sort of strange potion and died in their sleep, whereupon they were sacrificed to act as mediators between the Inca people and the gods.

I looked at the seven-year-old for a while, his head tucked between his knees, wearing his red funerary clothing, a white feather headdress on his forehead. I wondered what sort of parent would think it acceptable to poison their own child and leave him on the top of a volcano. It would never be allowed now. It made me feel a bit sad.

Anyway, short of looking at the mummified boy, there wasn't much else to do in the museum, aside from stare at a few photos of mountains in the Salta Province. Plus, all the English signs seemed to stop after the section with the mummies, as though the museum staff couldn't be bothered to translate any more. I got an ice-cream, walked back to the hostel and paid 380 pesos for a day-long trip to Cafayate. Which brings me to now. I've just got back. I'm exhausted.

You must go to Cafayate, said ... well, most people I've talked to who've been in this area of Argentina. 'The wine is so good and it's so pretty!'

I'll go anywhere for wine, as you know, and I was quite excited when the minivan pulled up at 7.30 a.m to collect me. It had to come early as it takes three hours to get to this wine-lover's paradise from Salta City, and another three to get back. I was also looking forward to seeing the limestone hills morph into the ochre-colored canyons and rocky arches of Quebrada de Cafayate along the way — supposedly some of the most impressive rock formations in the world.

Just before we set off, however, I was asked to leave the front seat of the minivan to allow a Colombian girl wearing a pink travel pillow around her neck to take my place. The other people on the bus were old. As you know, I love old people, they have lots of stories, but these people were so old they seemed to have lost the ability to talk. To me, anyway. I pulled out my Kindle but soon realised why I'd been asked to vacate my seat. No sooner had we set off than we were swerving to stop again at the side of the road and the Colombian, still with the travel pillow round her neck, was emptying the contents of her stomach onto the red gravel outside. Eventually her boyfriend climbed out and stood behind her, patting her on the back kind of awkwardly as she splattered another cactus.

Off we set again, through ever-changing spectacular scenery. It was obvious we had a tight schedule to adhere to and having someone needing to vomit every ten minutes was clearly not in our driver Bernardo's plan. Bernardo (also our tour guide) chattered away merrily, although as usual the non-Spanish speakers got the basic English explanations, such as 'this landscape has many cactus plants and red rock', whereas the Spanish-speaking old people were treated to a full historic run down and timeline of the Quebrada de Cafayate, complete with personal stories about his family, friends and pets, probably.

It doesn't matter how much my Spanish is improving as I

travel, when people speak really fast, it's so hard to keep up. These days I generally get the gist of a conversation and end up filling in the gaps with my own imaginings. Often I'll be so engrossed in my own idea of how, say, a man gesturing to the sky used to be an award-winning acrobat, or a pilot in Pakistan, that I'll forget he's only probably talking about rain, or leaves falling off trees.

When we stopped to look at some seriously gargantuan cactuses and some nice luminous red cliffs, I noticed that one of the old women was wearing an off-the-shoulder T-shirt with the words 'Dangerous Bitch' on it. She'd accompanied this with some diamante-studded thongs and was chain smoking at a rate that would put a chimney to shame.

When she finished her cigarettes she would simply flick them onto the ground, whereupon her husband — I'm assuming he was her husband — would bend down and pick them up. She even giggled at him doing it, as if to say, 'Oops, I forgot *again* that I wasn't supposed to do that.'

With all the desert dryness around us, she really was a Dangerous Bitch.

Next up, we stopped to see some llamas tied to a tree, which appeared to belong to three old women selling black cooking pots and bowls by the side of the road. Bernardo took huge delight in showing us a kissy pose beside the llamas, which we all copied instantly, and the poor things then found themselves at the centre of a paparazzi frenzy as we smooched them.

Both were cute with the thickest, woolliest, craziest, dirtiest hair I've ever seen on any living creature. Seriously, to get the sticks and twigs embedded into that fleece out, you'd need an industrial strength vacuum cleaner and *lots* of patience. I don't know how they make so many clothes from llama wool. Actually, I suspect the reason llama wool jumpers are so expensive is not

This guy had wonky teeth and bad breath. But he did have great hair.

because of the quality, but because it takes the average lady half of her entire, precious life to get the crap out of the source material.

When we were all back in the van, more fag ends had been collected and the Colombian had finally stopped spraying the scenery with her vomit, Bernardo said suddenly, 'They found some frogs with shells in the lake'.

'Frogs with shells?' I repeated. This was good news, as I was getting a little bored. There are only so many cactuses and old people you can surround yourself with before things get a little dry. 'That's AMAZING! When did frogs with shells die out? I never knew they existed.'

'Yes, many years ago. When the lake was a lake. Now it is a river.' Bernardo pointed out of the window at a sinewy river, winding its way between the craggy cliffs and cacti.

'But frogs with shells living anywhere is incredible,' I continued.

'Ah, I mean fossil,' Bernardo said then. 'Not shell. They find fossil frog.'

'Oh.' I sank back in my seat. So much for that.

When we finally reached the town centre of Cafayate, we were attacked as soon as we got off the bus in the main plaza by a guy waving a flier for a 45-peso lunch in our faces.

'Very good place, very good food,' Bernardo said, nodding enthusiastically. Not knowing of anywhere else in the vicinity and feeling rather hot and hungry, most of us sat down at a sidewalk table at his recommendation and ordered. And then wished we hadn't. What proceeded to arrive was probably the worst food I've ever been served, and that's no exaggeration. My meal of indeterminable meat, allegedly a *milanesa*, looked like a slab of dirty carpet. It was even gritty, like it had actually been used as a doormat before being slapped on my plate.

The Dutch girl on our tour, who'd humoured a starter of two folded slices of packet, economy-style sandwich ham, was given a salad for her main dish that consisted of just six sliced tomatoes and a boiled egg. I told the waiters that all of it was terrible and that I didn't think we should pay for what was clearly a tourist scam, at which point they laughed. One guy even said '*bueno*', before whisking my untouched plate away. The cheek!

To be fair, they didn't charge me, but everyone else paid. I felt a bit bad about that but, really, there's enduring a bad meal for the sake of being polite, and there's being served a dirty carpet tile. The moral, I guess, is beware of spruikers.

The Dutch girl was out for revenge. When she came back from the loo, she said, 'I threw my paper in the toilet, 'cause they deserve it.'

We all smiled smugly. That'll teach them. You're not supposed to flush toilet paper in toilets in these parts. Although, in fairness, a blockage might actually cause a flood or an outbreak of typhoid, so I wouldn't recommend you do this anywhere you've been told not to.

We all made Bernardo promise he'd never take people there again, but I have a sneaking suspicion he may have enjoyed a fine *asado* of succulent steaks with the staff out back, while we were picking bits of grit from our teeth on the sidewalk.

Regarding what Cafayate is so famous for — wine — we got to sip three tiny thimbles of it at the Bodegas El Transito after 'lunch'. The lady who hurried us around the barrels and explained the ways of the winery in about five minutes later told me she did ten tours a day. At one point, she even yawned.

It was such a long day for all of us. I'm not sure what was more disturbing in the end, the mummified child, the chain smoking Dangerous Bitch or the gritty *milanesa*, but I've signed up for another tour tomorrow nonetheless — to the little mountain city of Purmamarca. Let's hope the slice of carpet tile I braved doesn't repeat on me, or it'll be me vomming on the cactus plants in the morning instead.

20/10

Salt and battery ...

As I type, I'm sitting at a tapestry-covered table with salsa music blaring. There's only one plug in the entire reception area, so I'm taking my 'turn' to charge my computer. Opposite, I can see the Mama Coca Hostel manager smoking while bashing at a laptop, and a glass display cabinet featuring rocks and Andean relics against the wall. I'm not sure if the relics are real but it wouldn't surprise me as I'm in Purmamarca, a tiny Andean 'city', sitting in the beautiful glow of the Cerro de los Siete Colores (Hill of the Seven Colours).

The mountains I can see from the window are a number of colours; I'm guessing way more than seven, thanks to the varying mineral content in the rock walls. Hues of pink, orange, green and red swept into wispy layers by the hands of time have formed what look to me like Cadbury's Flakes set on their sides. It keeps distracting me from my screen. Mmm, chocolate.

I'm pretty far north in Argentina right now, making my way, as I am, up to the border at La Quiaca in order to cross into Bolivia. I got today's tour bus to leave me here instead of going back down to Salta. I figured this way I might meet some more happy travellers going in the same direction.

Purmamarca, from what I've witnessed so far, consists of the odd tourist wandering aimlessly about looking for something to do, and little old ladies selling handicrafts in colourful ponchos and top hats. The name of the town is a combination of the Aymara words *purma*, meaning desert, and *marca*, meaning city, which is pretty apt, although it's barely big enough to be called a hamlet, let alone a city. I really love it, though. It feels powerful somehow.

Every now and then a huge gust of wind will gush down from up high and whip the ground into a frenzy, making you think a tornado has struck. Everyone stops in their tracks to pull their clothes over their faces and, for a second, everything freezes like it's been paused by a remote control. Everything is so dusty, too. Forget wearing contact lenses.

Before arriving here, I took another tour from Salta. This one involved yet more time on a bus en route to Salinas Grandes,

Argentina's famed salt flats. We drove through more cactus-riddled scenery, gawping at swirling mini sand tornadoes around every corner. It was yet another arse-numbing journey that was so bumpy I feared my buttocks would be battered black and blue by the end of it. Our driver Jorge spoke way more English than Bernardo did, however, and I also made friends with a delightful couple in their late sixties from Wisconsin who've been travelling to amazing places all their lives and raised their youngest child on a US airbase in Germany. Hearing their stories made things a bit more interesting. And thankfully there were no travel sick Colombians hogging the front seat and forcing us to stop every ten minutes.

Today's most entertaining passenger, though, was a French man. I followed him down the steps of the van to admire a sight called Tres Cruces (basically, three nice rocks) and saw that his bum crack was fully visible above his slack trousers. He was clearly wearing no underpants. He tried to cover up this fact by yanking his trousers up quickly but by the sheepish look he shot me at the bottom of the steps I knew he knew that I knew. It changed things. At lunch I had to sit next to him, which was awkward.

Lunch was a beetroot, carrot, lettuce and tomato salad with olive oil (they're not big on fancy salads in Argentina) in a teeny-weeny town called San Antonia de los Cobres. After we ate, I went for a walk and met a sprightly 87-year-old lady called Lia who posed for a photo and then sold me a llama — a toy llama, I should add, although it was covered in real llama hair. This cost me twenty pesos, which I thought was a fair deal, until I found out that the man with no pants on had bought one for ten.

Moving on, we stopped to take photos of the Cuesta del Lipán (the Corridor to Chile), which is an impressive sinewy road that winds though the province of Jujuy, and from a distance reminded me of my brother Simon's old Scalextric race track. As we drove on around giant hills constructed of what appeared to be brownish gravel, I felt like an ant who'd crawled into the bottom of a jar of gravy granules, although I also noticed a heap of human detritus cluttering up the landscape here in numerous places. It was mostly plastic bottles, which I thought was a shame.

Once we reached the Salinas Grandes we were blessed with a slightly longer stop, a whole thirty minutes. Roughly twenty of these were spent in the vicinity of the toilet, because I was asked to pay two pesos to have my pee in a porta-cabin. Not having anything smaller, I apologised and gave the man in charge a 100 peso bill, thinking he'd probably let me off. He didn't and I waited fifteen minutes with my legs crossed while he scrambled around all over the place collecting change.

I was then free to use my new toy llama as a model on the salt flats, which were really quite striking: as cracked and dry as parched lips in the desert. I think the look of these places depends on the time of year you visit, though. People keep telling me Salinas Grandes is not as good as Salar de Uyuni in Bolivia and, if I'm totally honest, I saw a much prettier, less cracked and whiter salt flat in South Australia a couple of years ago in the Gawler Ranges. That one is so dazzling they film car commercials and movies set in cold places there because it looks so much like ice. It's much better. Call me a salt flat snob but there you have it.

You feel quite small when you're standing on Salinas Grandes. Clouds linger on distant hills like fluffy albino llamas, giving the whole place a rather dreamlike quality. I imagined a whopping great Monty Python foot coming down from the sky and hovering over me as I used my remaining few minutes to walk around the turquoise-coloured pools of water that occurred in places where the salt had been dug up. It was quite exhausting just walking about, thanks to the altitude. There are 6000 km^2 of salt flats here at Salinas Grandes at an altitude of some 3600 metres. Salar de Uyuni in Bolivia has 10,582 km^2 at an even higher altitude.

The giant heaps of salt laid out in rows ready for export (for cows, so we were told) looked to me a bit like the world's longest lines of cocaine for giants. I saw the no-pants French man getting his photo taken on top of one of them looking particularly joyful, and wondered whether he'd forgotten his pants because his mind had been racing too far ahead on another white substance that morning.

There's a small building made of salt on the site the tours all stop at, which was originally intended to be a restaurant, but, according to Jorge, it got rained on, and it melted. We saw it. It's only been partly rebuilt. It makes me worry a bit about the salt hotels you get to stay in for the night when you do the Uyuni tour. A quick change in weather and you could very well go to sleep in a hostel bed and wake up in a wet, sticky, freezing pool of water. Let's hope it's not the wrong season when we do that one.

Anyway, I have to pack up now, not only because my poor battered bum cheeks are hurting even more from sitting on a rock hard hostel chair, but because the lovely couple from Wisconsin have invited me for dinner at a restaurant near their hotel and apparently we can eat llama. I'm thinking why not? I've kissed one, bought a tiny toy one covered in real llama hair — why the hell not ingest one, too, and let it roam free-range around my intestines? Ah, Argentina. I'm going to miss you when I make it over that border.

24/10

Fifty shades of everything ...

Shortly after I returned from a dinner of llama meat with creamy mashed potatoes covered in grilled goat's cheese with my new friends from the tour group, I met Leandro. He was hanging out in the courtyard of the Mama Coca Hostel with a bunch of his Argentinean friends and two Germans.

We all got chatting and, thankfully, the slow, monocled hunchback who governs my dusty, musty internal language library allowed me to access enough Spanish to converse. This being Argentina and roughly 10.30 p.m., they asked me out for dinner. I told them I was already full of llama but went along anyway.

Copious amounts of red wine later, I found myself trudging up a darkened version of Cerro de los Siete Colores with the chatty Leandro at my side, plus even more booze and an assortment of musical instruments. The plan was to sing under the stars.

The walk to our destination was via a gravelly upward spiral, made slightly more strenuous due to the altitude, and overlooked by a grinning moon rising across a majestic Milky Way. We found a spot to sit high above the flickering lights of Purmamarca, as close as I'd ever been to shooting stars. A guitar playing, drumming and singing concert followed and I was instantly dumbfounded. These boys, all from Buenos Aires, turned out to be the most incredible musicians.

We sang in a multitude of languages and improvised new songs, all the while swigging from our red wine bottles as we sat on the cold dirt. Occasionally someone would sneak off to pee in the shadows and we'd all jump up, afraid of a random wee-trickle rolling back down the hill. As the wind whipped around us and I hugged a borrowed jacket over my knees, we talked between songs about the presence of Pachamama, the spirit of Mother Nature ever present in earth, wind, fire and water, which people here believe to be as real as their very own mother. I was fascinated.

It was one of those rare unplanned nights that make travelling alone seem like the only way to do things. Even though it gets lonely sometimes, had I been with anyone else that first night in Purmamarca, I probably would have bypassed the chatty group in the courtyard and taken myself to bed, happy and full of llama. You just never know what might happen when you start talking to strangers. The world can grow bigger and brighter in a second and doors can fly open that may have stayed locked otherwise.

Leandro and I formed a bond that night over singing and discussing the earth and, singing loudly as we made our way drunkenly down the hill. At one point, I fell and cut my knees, something I found weirdly thrilling because I don't think I've done that since I was about six. I felt giddy with wine and the altitude and even higher on the thought of Pachamama watching over us all. By day, the hill has seven colours. By night — *that* night at least — it had thousands more. We painted them ourselves with languages and music and laughter.

The next day, Leandro's friends caught the bus back to Salta in order to fly back to Buenos Aires. The Germans wandered off elsewhere, and Leandro, who was due to stay a couple more days, decided to take me to nearby Tilcara to check out the ancient *pucará*, or fortress, there. This pre-Inca fortress has now, however, been remodelled to the point where it's really not a pre-Inca fortress at all. There's even an entirely irrelevant pyramid at the top of it, close to the viewing platform, from which you can see for miles across the mountain towns, their slithering roads all silvery with mirages. The pyramid is a monument dedicated to two explorers who did a lot for the area, although I couldn't help but think of how they've now ruined it, a bit.

The cacti dominating the landscape were insane. There were way more than we saw the other day, literally thousands clustered together and looking from a distance like a spiky army. Leandro and I took photos of each other among them, some as huge and wide as ancient sycamore trees, and imagined they were people once, who'd had a spell cast upon them, destined to scorch forever in an environment as inhospitable as the evil witch who'd pointed her wand at them.

It can't escape your attention that everything in the *pucará* is designed to hurt you, from the sun to the dry air that burns your throat and the barbed wire gardens created by the cacti, but it's eerily beautiful, like stepping onto the planet from a distant galaxy after the apocalypse ... or maybe a life-changing visit from the *Maestros Ascendidos*?

We had a beer in a rare shady outside spot in Tilcara itself (even more dusty than Purmamarca but totally like being in Tomb Raider) and Leandro told me a story about a man who broke his horses in from birth by licking them all over and biting off their umbilical cords to make them believe he was their mother. Not sure where that came from or why, but it was interesting. I find Leandro very interesting. He's the kind of guy who can talk for hours about everything and nothing at the same time.

So you see, it was a lovely night, counting shooting stars, and it was a beautiful following day counting cacti. And on reflection, if I'd have left it there and not agreed to go with Leandro to a restaurant and order a large assortment of unknown meats, it would undoubtedly have been a lovely evening, too. But the fun stopped back in the hostel when, midway through a bottle of wine, my stomach began to churn. I had a vision of the blood sausage I'd eaten at dinner — and not enjoyed at all — laughing at me from the plate and, after a mad dash to the bathroom, there it was again, laughing at me in pieces from the toilet. Oh, the shame.

For nine straight hours I vomited until there was nothing left inside me to vomit, and then I vomited air. By 2 a.m. I had moved into Leandro's dorm room at his command and he spent the night making me drink water so that I could further clean my stomach by puking it up. The walls were so thin throughout the hostel I've no doubt I kept everyone up.

Leandro rubbed my back and told me it was OK and the next day, being a frank and direct Argentinean man, he told me I looked like shit and needed a cold shower. I obliged while he fetched me some medicine from the pharmacy: droplets which I was instructed to squeeze into water and drink every four hours to keep the nausea away. These rendered me a zombie. For the whole of that day I lay in that single dorm room bed like a dying hospital patient with Leandro in the next one, refusing to leave me.

He strummed guitar, read me poetry, wouldn't let me drink any old water with bubbles in it, because he said it would be drinking bad energy. He spoke of history and the myths of the land, and stroked my hair sympathetically as I groaned and writhed and generally acted in a way that was wholly unattractive. During my saner moments, we discussed at length love and relationships, the world and its infinite layers, and the fact that Pachamama was probably trying to keep me here in Purmamarca for some reason.

We discussed how, in spite of all of the colours, shapes and sizes in Argentina, there's no real racism here because everyone's the same; all subject to the same shitty politics and economic dysfunction. He even told me how Mama Coca, the hostel owner, had spent a good hour that morning while I was asleep, telling him that, although she's seventy-one, not a day goes by when she doesn't fall in love with her husband all over again, and she loves it particularly when they disagree over politics. She also told Leandro that every time she cleans the hostel, she plays a game with the wind, which she always wins when she succeeds in sweeping the dust from the floor into her bin without it blowing away first.

Leandro sang me his own songs in Spanish and played classics from Charly Garcia, the Argentine rock musician. We watched YouTube videos of people singing random notes at piles of salt and watched the salt move of its own accord into inconceivable patterns and shapes in response — I've never seen anything like this before, you must look these up! He told me that the frequency of the earth is F-sharp, the same frequency as that of our bodies, meaning we're all literally designed to be in perfect tune with this planet. He proved it by whipping out the guitar tuner and, as it hovered on and off F-sharp in the silent room, I almost forgot to want to vomit.

Honestly, it was one of the most incredible days for all the things I didn't do while lying in that stuffy, darkened dorm with Leandro. The sun continued to scorch the life out of the desert world beyond the doors but we stayed there till dusk, when my stomach was empty and I hadn't vommed for roughly six hours and it was high time for an empanada.

Even though it was a brief exchange, Leandro and I discussed the connection that we both noticed instantly, and discovered our birthdays are just four days apart. Sure, I could have done without the embarrassment of puking all night or falling down the hill and cutting my knees, but as he noted so eloquently, sometimes Pachamama forces her hand ... especially when she really thinks you should be doing something differently.

I considered that perhaps we were supposed to connect right there and then, to meet in the middle and share our thoughts, to slow down and look at the world in another way for a while. It's nice to believe that cursed people can take the form of cacti, that every human can harmonise at F-sharp and paint fifty shades of colour over a seriously grey day.

I waved Leandro off as he left to return to Buenos Aires. I wished him well, as he did me for the next step of my journey into Bolivia, said goodbye and watched his bus roll away in a cloud of dust that I have no doubt Pachamama made twirl and dance around him as a final serenade. Sometimes life throws the most incredible, kind and inspiring people into your path just when you need them most. And sometimes, I think, at least when Pachamama gets involved, the things you think you want to forget, like dying in a hostel in the sticks of northern Argentina, are the ones you end up remembering quite fondly, forever.

**By the way, if you're wondering about the llama, it was all right. A bit like a tougher version of beef, really. I much prefer their woolly jumper offerings than their flesh on a dinner plate but the Americans enjoyed it.

27/10

Ready salted trips ...

I followed the masses off the bus when we arrived in La Quiaca and found myself standing on a bustling sidewalk, with Winnie asking 'Where's Bolivia?' I walked around for a bit and then got worried. I wasn't entirely certain I wasn't already in it. Maybe I'd slipped through some unofficial border as I wheeled my suitcase around and had actually already left Argentina? Wondering as to the location of a country from a street corner was not my finest travelling moment. I was just about to pull out the *Lonely Planet* when a teenager called Diego from Buenos Aires noted my consternation and came to the rescue. He offered to share a taxi with me to the border, which took about seven minutes in the end.

Once there, we checked out of Argentina, walked two metres more along a ramp and checked into Bolivia (I'm aware I'm using Foursquare terms here but, seriously, it was that simple), whereupon my teenage friend pointed the way and we walked the five or so blocks together towards the Villazón bus station, stopping for a freshly squeezed orange juice along the way.

This one road was packed with stalls selling much the same stuff as those in Purmamarca, but it was clearly a world away from Argentina. Women in giant, voluminous skirts, tiny pork pie hats and colourful jackets, with long plaits down their backs, were sucking on oranges or cramming wedges of coca leaves into their mouths. Bags of the leaves were everywhere, as was an array of cheap and alarmingly ugly pyjamas dangling from coat hangers. Walking wasn't easy. It felt like every breath was difficult to inhale and my heart was pounding. Then I remembered Villazón stands at 3447 metres above sea level and any form of altitude sickness was only going to get worse from here.

I was all prepared to get the train to Tupiza, where I'd made a booking at the recommended Valle Hermoso II Hostel, but Diego said there was a quicker and cheaper way to go. Before I knew it, I was crammed into the back of a van with a family of five and numerous bags of what looked like papayas wedged into every available gap. We paid our twenty bolivianos each (well, I paid for Diego because he'd been kind enough to help me find the country) and off we went.

Which all brings me to where I am now, sort of — hard of hearing in the middle of nowhere, at the end of day two of my four-day jeep tour to the salt flats of Uyuni.

I remember the moment it happened. I was shuffling what was left of my tattered silicone earplug in my ear in order to permanently block the intolerable snorer keeping me awake in the hostel when I did just that. I blocked her (yes, her) permanently. With a tricky finger manoeuvre that went awry, followed by a swift bout of panic, I managed to lodge the tiny remnant of earplug in a totally unreachable part of my ear canal. So I'm now deaf in my right ear. I can't hear a thing, which of course was my initial aim, but I kind of hoped it would be reversible.

When I realised I couldn't hear, I dashed to the bathroom in the darkness, soaking my socks on the grim, flooded floor and desperately rinsing my ear over the tap in the hope that I would dislodge it and hear that blessed little pop you get when balance is restored. But then I realised the cold air and water were probably setting the silicone even further into a hardened mass in there and that all hope for a continued Bolivian tour in stereo sound was sadly lost.

I know now that you're not supposed to insert tiny pieces of this stuff and that the only safe way to use these large shape-shifting globlets of white putty is to shove them in whole over the top of your ear openings (never in fully, you see), but really, when it's 2 a.m. and you can't sleep and someone's doing a vocal impersonation of a machine gun across the freezing dorm room, you don't remember the details. When you're dizzy from lack of sleep at 4000 metres in some off-the-map Bolivian village and your heart is beating like a hummingbird just from turning over in your hired sleeping bag, and the machine gun's getting louder to the point where you start to doubt that such a sound could actually be coming from a human (let alone a girl), the last thing you're thinking to yourself as you reach for those sweet silicone saviours is, 'Oh, I should probably read the health and safety warning on my earplug container.'

So, day two dawned on a deaf ear for me, and whereas day one was about nine tedious hours of driving, stopping for photos and getting to know the others in my jeep — a permanently smooching/snuggling Belgian couple from Brussels who are very nice when they separate lips and take on their own individual forms, and a single and slightly annoying French-Italian guy — today we were promised spectacular sights within the Reserva Nacional de Fauna Andina Eduardo Avaroa. Understandably most people just call it 'the park'.

This was declared a protected area in 1981 for the benefit of native animals like flamingos, ostrich-like rheas and vicuñas. It cost us 150 bolivianos each to enter yesterday evening at around 5 p.m. — another hidden extra in the price of the trip from Tupiza, which will culminate in a visit to the world's biggest salt flat, Salar de Uyuni.

Unlike most, who'll be deposited in Uyuni city when we get there, I've opted to go back to Tupiza in the jeep afterwards so I can do a horse-riding tour via the hostel with some fun girls I met in the lobby. We were all waving our phones in the air, trying desperately to get a decent wi-fi signal like some mixed nation, uncoordinated girl band (Internet is near non-existent in Tupiza), when we got to discussing the potential awesomeness of two full days on horseback. Still high from my gaucho and wine-fuelled adventures at Estancia Los Potreros, I wound up paying the equivalent of $230 for the two tours (salt flats and riding), plus two nights at the hostel, and I've a sneaking suspicion I was overcharged a bit, as the hostel manager assaulted me in a flurry of Spanglish at lightning speed and bashed numbers into a calculator.

Anyway, first, here I am off on another salty expedition. In the jeep. I can't explain to you the arse-pummelling bumpiness of these South American road trips, by the way. Most of the time you're on roads so rocky it's a wonder the tyres don't burst. Doing anything other than looking out of the window is near-on impossible. I couldn't even read my Kindle. I shoved more coca leaves in my cheek, as they really do help combat the motion and altitude sickness, even if they make you look like a hamster.

Unfortunately, sucking and then chewing the leaves did nothing to aid the unblocking of my ear, but on the positive side, this means I can only partially hear the God-awful Bolivian music our guide insists on playing as he drives ... which I'm sure I'll come back to. I really can't talk about it right now because, to be honest, just the thought of it irritates me to the point of wanting to slam my other ear into a cactus bush.

My group is discovering that there's a vast difference in the quality of this trip, depending on the guide and cook you have travelling with you. Our guide is a smiley Bolivian man called Santos, who has a big bulging belly full of Coca-Cola. I know this because, as he drives, he swigs it from a two-litre bottle and consequently grows fatter by the day, probably. He doesn't speak any English but, according to the Belgians and the French-Italian, all of whom speak decent Spanish, he doesn't offer much information in any language, really. He's very nice, though, and drives the jeep very carefully — as you would if you were permanently caffeinated to the max and in danger of locking the steering wheel with your stomach.

Our cook, assigned only to us four, is a very sweet and wrinkled lady called Ilda, who's incredibly quick with a warm smile and a laugh but not so speedy with the food. Last night, everyone else at our shabby new hostel had eaten and gone to bed before our food showed up, by which time we had all stuffed ourselves silly with biscuits to stave off the hunger. Watching the others tuck into offerings of fried chicken, chips and salad, all smacking their lips and leaning back in satisfaction, we played and sang along to a French guy's guitar to pass the time and looked forward to our own feast. But when the food turned up it was … well … how can I say this without sounding ungrateful? It was instant mash and chewy beef bolognese in a watery sauce. Make what you will of it.

Of course you can't complain, can you? This is Bolivia. These cooks are probably being given a set amount of money to cater for their jeep and in some cases they spend it all on delicious food; in other cases they spend most of it on a new llama for their family and use what's left to feed their tour group. Anyway, we ate it all, along with yet more stale bread (as seems to be the norm for bread in Bolivia) and sloped off to bed dejectedly.

So here I am, about to turn the lights out on day two in another random room in a Bolivian village I don't even know the name of. It's cold but they've given us numerous blankets and, in spite of there being no plug sockets and no flushable toilets (you should see the disgraceful turds people have dropped in them anyway — tut), it's not actually too bad. And what's even better, I guess, is that I only need one earplug tonight.

29/10

Flamingos, Maroon Five and a French-Italian ...

After a breakfast of yet more stale bread yesterday (honestly, I cannot figure out why the bread is never fresh in this country), we set off across vast expanses of red, rocky and rolling scenery and drove around iridescent aqua lakes polka-dotted pink with flamingos, all still within the Reserva Nacional de Fauna Andina Eduardo Avaroa.

Stopping on the edge of an aquamarine lake, we bounced on welts of salt and mineral collections so squishy they could almost have been used as trampolines. The French-Italian broke through one and seriously muddied his trainers. He was quite irate about it, which amused me. He's over six-feet tall and devilishly handsome but he is so blunt about absolutely everything that we don't get each other at all. You know when you just clash with someone? At first you let things slide because, after all, these things happen sometimes when you dare to travel with strangers, but then the little comments and quips start to bug you, until everything they say is annoying. Yesterday he told me I look like 'an ugly Katy Perry'.

He never lets me control the music in the jeep, because he thinks my taste in music is shit. This is because I put one Maroon Five song on, once, and this is in spite of the fact that, since we set off, we've been using my iPod to provide the driving soundtrack. Clearly I must have some good music on there. Honestly.

Anyway, last night as we bundled into our beds at yet another hostel of questionable hygiene in the middle of nowhere, I noticed he had seven books on his dresser. Seven! As we all started reading, I commented that he needed a Kindle, preferably one with a nifty light on it like mine, at which point he glared at me as though I were insane and replied with something along the lines of, 'We don't all need modern gadgets, you know, some of us like to actually hold a real book.'

Shortly after, the electricity died and I was the only one who could carry on reading. I felt quite smug about that. Even though I was still deaf and hungry, thanks to another largely inedible dinner by Ilda of neon pink Frankfurt sausages spliced into three fronds, surrounded by minced beef and sauerkraut all piled onto sopping, uncooked French fries, I went to sleep happy. Oh, by the way, to follow that dinner we had some sort of unset flan of an indefinable flavour in tiny metal bowls. I'm starting to enjoy meal times here in Bolivia, if only for the fact that I'm getting thinner with each one.

As we drove across the park, we tried our best to finagle some information out of the mute, Coke-swigging Santos and he eventually told us how some of the salts and minerals found in the area are used as the main components in laundry detergent and also as the shiny coating you see on porcelain units, like toilets and sinks. Interesting. When we stopped at Laguna Kollpa, a lake rich in sodium carbonate minerals, we learned how the Incas used deposits from it as shampoo. There were woven bags of white and grey powder everywhere, for export to Chile — they buy a lot of it, apparently. A guide from another jeep hopped out and started scooping vast amounts of the stuff from a pile into plastic bags, probably for his own use. I wouldn't have minded trying it. I didn't have a container, though.

Santos also told us, a bit more willingly, how since the age of fourteen he's trekked from his tiny village south of Tupiza into Argentina with llama wool draped across the back of donkeys, just to make money. He makes this seven-day journey once a year during November, when the border is open to Bolivians due to an Argentinean holiday. Hearing this made me quite glad I didn't bother questioning the suspicious pricing methods for these adventure tours back at the hostel. I mean, no foreigner likes to feel ripped off but, really, if I'd been hurried into the blistering desert with a herd of donkeys at fourteen I'd probably be working with more of a 'screw the over-privileged, let's milk them for all they're worth' mindset, too.

Next to blow my mind: Laguna Colorada. This is one of the most impressive sights you'll see on the salt flats tour in Bolivia. It's a shockingly bright red lake over 4300 metres above sea level, so-coloured by sediments and the pigmentation of algae. When we arrived, we were accompanied by a fierce wind, the kind that stings your eyes and deafens you, if you're not deaf already.

Andean, Chilean and rare James's flamingos were feeding on the borax islands, seemingly oblivious to the gale. I diligently stuffed my cheeks with more coca leaves, battling to take a decent photo in what had become a veritable dust tornado. The fact that I could only hear out of one ear totally threw me off balance, too.

About that: ever since the ear plug got stuck, little bits of the silicone have taken to springing up in my ear unannounced, so I think my canal is actually fixing itself. The human body is a remarkable thing! I'm still deaf but, at this rate, maybe I won't have to head to some backstreet Bolivian ear doctor for a probing when I get back to Tupiza, which is nice.

Unfortunately I could still hear Santos's heinous music in my good ear when I headed back to the jeep early to escape the wind. I've been meaning to come back to this. I think it's called Cochabamba. It has to be the most soul-splintering music in God's galaxy and I don't say this lightly. Imagine a cross between a Jewish wedding, an unsigned 80s synthesised disco act and the sort of tune you might hear pounding out of an empty nightclub somewhere weird, like Kazakhstan. There seems to be only one tune that plays on repeat in the entire genre of Cochabamba, although occasionally you can detect a slight adjustment in vocal arrangement (usually nasal off-key singing), which is how you know the song has changed. Listening to it feels a lot like being stuck in a bad kid's cartoon, or a jingly Nintendo game where the cheat mode's on and you can't die.

Santos would sneak this hideous music on whenever we were off seeing the sights, and had we not brought our own tunes to plug in through the speakers I've no doubt we would've had to endure four straight days of Bolivian musical torture. The French-Italian would have been begging for some Maroon Five. Go ahead and look some of this Cochabamba stuff up on YouTube if you think I'm being unreasonable. And then picture being stuck in a jeep with it for nine hours with an annoying French-Italian and some kissy-kissy Belgians as you trundle along through the bumpy wilderness, getting a numb bum.

If you need to soothe that bum, you should probably have a dip in the thermal pool at Laguna Polques, which was a nice pit stop yesterday. Situated in what feels like the middle of nowhere, it's the perfect place to bask in the sunshine while gazing out at flamingos in the hot healing waters. We ate our lunch in what looked like a classroom nearby and Ilda cooked cauliflower florets and flat flaps of beef that looked like skinned elephant's ears in the adjoining kitchen.

'You have a weird imagination,' the French-Italian stated in disdain when I made this elephant ear observation, before putting down his cutlery and abandoning the meat. I felt quite smug about that, too.

A word of warning. At Polques I was charged three bolivianos to use yet another insalubrious cesspit in disguise as a toilet, which upset me greatly. Even India doesn't do toilets as repugnant as this one. A bored teen looked me up and down as he counted out my change and went back to studying his phone, while the shit-smeared hole in the floor I was expected to crouch over went on festering in its own stench. Pee in the bush if you're desperate here. Or in the thermal pool; no one will know.

On we bumped, to the skyrocketing geysers. These boiling mud pools and fumeroles, which we got to stop at on day three, were amazingly scary. Each perniciously frothing pit spat at us with the ferocity of a giant mutant camel and, combined, they made up my favourite sight on the whole trip. For about an hour we were free to walk around bubbling brown pools and stroll through clouds of noxious sulphur fumes at our leisure. The loved-up Belgians must have taken at least 900 photos of themselves smooching against spitting fountains and the French-Italian did a great job of wandering off on purpose into a fog of steam when I suggested a group photo. He really does try to do everything in his power to annoy me.

A few years ago, when I went to Rotorua's Wai-O-Tapu Thermal Wonderland in New Zealand, I was comforted by the number of cautionary ropes and hazard signs around springs of cyanide, expansive simmering waters and ominous volcanic craters. Here in Bolivia, there's no bothering with any of that. At any one point you're two steps away from falling to your doom and boiling alive while everyone takes photos from the perimeters; the prospect of which, to me, was actually only slightly more frightening than the thought of falling into that toilet at Polques. Exhilarating, though!

Several people got sick during the third day and night … including the French-Italian, after a session drinking Fernet

Early morning on Bolivia's Salar de Uyuni.

with another tour group in the salt hostel. I felt smug again when he told me he had a headache on the way to Salar de Uyuni, although the more the morning went on, the more I actually felt sorry for him. Drinking at high altitude is never wise and Fernet is the kind of bitter, leafy-tasting spirit that recurs on you in sicky burps when you'd really rather it didn't.

But back to the salt hostel for a moment. The tour guides will have you believe that there's only one and that it's very special and that the price of the tour is higher than others because it includes a stay here, but in actual fact, there are several salt hostels in the park. It's true that everything in them is made of salt, though, even the bed frames are giant, compressed blocks of the stuff. I licked a wall, just to make sure. I wouldn't recommend you do it, however: I felt a bit sick afterwards. I felt even more sick when I went to line up for a wash (the first proper wash in three days) and heard a German couple having sex in the shower.

Anyway, our final destination, Salar de Uyuni was well worth the wait, worth getting up at 4 a.m. for, and it made a suitably showbiz finale as we sipped coffee, watching the sun rise over its sparkly white surface. As the world's largest salt flat (and ex-prehistoric lake) at 10,582 square kilometres, the sheer scale of it is mindboggling. It totally blew me away with its nether-worldly sheen and, as predicted, it was way more impressive than the Salinas Grandes in Argentina.

The salt at Salar de Uyuni, as well as holding seventy per cent of the world's lithium reserves, is over ten metres thick in the centre, and in the wet season the whole thing is covered with a thin sheet of water that you can drive across. During this time, people say it reflects the sky and makes you feel like you're driving in the clouds. I kind of wish we could have seen it like that, but cruising along I noticed how the salt flew up around our wheels and sparkled in trails, like a troupe of drag queens might have brushed across it in Rio Carnival costumes shedding glitter, and it was mesmerising all the same.

We stopped to take photos for at least an hour. I wandered away from the smooching Belgians and the French-Italian at one point, and I wondered at how the salt caught the light in heavenly droplets; miniature sunbeams piercing the earth like pinpricks. I sat for a while among the huge hexagonal flats, all with puffy edges as though someone had been cementing tiles together, painstakingly, day in, day out, for centuries. And, in spite of my semi-deaf condition, I felt suddenly overcome by a sense of contentment.

It's so white out here, so pure that you half expect to see Jesus walking towards you from infinity. I would have believed I was in heaven itself … if it wasn't for that fucking Cochabamba music, which Santos suddenly decided to crank up from his place in the jeep. I swear, the sound of that was probably what caused the lake to recoil and dry up in the first place.

Having snapped the hell out of the flats, with hundreds of trick photos on digital cameras to prove we were really there, we piled back into the jeep and began the long drive to Uyuni city.

'I'm going to put a good song on now,' said the French-Italian over the Cochabamba, reaching for my iPod between Santos and Ilda.

'No problem,' I told him, snatching it before he could so much as touch it. 'But let's listen to the Maroon Five album all the way through first, shall we?'

30/10

Horsing around …

When I was fourteen I landed my first job earning £1.50 an hour in the local Spalding chippie. My shifts were Saturdays and Thursday nights after school. Everything went well until one day when an old man came in and asked for a fried egg with his haddock and chips. I panicked. I had no idea how to fry an egg. No one had ever asked me for one and no one had ever shown me how to fry one, so I told him we didn't have any.

When he'd finished his meal sans eggs and left, my boss called me downstairs. He was not pleased.

'Why did ye tell tha' man we've go' no eggs?' he asked, pointing to the store room. 'He always 'as eggs. We've got tons of 'em out back.'

Of course, I didn't want to admit I'd reached the mighty age of fourteen without ever frying an egg for myself, so I did what any other embarrassed schoolgirl would do in the face of an angry man: I burst into tears. I think that was when he realised he'd hired a child.

However stressful my job was at such a young age, it was nothing compared to what our horse riding guide Juan Luis has had to endure. For the past two days, Juan Luis has accompanied myself and a group of four other girls (two Australian, one German, one Austrian) on our horse trek through the valleys surrounding Tupiza.

Trotting through dust clouds and sporadic fields of green encircled by perpendicular scarlet cliffs, Juan Luis, now just sixteen, told how he started leading horse tours at the age of seven. At that age, he says, he was working with his father, but when he got to fourteen he was taking groups of up to ten adults across the valley all by himself.

Imagine leading tourists on horseback when you're seven. How can you even stay in the saddle when you're only as big as the saddle yourself? The story was not unlike that of Daniel at Estancia Los Potreros (who was put on a horse as a baby), or Santos with his llama skins. But looking at this waif-like schoolboy in front of us in his Adidas jacket and baseball cap, denim legs wrapped round his rather unruly pony, it was like watching a scene from a cowboy movie before the kid grows up to be a jaw-droppingly handsome horse-whispering/herding champion with an insatiable appetite for women in jodhpurs with foreign accents.

Aaah ... he has so much ahead of him. But yet so much to learn. Juan Luis, like so many landlocked Bolivians, has never even seen the sea. I should mention here that Bolivia is in a bit of a state. They've had over 190 different governments in the years since claiming independence from Spain almost 190 years ago and it's never really had much independence at that. In 1883, it lost its part of the Pacific coast to Chile, who nabbed the Atacama Desert while they were at it, making the most of the nitrate there. Brazil took the rubber-producing Acre region of the Amazon and, as recently as 1935, Paraguay laid claim to the fertile, forested territory of Chaco. War and corruption have taken their toll on poor Bolivia, but luckily its most recent leader is much-loved.

Evo Morales, Bolivia's first indigenous president, pushed through a groundbreaking constitution in 2009, giving new hope to the indigenous majority. He is constantly working to manage the country's untapped reserves, like lithium — evidence of which we saw on the salt flats, and eco-tourism opportunities are on the rise, especially in the Rurrenabaque area. Mention Evo Morales to any Bolivian and chances are they will hail the skies as though he is some sort of God.

So … my bum-cheeks had barely recovered from the jeep and there I was, about to endure a full two days on horseback. It was an interesting journey back to Tupiza from Salar de Uyuni the previous day, too, not least because we deposited the Belgians and the French-Italian at some crappy looking hostel in Uyuni city (which is a total dump, by the way, don't stay there, ever) and then stopped to collect a family of four with two babies and another older woman to share the jeep ride back with us.

After five long hours with my iPod on full blast in my ears to drown out more Cochabamba music, and staring in disappointment at miles and miles of plastic bags clinging like flags to desert shrubs and cacti constituting what has to be the biggest open rubbish dump in the world, we stopped and dropped them all off round the corner from the hostel. I watched

Santos take their money and pocket it slyly. I contemplated telling the hostel managers that their driver has a side business at their expense, but then I remembered a young Santos was shifting llama fur on the back of donkeys across the desert when kids in other places had been stomping their feet in Toys'R'Us, and decided not to say a word.

It was just before the riding tour, during breakfast at a little cafe opposite the hostel, that my ear unblocked a little more, too. Not fully, mind you, I'm still about thirty per cent hard of hearing, but it cleared enough to restore balance. Breakfast, by the way, was a semi-soft roll with a fried egg in it. I think we must have caught the roll in the two-second window they all seem to enjoy here between being squishy, doughy balls of joy, and door stops.

A hungover teen, perhaps Juan Luis's friend or brother, met us in the lobby shortly afterwards, clad in a baggy jumper and tracksuit bottoms. He refused to speak, as many teens do, but pointed the way to our bus stop, at which we had to clamber on board a local bus to the paddock to meet our horses.

There was no mention of any helmets, although we were given some cowgirl-befitting hats before we each hoisted ourselves aboard our respective equine rides and Juan Luis cantered up to greet us. Unlike at Estancia Los Potreros, there was no checking if our stirrups were adjusted correctly, no stopping to double check the girth, or even asking if we could ride, for that matter, but I suppose as this is Bolivia, there are different rules. Or perhaps none at all. Oh, also unlike at Estancia Los Potreros, there was no mid-morning coffee break with biscuits and absolutely no mention of fine Argentinean wine. We got no food all day. Apparently we were supposed to bring our own, but Mrs Spanglish had neglected to tell me this.

We trekked for about seven hours the first day, stopping only for lunch on a grassy playing field in the shade of even more huge copper-coloured cliffs. The girls shared their melon and papaya with me and I contributed some Vegemite and crackers, so I was able to climb back on my horse, a dusty red mare called Colorado, with a relatively full stomach. The sky remained cloudy, so my hopes of a day bouncing rays off my pasty white arms were dashed, but on reflection it was probably a good thing. I've heard of people doing this tour in forty-degree heat, which wouldn't have been fun at all.

It was a fairly relaxing journey, just taking in the scenery, trotting through tiny Bolivian villages with mud houses sitting in crumbling clumps behind donkey paddocks and goats clattering on tin roofs. At around 5 p.m. we stopped at our overnight camp — the most random house I've ever seen (with the exception perhaps of a guerilla pop-up Ramadan house in Dubai, which was truly marvellous). This house appeared to be half finished and furnished sparsely with the Bolivian equivalent of IKEA. Except for one room with a few beds in it, which we were to share, other huge rooms had maybe one wooden chair in them, meaning our voices echoed about the place every time we spoke.

It was like one of those houses you visit in dreams — you know, with doors that go nowhere and windows with views of walls, and it was all set against a backdrop of those towering russet cliffs. Our host for the night, a chatty Bolivian lady, just twenty-six years old with an enormous eighteen-month old baby strapped to her bosom, showed us up to our room and proudly opened the door onto the 'balcony'. This balcony was in fact a ledge above the front door, strong enough to hold those brave enough to sit on it, with no barrier, some ten feet above the ground.

We all crammed on, had a beer and watched Juan Luis untacking the horses and carrying mammoth bales of hay three times his size to the paddock from a nearby field. This field was populated by two scary-looking cows and a frisky calf with red ribbons hanging from the tips of his ears.

Dinner was chicken and rice. It was OK. Breakfast this morning was one stale bread roll each (naturally) and off we set for day two with no extra food for our saddlebags. Maybe I was spoilt at the Estancia Los Potreros but, really, it did feel a teeny bit like we were paying a lot of money for nothing but a bed in an unfinished house and, of course, our horses. I'm not really complaining, though (I'm really *not*), because again … this is Bolivia and you don't come here for gourmet cuisine, do you? You come here for an adventure. And possibly food poisoning. Or a deaf ear.

Speaking of adventure, it wasn't long after a lunch of yesterday's leftover papaya that the heavens started rumbling with an even greater frequency than our stomachs. We looked up at the ominous grey clouds, packed up our rucksacks and clambered back on our horses to a worried '*Vamos!*' from Juan Luis, but it wasn't long before we were deep in the wide open valley being pelted with hailstones and dodging lightning bolts, which streaked across the sky in thin, evil-looking strips like Thor poking his fork down at us from his dinner table. The wind picked up, sending clouds of dust into our eyes as our horses waded bravely through quickly expanding and rising streams. I honestly thought I was going to die.

As another crash of thunder almost split the sky, Colorado sped up and before I knew it we were cantering across the grass, over rocks, across the valley and I was holding on for dear life with my eyes shut, thanks to all the grit getting into my contact lenses. I have to tell you, even though I was fucking terrified, it was one of the most thrilling moments of my life! Finally, I was a cowgirl! Yeee-haaa! Behind my eyes I saw a thousand endings involving crashes and lightning bolts and burns and falling with my feet still in the stirrups, being dragged across the ground, turning redder with my blood by the second. Not that I'm a drama queen, of course. I'm just saying.

After a good hour of being pelted with hailstones, rain and all the filth kicked up by both the horses and the howling wind, the thunder lessened, the lightning ceased and we were free from nature's wrath; we were survivors on horseback, coming home from war.

We arrived back at the paddock, having come more or less full circle, exhausted, soaked, hungry, but alive. We each handed Juan Luis 30 bolivianos as a tip for his efforts (even though, to be fair, he'd done nothing but lead a group of frightened tourists out into the middle of an open valley and through bodies of water during a lightning storm) and wished him well for the rest of his career.

A bit like when I was fourteen, going home and demanding that my mum teach me how to fry eggs so I could sleep at night (or maybe not like that at all, really) the young Juan Luis can sleep just as soundly, knowing that, by sheer luck, he didn't help to fry five tourists in the wilds of Bolivia's Tupiza.

03/11

Day of the Death Road ...

The North Yungas Road is beautiful by anyone's standards. Winding through the Bolivian Andes, it provides sweeping views of lush rainforest, soaring birds, billowing clouds and loud, gushing waterfalls. But all of this is marred somewhat when you're on it, because this rocky road is undisputedly the most dangerous road on the planet. It's so dangerous, in fact, that a multitude of Bolivian tour operators beckoning you to come ride it with them on extra stable 'super-hydraulic' bicycles call it the Death Road.

Bolivia's Death Road spans a near seventy-kilometre stretch between La Paz and Coroico, boasts a mad descent of some 3600 metres and includes over 200 hairpin bends. At any one time, you're pretty damn close to a sheer 800-metre drop into the abyss. Stone and wooden crosses decorate the route, sometimes almost completely masked by flowers, and each one serves as another sinister reminder that someone attempting to make exactly the same trip as you quite literally reached the end of the road.

Naturally I thought 2 November, the official 'Day of the Dead', was the ideal day to take one of La Paz's Death Road tour operators up on the offer of a cycling adventure. (I'm actually kidding — when I signed up, I had no idea of the significance of the date, but it seemed as good a day as any for a dangerous downhill bike ride.)

The idea of cycling on this hair-raising road was turned into a touristic money-spinner in 1998, by a thirty-nine-year-old New Zealander called Alistair Matthew. He started the company Gravity Assisted Mountain Biking, although I was warned against doing the tour with them, purely because they're now more expensive than the rest. That's what being a *Lonely Planet*-favoured business will do, I'm discovering. The more popular you get with budget travellers, the less budget travellers can afford you.

Up to 25,000 backpackers a year are known to join the Death Road thrill ride, all of whom, like I was, are keen to see if it's as nerve wracking as everyone says. Let me clear this one up for you.

It's fucking terrifying. Even now as I think back to what I did, I can barely believe I was so stupid. And neither can my mum. The only thing more stupid would have been riding down it (or up it) on a juddering public bus. But then, everything seems dangerous here ...

After much deliberation I decided not to join the horse-riding girls in Potosi — a UNESCO World Heritage site and the world's highest city at 4090 metres — for a Cerro Rico mining tour, even though it featured the option to buy and ignite sticks of dynamite. As yet another popular experience in Bolivia that's clearly designed to kill you, I've heard it's well worth it for the fact that, while crawling through the tunnels as thousands of miners still do, you learn an incredible amount about the colonial and corporate greed and corruption that made much of South America what it is today.

It was in Potosi that the Spanish found what they were seeking back in 1545. Silver. The Indians found it first, actually, but being more interested in their llamas at the time, it was the Spanish who thought to mine it, turning Potosi into the heart of the Spanish colonies here and one of the richest and biggest cities in the world.

I'm sure the experience of the mine would be as eye-opening as it would be horrific (the lung-eating dust claims many workers after ten years, and kids as young as twelve still work down there), but I'm kind of on a deadline to reach Cuzco in time for my Inca Trail expedition. So, having taken a hideous sixteen-hour bus ride from Tupiza to La Paz, I signed up with Barro Biking for the Death Road instead. This company won me over in the booking office with their slideshow of on-screen photos, a promise of a CD and video documenting my own personal experience, plus the essential 'I survived the Death Road' T-Shirt.

I paid 450 bolivianos all up, which included breakfast, lunch, all my gear and a bike with double suspension, which is apparently better. I wouldn't know too much about suspension on bikes, to be honest, but I wasn't about to go cheap on a tour with 'death' in the title, so I paid what the lady asked me for … and still worried about my imminent doom all the way back to the hostel.

'Oi don't normally get loike dat, oi don't,' the Irish lad protested at 7.30 the next morning, as he sat with his head in his hands next to me in the minivan.

'Yeah, right!' his British mate laughed, slapping him on the back and making him go so green I thought he might actually be a leprechaun. I recoiled slightly against the window, gulping in air. The pair of them, both no older than twenty-one, had brought with them into the vehicle a smell of alcohol so strong I'd have believed them if they'd told me they'd slept in a beer barrel. Apparently, they hadn't slept at all.

The Irish lad had participated in a game called Drunk-Fucker, or Shot-Shitter, or something equally inebriating and had consequently wet the bed at around 3 a.m. and wound up in a heap on the floor. Shortly before we'd collected them from The Wild Rover Hostel (a hostel in La Paz which is famous for its parties), he'd actually come close to being evicted.

'I can't believe they had to drag your mattress out into the corridor! You dickhead, they're gonna make you pay for that when we get back!' the Brit chastised. Both were completely oblivious, of course, to the fact that the *rest* of us in the van couldn't believe they'd come on a day-long cycling tour of the world's most dangerous road, still half drunk. Myself and a French couple had to sit in the abhorrent stench of their hangovers for over an hour, while they nodded off and drooled on their own chests.

When our van arrived at our high-altitude starting point, we started pulling on our supplied knee and elbow pads, plus waterproof and windproof jackets and trousers. We quickly discovered a group of equally hungover backpackers had been in another van behind us, so in actual fact there were around ten 21-year-old Irish and British lads on our tour, all suffering immeasurably and about to hurtle themselves around more than 200 hairpin bends.

Still, all credit to them, they were definitely chirpy and polite as we went through the safety instructions. They also seemed to be less visibly intoxicated by the time we set off. And each set off with the determination and velocity of Lance Armstrong with a rocket up his arse.

The first part of the cycling experience, on the way to the Death Road itself, was all perfectly paved and smooth. A chilling fog descended and gripped my fingers in spite of my gloves, though, and thank God for the Power Rangers-style cycle helmet covering the majority of my face, else the brutal wind probably would have given me frostbite. I found myself trailing behind the rest, and then I lost my group altogether as the clouds pulled in around me. I tried not to panic. It was all downhill, so all I had to do was sit there, avoid the traffic and steer, and it wasn't like I couldn't still see the curves in the road.

Octavio, our guide who's been doing this for seven years, had told me he expected the boys to go fast. Apparently, the people who ride the fastest on the Death Road are the young Brits and Australians. The ones who get themselves killed most are the Israelis.

'They have no sense of fear,' Octavio told me in his perfect English. 'The Israelis have to do military service when they're young, so after that they do crazy stuff and they just aren't scared of anything.'

When we finally reached the Death Road, we stopped for yet another safety briefing and it was instantly apparent why the road claims so many lives. You can see it narrowing off instantly in front of you, like a thin brown ribbon wrapping itself around the mountains, or a slippery snake slithering off into the distance. The fog had cleared and cars were sparkling in the sun like beacons at random points. Octavio said there might be more on the road today, it being a public holiday. Everyone's out on the 'Day of the Dead' in Bolivia, travelling to the cemeteries with picnics to share with their deceased ancestors. I shivered in my Power Rangers headpiece.

'Let's get another photo with our cocks out next time we stop!' one of the British guys yelled as soon as we'd set off again. The rest of his friends cheered.

'Yeah! Man, isn't it sick how we've got all these, like, photos of us, like, giving the finger to nature?' another guy replied, pedalling furiously to build up speed. 'Like, fuck you, Machu Picchu! Fuck you, Death Road! Yeeeaaaah!'

He was hollering this last part loudly, getting faster and faster in front of me. And then he promptly fell off the cliff.

That's right. He fell *off* the cliff, on the Death Road. He hurtled over a rock (of which there were many), tumbled down the slope and took his bike with him.

Of course, we all thought that was it. He'd been taken by the road, or perhaps by Pachamama, in light of his blatant disrespect. But by some decidedly un-small miracle, his hands appeared around tufts of grass. Then appeared his helmet. Then his body as he hauled himself up onto the road again.

'Fuck me,' he said to no one in particular. He stood up straight and dusted himself off, visibly shaken. Then, with the help of two of his friends he turned to pull the bike back up, which had also landed miraculously within reach of the road, saved from an 800-metre drop by some springy vines.

Moving on, all slightly slower, we stopped to get a group photo taken sitting on the edge of a mammoth cliff. I couldn't even see the bottom, just a jungly mass of green. At another point, Octavio told us to stop and look over the edge at the twisted wreckage of a black car that had rolled over and smashed almost beyond recognition some four years before. Octavio said that no one knew the car was there or where the people in it had gone until they noticed the vultures circling almost a month afterwards.

After that we heard all sorts of horror stories. We ate a breakfast of bread rolls (pleasantly fresh ones) filled with eggs as we sat around a fancy memorial, which was erected by the family of an Israeli girl who died on a similar tour in April 2001. She was waiting for a bus to pass her when she misjudged the distance to the edge and fell 50 metres to her death. Strangely, another Israeli girl died in the exact same spot on the road, on the exact same date in April, in 2010.

In another incident, two guys riding side by side on the road, instead of single file like you're supposed to, were mucking about when one decided to stick his leg out and 'pretend' to kick the other. You can imagine what happened next.

Back to our journey. Several naked man shots later (yes, the boys really did take pictures lined up with their anatomy out), and a good few hours of cycling alone with the van behind me as I struggled not to hit a rock and hurtle forwards over my handlebars, we reached the end of the road. I've got to say, in spite of taking it relatively slowly with the bike, anything more than walking on the Death Road is enough to scare the shit out of someone. My hands were moulded into the shape of the

You never know what you might see on
Bolivia's Death Road.

handles when I was done, and moving them hurt where I'd been gripping the brakes so tightly. Half the time, I didn't even notice the scenery because I was too terrified of missing a bump or a boulder to look up from the road.

On the way back to La Paz we stopped at a hotel with a swimming pool for a buffet lunch, during which the boys refrained from yet another naked photo and it rained. The air was balmy and tropical, the pool was lined with palm trees and people lazed in hammocks. We'd reached more or less the Amazon basin, a totally different microclimate to the one we'd set off in that morning, when we were smothered with clouds at over 4000 metres. The Death Road tour takes you 95 per cent downhill and though several seasons in one day.

Back in the minivan with the boys asleep (but alive), Octavio told me a story about a driver coming home along the road one night. It was pelting with rain. He was tired and shoving coca leaves in his mouth to stay awake when he saw a little girl walking along the cliff edge. He stopped, obviously concerned, and asked where she was going, to which she replied that she'd been chasing an animal earlier in the day, taken the wrong path and got lost. The driver was confused but offered to drive her home.

When he got to the house (pretty much the only one built on the Death Road), it was still raining, so he offered her his jacket and said he had to drive the same way the next day and would pick it up then. Sure enough, he arrived the next day in bright sunshine to find an old woman working in the garden. He asked about the girl, but the woman freaked out and started praying.

'There's no girl here!' she told him, shooing him back towards the gate.

Just as he was about to leave, he spotted his jacket hanging on a post across the garden and, thinking the woman quite batty, went to pick it up.

It was then that he realised the post wasn't a post. It was a stone cross. The little girl had died along with her parents years before in a car accident.

Drivers on the Death Road are so scared that they often stop to pour libations of beer into the earth. These are intended to appease the goddess of nature, our good friend Pachamama, in the hope that she'll grant them safe passage. But with a fatal accident occurring on the road every two weeks and up to 200 people perishing on it every year, it doesn't matter how qualified your guide is, how many mountain biking expeditions you've endured and survived, or how much Pachamama likes your beer.

The Death Road is in a league of its own and the only person who can really keep you safe on it is yourself.

Witches, warnings and the spirit of the vine ...

La Paz is the world's highest capital city and when you approach it from a height of 400 metres, overshadowed as it is by the snow-crested, 6438-metre Illimani, it looks like a city that fell into a hole from the sky. You think: *Wow!*

La Paz has a distinct Andean yet 1960s feel to it, thanks to the ugly beige tower blocks and dangerous low-hanging cables threatening to tangle in the hair of passing pedestrians. Short and stocky, leather-faced *campesinas* (local women) huddle on every street corner drinking *mate de coca*, or hot leafy drinks known to help with altitude from silver cups, wearing infinite layers of ponchos and scarves and the obligatory pork pie hats. They all seem to sell, as far as I can see, bars of Dove soap, loofahs and phone time — whereby you pay by the minute to make a call on one of a collection of mobile phones laid out on a table.

It's hard to breathe and the people seem to be indifferent to the point that it's verging on mean. Or maybe that's just a reflection of my mood at the moment.

I'm still the tiniest bit deaf in one ear and, also, I've not really been sleeping well. Perhaps it's the altitude, but I've been having bizarre dreams for the last couple of weeks, the sort that linger with you all day and unsettle you like a tiger crouching in the shadows.

Anyway, I've managed to pass a couple of days here before I take another bus to Cuzco in order to begin the Inca Trail. I started by checking out the famous Witch's Market. I was, of course, hoping for something akin to Diagon Alley, with women in pointy hats stirring cauldrons and casting spells, and perhaps the odd hole-in-the-wall pub with a kindly wizard splashing ladles full of cold Butter Beer into giant mugs. But no. You should know that La Paz's Witch's Market is nothing like Harry, Ron and Hermione's hangout.

Instead, I found a strip of rather uninspiring stalls selling shriveled up llama fetuses and lucky charms. The lucky charms looked more like little jars of cotton threads and Skittles sweets sitting in water. Disappointing. Don't bother. Unless of course you really need a dried llama baby, or you want to stir up the scene a bit more and go dressed as a witch yourself.

I like this idea. If this Witch's Market was a staple tourist spot in England, as it is in La Paz, it would have been hyped to the max already with people dressed in costume, juggling with fireballs, selling jellied candy-sheep's eyes and reading tarot cards on every corner. Bolivia is keeping it real and, I'm afraid to say, it's all the more boring for it. You can't even buy a cape.

I spent a couple of hours in the tiny Coca Museum, which is actually great. They hand you a mammoth booklet when you enter, containing all the English translations for the exhibits, which hilariously have been copy-checked quite visibly and numerous times in pencil on each page. I thought it was quite funny how someone's taken the time to do this, but hasn't yet printed a new English booklet containing the changes. I would have offered but, you know, I'm quite busy. If you're in the area and you're looking for a little project, and perhaps some free coca products (ahem), you know where to go.

As well as learning all about how Coca-Cola derives from an alcoholic drink containing cocaine, which was promptly banned (shame), I learned that Sigmund Freud was the first famous European cocaine user. I didn't know that; did you? Mind you, it does explain a few things. Doesn't coke give you a giant ego? You'd have to be pretty aware of an ego to sit down and develop all those theories about it.

We could produce a book in itself about Bolivia's cocaine issues but suffice to say this country is riddled with it and La Paz is renowned as the top place to try pure cocaine for the first time. Apparently, there are over 9000 factories hidden in three-by-four metre spaces throughout the country.

I heard rumours before arriving in La Paz about a cocaine lounge called Route 36. The problem is, it keeps shutting down and moving. The owner regularly pays off the local police, but they're still at risk from other officials barging in, so now it's gone so underground that few tourists can ever find it. I quite fancied popping along, just to talk to some of the clientele about this interesting 'holiday experience', but no amount of asking got me any closer.

There are others, of course, in which you're served the stuff on giant silver platters like canapes at a cocktail party, but it seems the mother-of-all is gone for good. Perhaps I just don't look trustworthy enough to tell. Either way, I'd probably be careful who you ask if you're looking for the same thing. You never know when you might find what you're *not* looking for.

I also tried to get inside the San Pedro Prison. This gargantuan penitentiary in the middle of La Paz is famous for housing criminals convicted of drug-related crimes, yet allegedly it produces some of the country's best cocaine at night in its factories. You used to be able to take tours and embark on cocaine benders with the infamous British prisoner Thomas McFadden, but these trips are no more, and not just because he's since been released. A movie version of *Marching Powder* (the book written by Australian Rusty Young about McFadden's life in the prison) was planned with Brad Pitt in the director's seat and, with the fear of Hollywood's invasion upon them, officials at San Pedro began improving its public image.

The media will tell you now that all tours and all cocaine production lines have ceased inside San Pedro but, if McFadden's words are anything to go by, chances are they're just being even more sneaky and you simply have to find the right people to bribe. There's too much money to be made in cocaine production for them to stop completely. Stopping the tours has dented the economy in the prison enough as it is.

Read the book, if you haven't already, especially if you're considering a trip to Bolivia. It's one of the most interesting portrayals of South American drug culture I've ever read. McFadden told Rusty everything about the corruption that powers what's essentially a microcosm of the Bolivian capital. Prisoners at San Pedro are expected to pay for their own cells and food. Their wives and children can live alongside them. There are shops and restaurants inside like any other town, and prisoners live by their ranks, as in the most fortunate and rich can afford giant cells with TV systems, in-built kitchens and en-suite bathrooms, while the poor eat next to nothing, live in shared cells and have to rely on the wealthier prisoners to survive by taking up employment in their various ventures.

According to McFadden, being a prison officer is one of the most highly desired jobs in Bolivia, because of the money to be made by accepting bribes. Some prisoners are allowed to pay to go out for the night, accompanied by a minder, to dance and eat and gamble and drink in La Paz, which is how McFadden got to meet his Israeli girlfriend, a tourist who spent many nights with him in the prison and who, in the end, encouraged him to start the tours. These prison tours were eventually recommended by *Lonely Planet* as one of the most bizarre and exciting ways to spend a day in Bolivia.

Good luck getting in now, though. Brad Pitt would be a wanted man in La Paz and not for the usual reasons.

At my hostel (the Adventure Brew, which is huge), I got chatting to a British girl called Anna who was sitting on the edge of her bed, staring forlornly into her rucksack. It transpired she'd packed for her travels in a drunken stupor after a goodbye party with her friends and, having created two piles of clothes — a 'maybe' pile, and a 'definitely pack' pile —she had actually packed the 'maybe' pile, and now found herself hungover in freezing-cold La Paz with nothing but a collection of sparkly, strapless party dresses, some high heels and her hair straighteners. I tried not to laugh and told her it was better than what happened to a bloke I met in Argentina, who'd packed in a state of blind inebriation and turned up in wintry Buenos Aires with a pair of IKEA bedroom curtains in his bag and nothing to wear at all.

I also got chatting to a guy called Mobi from Argentina. The more we got into our beer, the more he opened up about his travels. Chats about the cocaine industry and our opinions on the book *Marching Powder* led to the subject of ayahuasca. It's funny, but on the Bolivian salt flats tour, a girl called Claire was talking about it over dinner and I overheard her say, as I had heard several times before now, that 'the spirit of the vine' will call to you when you're ready.

'When you're ready to take it, you will know,' Claire had said and I panicked, because simply by hearing her talk about it, surely I was receiving yet another sign of readiness myself?

For the past month or so I seem to have been hearing more and more about ayahuasca, at the strangest times, without ever asking. And I'm not even in Peru yet. Of course, there were those German guys on the jungle tour in Ecuador way back, who did a ceremony one night with a shaman and spoke of heaven, hell and almost crapping their pants, but even though I was intrigued back then, I never thought to try it.

'It sounds like Mother Ayahuasca is calling to you,' Mobi said when I told him all this. 'How much do you know about the sacred medicine?'

At his words, I was swept immediately back to Ratu Bagus's shaking ashram in Bali. I spent a week there last year surrounded by hippies and while there was no ayahuasca there, they shot a 'sacred medicine' containing blessed tobacco up their nostrils before shaking on the spot for six hours every day, searching for a Divine Energy. I left early.

'I've had some experience,' I told him. 'But not with the ayahuasca kind.'

'It's one of the strongest hallucinogenic substances on the planet,' he said. 'No one really knows if it was created by accident, or if, like they say, the plant spirits directed indigenous Amazonian people to create it, but it definitely changes your life when you take it. I know it changed mine.'

At the widening of my eyes, Mobi went on to tell me stories of his time at a retreat called Hummingbird somewhere near the Peruvian jungle city of Iquitos, including an alarming tale of a lady who got so off her face she drank a man's sperm from a cup, after he pronounced it the absolute essence of himself, endorsed by Mother Ayahuasca herself. Apparently, for reasons I still don't quite understand, this hippy also drank his own urine every time there was a full moon.

I finished at least three beers as he spoke and, thanks to the altitude, felt like I'd drunk double. Mobi told me the ayahuasca had helped him to heal emotionally after his friend died in an accident. He saw visions of heaven, a place so beautiful it was difficult to return from, but he also saw death: an infinite black hole filled with screaming demons that he fought his way out of for what felt like hours. He emerged, so he told me, with a greater appreciation for life and a total understanding that every moment, no matter how bad it might seem, is worth living. Even the sperm-drinker felt refreshed afterwards, he said. I was mesmerised. I wanted to know more. I took it as yet another sign.

'Be careful who you do it with,' Mobi warned me. 'It's getting more popular with gringos and there are con artists who will try to take your money. The right shaman will find you once you start putting your intentions out there.'

I nodded, deciding to start my research at once. And then I told him, probably because I was a bit tipsy and he seemed like the kind of guy I could tell, about all my weird dreams — the swirling shapes and creepy voices coming from floating orbs instead of visible bodies. Mobi smiled knowingly.

'Sometimes, the plant spirits find you first and try to help prepare you. They know you're ready. They know you're coming.'

'But I've not been dreaming about ayahuasca,' I reminded him.

'No, but you're remembering your dreams, which means you're getting more in touch with your subconscious mind. It's all part of the preparation. Have you dreamed of any jaguars?'

'No.'

He looked disappointed. 'Well, if you dream of jaguars, or snakes, they are signs of protection. Look out for them.'

Whether the stuff about dreams is true or not, ayahuasca seems to be calling me with a force like no other spiritual ritual or practice last year in Bali ever did. While I don't much like La Paz, cocaine seems like a stupid waste of time and money and the Witch's Market is about as spellbinding as a broken wand, I can't deny that the 'spirit of the vine' has found me once again, where I least expected it.

07/11

Pots, potatoes and preparing for Machu Picchu ...

I met a girl from Australia in the hostel today, who chose to come to South America purely based on a series of dreams she's had since the age of ten. In these dreams, she sees herself as a curly-haired, partly dreadlocked teen in a white dress, running with a female friend through Machu Picchu, surrounded by goats.

She remembers it vividly as a whole place at the heart of the Inca Empire, before the overpriced gift shops and pole-toting hikers cluttered up the landscape. In her dreams, she sees the buildings as they were, she says, their polished dry stone walls and three perfectly intact primary structures: the Intihuatana, or Hitching Post of the Sun, the Temple of the Sun, and the Room of the Three Windows.

The funny thing is, this girl never knew what it was she'd been dreaming about until one day when she turned the TV on in Melbourne and saw a documentary on Sun Temples. She was even more shocked to hear that the Incas believed in reincarnation. Some ten years later, she's come to Cuzco with the sole purpose of standing amid the wonder that is Machu Picchu for herself and seeing if she remembers even more from what she's sure is a past life she must have led in the fifteenth century.

Unfortunately, this girl is not on the tour I'm doing with Gecko's Adventures. I'm signed up for a four-day trek, which cost almost $500, including a night in a hotel either side. You can do the Inca Trail cheaper but I've heard horror stories about bad guides and not getting fed properly, so it looks as though it's definitely worth doing some research and talking to other travellers before booking anything.

I shared a taxi to my hostel in Cuzco with a doctor called Al from South Africa, who told me he'd been held at gunpoint in Ecuador and had $500 in cash stolen, on a bus. I decided after that not to carry my iPhone around with me anymore and also to keep all my money in my bra when travelling on buses.

Before arriving here in Cuzco, I had a quick stopover at Copacabana by Lake Titicaca. Twelve kilometres northwest of that town is the Isla del Sol, which has been welcoming pilgrims and visitors for hundreds of years and is really easy to reach on a day trip. It's an important island in the Andean world of religious sites, as it was here that the Inca dynasty was born, although these days, strangely, it seems to be populated by a large number of filthy, snuffling pigs, a few wild cats in cruel cages and sunburnt tourists looking as I was, I assume, for the Sun Factory.

The Incas believed that the god of creation, a heavenly being called Viracocha, rose from the immaculate waters of Lake Titicaca and commanded the sun and moon to light the whole world. I caught the boat over with a crowd of lobster-red backpackers and spent the day learning interesting things, like the fact that the most famous beach in Brazil, Copacabana

Beach (which I'll see in February, as my plans to go to Carnival are set now), featuring scores of women in thong bikinis and the hottest men in the world, so I'm told, is actually named after Lake Titicaca's Copacabana. I never saw the Sun Factory but I have my suspicions it was crafted under the lake, which is why it's so big — the biggest and highest lake in the world at almost 4000 metres.

Another touristy site is the shrine of the Virgen De La Candelaria, where you'll find Our Lady dressed in lustrous garments and residing in a glass box in the Moorish Cathedral. She's worshipped there like a living lady, and is only moved at very special times during festivals in case she gets annoyed and causes a flood. I don't know why it's called the Moorish Cathedral. It was a bit dull. One visit was enough for me.

There's nothing really moreish about Bolivia's Copacabana in general, to be honest. It has awful Internet connection and bad food and most people, like me, just use it as a transit point before boarding a bus either to Bolivia or Peru. The lake is very pretty, though. And I had a lot of fun when I rode a peddle-powered boat shaped like a swan out across the water with a hot man called Boti, who I met while eating a greasy plate of spaghetti and being sad at having no wi-fi in a restaurant that advertised wi-fi.

But I digress. Onwards from Copacabana, I enjoyed another horrible night bus over the border into Peru (during which at one point I had to get off the bus and actually pee on the road in front of oncoming traffic) and two nights of debauchery at the lovely Pariwana Hostel in Cuzco, where I've just met my group for an Inca Trail briefing. I'm scared.

To be honest, when I signed up for the Inca Trail several months ago, I had no idea what to expect, really, aside from a lot of walking and some nice scenery. They only let 500 people on the trail each day, so you must book ahead. I've just been told that contrary to my imaginings, we're not staying in cozy hostels along the way. We will not be sleeping in warm beds, taking hot showers at the end of each tedious day, or using handy plugs for charging camera batteries. We will, in fact, be *camping*!

On the plus side, our guide Elias seems quite lovely and speaks excellent English. It's going to be his 150th time on the Inca Trail and he's absolutely certain (from looking at us for twenty minutes, sitting on chairs) that we are all physically fit enough to be able to cope, which is comforting. I told him that I didn't have a sleeping bag just now, to which he chirpily responded that I could borrow one (for 45 soles), along with the hiking poles I'll also need (for 45 soles). Then I asked him, 'What about a pillow?' and he made a rolling-up-clothes motion with his hands, looking at me sheepishly.

I wanted to say all sorts of things, of course, mainly along the lines of, 'Isn't there some sort of luxury version of this, involving llamas carrying us up beneath glitzy umbrellas and sleeping beneath goose-down comforters in heated tents, and if so, can I get a refund and do that one instead?' But in the end I bit my lip and smiled because I don't want my fellow hikers, who all look very nice and excited, to know what a snob I am. At least Autumn left me with the travel pillow, so all is not lost. Its U-shaped squishiness is a little victory I shall cherish when everyone else is sleeping on their rolled up, mud-spattered hiking pants.

Elias just handed us all sacks that we're to fill with a maximum of five kilos, although the sleeping bag I'm having to hire weighs two. The porters will carry these, containing our clothes and toiletries and, in my case, travel pillow, scented feminine hygiene wipes and emergency Toblerone stash, so all we have to carry on the trail is a day pack.

I still can't believe that for once I'll be doing something at just the right time of year … even though the Incas built the end prize so far away and I'm really not much of an outdoors adventure type person. Let's think about Machu Picchu, though, the reason I will undertake this treacherous journey. I've always wanted to see it with my own eyes.

The Inca people first came onto the scene around A.D. 1150 in what's now modern-day Peru. The Inca Empire spanned 3500 miles at its height in the 1520s, from what's now modern Colombia, through to central Chile and quite a lot of Bolivia, Ecuador and Argentina. It's believed that Machu Picchu itself was abandoned around 1572, when those brutal Spanish rulers marched in, stomped all over their traditions and went about destroying most aspects of the Inca culture.

Machu Picchu is called 'The Lost City' because it quite literally got lost in the jungle until a lucky American explorer called Hiram Bingham III brushed some wild vegetation aside and rediscovered it in 1911. In 1983 the site was declared a UNESCO World Heritage site and now thousands of visitors every year get to witness what's known as one of the New Seven Wonders of the World. Not all of them walk there, though. The cheater's train only takes a couple of hours.

In order to feel more excited about seeing Machu Picchu for myself, I went to the Inca Museum in Cuzco yesterday. It was pretty good, although, as usual, the English translations left a lot to the imagination. Also, like many museums about ancient civilisations, it was probably about eighty per cent pots. I'm always suspicious of museums that feature vast collections of pots. Sure, you've got your mummies in a dark room, conveniently shrouded in cloth and lit very dimly by a two-watt red bulb behind a glass door, and you've got your combs and other tools crafted from flint and promiscuous hooker bone, welded together with dinosaur semen and what-not, but mostly what you pay to see in these places is a whole load of pots.

I don't know about you, but to me this just screams, 'We don't know anything about these people at all, but hey, we found some pots, so we'll make a museum out of them and pretend they tell us loads, till we figure out something else. That'll be ten soles, please.'

I wonder, if the human race as we know it dies out, whether future civilisations on earth will pay to visit museums filled with the remnants of our Crate and Barrel eighteen-piece dinner sets and Betty Crocker frying pans and cake trays. Will they all go, 'Ooh, weren't they clever, would you look at the decorative artwork on that Harvey Norman kettle!' completely oblivious to the evidence of all that quantum electrodynamics/nuclear fission/laser technology we dreamed up later? It's a bit daft, when you think about it. The Incas must have made so many wonderful things, but the average tourist coming to Cuzco judges them on their giant pots.

I suppose it's their fault really, though … they didn't write anything down. I found out that the Incas kept records by tying knots in bits of string that varied in size and colour, which we can only guess the meaning of in most cases. They communicated verbally, of course, but as for taking a pen to a piece of paper … well, they just drew pretty pictures on all those pots. Even the reason for the existence of Machu Picchu itself is open to debate, and I'm looking forward to learning more about these debates on the trek.

Somewhat disheartened and not much the wiser as to the *real* way of the Incas, I had an excellent lasagne at Cuzco's Paddy's Pub, 'the highest 100% Irish-owned pub on the planet at 11156 ft', according to the sign (shameful, I know, but someone told me their lasagna was excellent, which it *was*). Then I paid three soles to enter the Museo de Historia Natural, which is basically a large room that smells like disinfectant, full of fossils and creepy dead things.

I couldn't make out if this was Peru's ugliest collection of animals, or if they've all just been stuffed so badly that they're now grossly contorted. I swear, there's a member of the puma family in this museum with the tiniest head ever and a body so long it looks like it's been tied between two buses driving in opposite directions. All have ghoulish, bulging eyes, too. You wouldn't want to get stuck in here at night.

Like a lot of South America, the Museo de Historia Natural also needs to invest in some more light bulbs. A lot of the exhibits were shrouded in such a cloak of darkness I could barely tell my dead Homopteras from my dead Orthopteras, two types of what appeared to be giant winged insects, fastened cruelly to red tabletops with large pins. However, if you want to see a pig fetus, a double-headed calf, a Siamese goat or a six-legged lamb, this is the place for you. Most of these oddities from the animal kingdom are crammed into Tupperware boxes, or floating in tanks full of formaldehyde. I stood for a while in front of what had to have been the world's biggest toad wedged like a strange balloon into a screw-top jar and wondered whether there was more point to a room full of Inca pots, or whether both were irrelevant and I was just a silly tourist throwing my money at whatever I was told to.

Oh. If you're a corn fan (the vegetable, not the band) there are twenty-one different types in here. I counted them. Corn is very important in Bolivia and Peru: they do everything with it. And while we're onto veggies, the Incas were the first to cultivate the potato in Peru and there are seventy-eight kinds of fake potatoes on display for your enjoyment as well. I counted them, too.

They're not really good fakes, though. I couldn't help but think that if the people of Cuzco put half as much effort into producing their fake potatoes as they do their fake North Face and Columbia weatherproof hiking jackets, there might have been more than one person in the museum. As it was, it was just me … counting veggies and scribbling notes like some weird plastic food fetishist from afar.

We've got a 5 a.m. start tomorrow and then it's time to shove everything I own, bar my five kilos, into the hotel storage room and begin the Inca Trail. I'm kind of hoping I get some sort of dream recollection of my own past life in Machu Picchu overnight, so I can have something more to look forward to, like my friend from the hostel. Knowing my luck, though, I'll dream of getting stuck in a tent with dead toads stuffed into Inca pots, all lit dimly by Mother Ayahuasca holding a red two-watt bulb.

8/11

Inca Trail. Day One.

Dear Diary,

How are you? I'm OK but I'd prefer it if I was in a hotel room and not a tent. Today I counted sixty-nine donkeys. I thought if I gave myself a task other than trying not to faint, it might make walking in the rain up vertical slopes with a rucksack more bearable. Did I spell 'bearable' right? It looks weird written in pen and I have no way of checking. No wonder the Incas didn't write anything down. They seem like they were very clever and they probably didn't want to be associated with grammatical errors of any sort.

I hope my laptop is OK in the hotel safe. I'm quite worried about it, although I should probably be more worried about the fact that my tent is on a slope on a mountainside and every time I move, I seem to roll a little downhill in my sleeping bag. I also need a wee, but I don't want to go because the loo at this campsite is miles away and there are lots of big animals snuffling about. One of the guys said he was holding in a poo because he didn't want to walk through 'the donkey shit gauntlet' just to get to the toilet. There really are a lot of donkeys up here — I swear, half the world's population must live on the Inca Trail.

Anyway, today was OK. There were only a few hard bits, really. Elias says we've made it through the easy day. All up, the Inca Trail is forty-three kilometres and I'm not even sure how many we walked today, but we were hiking for a good six hours after making it through the checkpoint. My legs hurt a bit but already the scenery is mind-blowing and our chef, another Octavio, is a genius. He made grilled trout for lunch with rice and some sort of spinach quiche. For dinner we had stir-fried beef.

To think that someone had to carry the stove all this way ... it's insane. I saw one porter rush past me with eight stools tied to his back today, too, and another guy with a bag of heavy tent poles. You're not allowed to leave anything at the campsites on the trail, so everything has to be carried in and out and re-erected by the porters, every time.

You should see these guys. There are fifteen of them in our crew and just eight of us 'trekkers', including Elias. These porters range in age from twenty years old to fifty-three, all of them as strong as mules. Elias said the oldest porter working the trek is sixty-three but he's not in our group. That's the same age as my dad. It's almost too much to imagine my dad carrying a bag of tent poles up near vertical slopes in Peru. He gets grumpy enough pushing a trolley round Sainsbury's.

Each porter carries twenty-five kilos, but Elias told me that, before regulations put a stop to it, some used to carry over forty kilos! That's only a little under what I weighed before Buenos Aires.

I like Elias, Diary. He's always smiling and he totally loves his family. He told me how he is saving up to build a house and how his six-year-old son wants to do the Inca Trail with him at Christmas. He also said that last month he did four treks back to back, which is sixteen legs. He's a machine. We discussed Peruvian politics (as corrupt as Bolivia's by the sound of it), the weather in Iceland, Will Smith, Inca pots and the merits of Vegemite, which he likes, even though no one else he knows in Peru can stand it. I told him I would post him some Vegemite when I get back to Australia, and he told me that in return he wouldn't let me die on the Inca Trail. It's funny what you talk about when you walk with a stranger all day, and how much you can learn from each other.

The three Aussie guys in my group — Josh, Zack and Ben — are all AFL footie players and seem to walk at the pace of a herd of giraffes. They're always ahead by at least an hour. I've barely seen them all day, except for meal times and a competitive game of Uno in the dining tent tonight. I like Uno. I remember once on a holiday to Mexico, me and my friends Hannah and Kirsty played Uno all day every day in a hotel bar for about a week while drinking through the cocktail menu with a bunch of Texans. There was nothing else to do because it was rainy season. I remember

watching the deckchairs flying across the beach and landing in
the swimming pool as a hurricane destroyed everything around us,
thinking, God, this was a terrible idea, no wonder it was a cheap
all-inclusive, last-minute deal. I've never been very good at travel
planning, now that I think about it.

There are two very nice Asian–Australians in the group, too, both
called David; and an Aussie girl called Emma, who's doing the trek as
a kind of last hurrah before she gets reconstructive knee surgery. She
says she has the knees of an eighty-year-old, even though she's thirty-
two. She's still faster than me.

Elias told me today that our final destination is actually
pronounced 'Machu Pick-chew' which means 'Big Mountain',
whereas 'Machu Pee-chew', the way most visitors pronounce it, means
'Big Penis'. How funny is that?

I have nothing to do in this tent apart from write in you, Diary.
It's easy to see how the Incas got so much done. I wonder what kind of
empire I could build if I didn't spend seven hours a day on Facebook?

Goodnight, Diary. Sorry for never writing in you before now.

I wonder what font my handwriting would be in if it was on a
computer …

9/II

Inca Trail. Day Two.

How's it going, Diary?

I've been thinking very carefully about whether to say something
as casual and seemingly flippant to you as 'today was the hardest day

of my life', but really, I honestly think it was. I'm here in my sleeping bag on yet another perilous slope and it's only 7.30 p.m. Camp is deathly quiet beyond this canvas. Everyone's crashed out in recovery mode because today was hideous. Truly horrendous, Diary. I even cried at one point.

Of course, I did it very discreetly behind my sunglasses as Elias puffed diligently along behind me, but as the steps kept on coming, so did my tears and I thought my lungs were about to collapse along with my dignity. I can barely convey the difficulty that comes with heaving your wobbling thighs up an endless rocky staircase at high altitude, carrying a rucksack, two litres of water (and a half-eaten Toblerone).

I have never seen so many stairs, Diary. Scaling them was like one of those dreams where you try to move but you can't ... you know? When your limbs become heavy and the air thick, like sludge? Every time I thought I'd reached the top, more steps sprang into view, each one at least a foot high and a foot deep.

Yesterday, the less fit among us stopped regularly to 'admire the view', but today there was no disguising the desperate panting coming from all corners as people stopped, hunched over beneath their rucksacks, slugged back water and struggled for air. I was huffing and puffing all day, but still, something made me want to hold my breath as the porters passed me and it wasn't just their body odour. I felt so guilty even conveying my discomfort when they were carrying so much more. Loads of them were doing it in open-toed sandals, too. Some were even running!

Two of the guys in my group got sick today: one of the Davids and AFL Ben. Ben says it was the food (he did rather overindulge in

Octavio's offerings last night), but it was more than likely altitude sickness that made him hurl his guts up first thing this morning, outside his tent. It made a nice breakfast for the chickens, and a good wake up call for the rest of us, at least.

The second day of the Inca Trail is known to be the most difficult, as you have to scramble all the way up to Warmiwañusqa (Dead Woman's Pass) at 4198 metres, and then walk all the way down to Pacaymayu Camp at 3580 metres. While battling to control first your protesting quads and then your quivering knees and calves, you literally have to climb a mountain, stop at the top and scramble down the other side. Those Incas were either deranged or made of stronger stuff than your average twenty-first century human. Why they didn't build Machu Picchu there instead, I will never know. It would have saved a lot of effort on everyone's part.

I went through all the clichés and songs in my head, weighing them up: 'I'd climb a mountain for you' (but not this one, ever again); 'don't make a mountain out of a molehill' (because molehills can be jumped over in one second); 'ain't no mountain high enough' (yes there bloody well is, it's this one). Every one of them annoyed me.

The mountaintop is called Dead Woman's Pass because apparently it looks like the contours of a horizontal woman, when you look at it from the valley below. I couldn't see it myself. I was too busy crying. I chewed so many coca leaves today I'm surprised I didn't fly off the pass when I finally made it up there, and perhaps because of them I didn't feel the altitude as much. I didn't get sick anyway. Just knackered.

I made it to camp at roughly 4 p.m. and promptly collapsed on the blue tarpaulin laid out on the floor by our tents. Elias called Happy Hour (popcorn and hot drinks) at five o'clock and we all dragged ourselves begrudgingly to the dining tent, practically falling asleep over coca teas and a halfhearted game of Uno.

Apparently, tomorrow isn't as difficult. I hope not; I don't think my legs could take it. Machu Picchu still feels like a distant dream, and not from a past life, either, sadly. Goodnight, Diary. Thanks for listening. You're helping me not to feel so alone. Sometimes when I'm alone for long spells I go a bit mad, like last night when I couldn't sleep for a while in my tent because I kept thinking about my eyes just looking at the back of my eyelids. It's a bit weird how eyes never really switch off. I'm starting to like writing all my thoughts in you, although I do still miss my laptop, so I don't think this relationship will last. Don't get any ideas.

10/11

Inca Trail. Day Three.

Oh my God, Diary,

Today I learned even more more about how the Incas made human sacrifices — child sacrifices, too — during or after important events. Elias told us that as many as 4000 people were killed when the chief Inca Huayna Capac died in 1527. That's like the US government ordering a mass hanging after the death of a president, just to show acknowledgment for what he did/didn't do. Mental.

Cranial deformation was also popular with the Incas. To do it they'd wrap cloths tightly around the soft heads of newborn babies in order to change the shape of their skulls. The result of this was a line of people we'd call Coneheads today (probably), who, instead of being laughed at and made to feature in local carnivals, were regarded as a higher class. Only the most noble of Incas were Coneheads. Again, mental.

The Incas also tested the intelligence of their children at an early age and, based on the results, kids were either sent to school in order to become part of the nobility, or taught a trade. Personally I think this is terrible. My GCSEs were enough pressure at age sixteen, but imagine if a pass or fail was the difference between living in a palace eating delicious roasted guinea pig with a noble future ahead of me, or living in a slum with the cockroaches, learning how to make yet more pots. Maybe that explains why there are so many of them (pots, that is)? It must have been a hard test to pass.

All of this further cements my theory that the Incas knew full well what they were doing when they got the aliens to help them build Machu Picchu. They're probably looking down on us from their spaceships, laughing as we struggle to follow in their footsteps, saying things like, 'I can't believe they think we did that fucking walk. What fools!' The Incas were clearly very smart, but very cruel.

Anyway, Diary, today was pretty interesting. It was tough because my legs still hurt from yesterday, but nowhere near as challenging. We started early, as usual. Our wake-up call was at 5 a.m., and after another of Octavio's feasts (this one featured omelettes, fresh fruit salad and steaming tins of hot chocolate), we started our ascent to Runkurakay Pass, which lies at an altitude of 3950 metres. It took the AFL boys about an hour. It took the rest of us two. On the way up, we saw a few lagoons and the mosquitoes started to attack, but luckily I'd replaced my now-eaten Toblerone with a can of mozzie spray in my day pack.

Once over the pass, it was mostly downhill again for about five hours. My calves feel firmer than they have in years, which is kind of cool. I keep squeezing them and, yup, they're definitely not as wobbly as they were. I wonder if that's because I'm fitter after just three days or if my muscles have seized up in self-defence. I guess I'll find out soon enough.

We saw some amazing Inca ruins on the way to the Wiñay Wayna campsite (where I am now, in yet another sloping tent close to a dodgy cliff edge). The first was Sayacmarca — a fort-like ruin that was once the old control point for those heading on the trail towards Machu Picchu. Getting to the top of it involved an optional climb up even more stairs, which Emma and I declined in favour of finally beating the AFL boys to our designated snack spot at Phuyupatamarca. They overtook us about twenty minutes later.

The best thing about today was seeing the ruins of Intipata, which is a complex and impressively steep set of terraces slap bang in the middle of a sloping mountain. The Incas used advanced farming techniques, we learned, and this kind of terraced system was designed to capture the sun, grow different produce at different altitudes and irrigate crops. Canals and ditches helped to harvest all the rainfall. Before reaching it, we looked down on the emerald green ridges from up high and marvelled at how they could have done all that in such a precarious position, with not a motorised digger or lawnmower between them. And then I remembered the aliens again.

Elias pointed out a section of the construction that's still covered in dense vegetation and can't yet be seen from afar. It's crazy to think of how much is still undiscovered up here. As well as more pots, I'm sure there are millions of trinkets you could unearth if you weren't busy gasping for breath and struggling down slopes, jabbing rocky pockets of the trail with a set of hiking poles. Most of the time you can't even look up at the scenery because you're so busy figuring out where to put your feet.

The architecture involved in creating all these terraces is quite incredible, as they're comprised of dry stone walls built with mountain rocks so tightly locked together you can't even pass a knife blade between them. Their structures were built so well, in fact, that they, including Machu Picchu itself, remain pretty much earthquake proof. And the Incas didn't even use any mortar.

Me, Elias and Emma took photos of each other and some random llamas against the deep green and brown valley with our final campsite, Wiñay Wayna, in the distance and then made our way down to it, to find the boys had been taking showers from dishes of hot water while they waited for us. They said they'd tried to buy cold beer, but the price at the camp was the equivalent of something like $8 a bottle so they just had some more coca tea instead. Octavio made us roasted chicken stuffed with cheese, accompanied by mashed potatoes with herbs and empanadas, followed by a cake. God knows how he baked the cake. I'm starting to think he's been sent down from a spaceship by the Incas themselves. Maybe the noble Conehead ones?

We're not at such a high altitude now, so our lungs can relax a bit. Tomorrow we have to get up at 4 a.m. in order to make the final hike to Machu Picchu. Gotta say, I'm pretty excited at the thought of seeing it, finally. I hope it's as good as it is in the photos. I want my own smug 'here I am in front of this wonder of the world' photo, preferably without an annoying Asian tourist in the background, flipping the V with her fingers. There's always the risk of that wherever you go but, after all this, if anyone threatens to ruin my smug photo I am shoving them and their fucking hiking poles off the nearest Inca terrace.

Good night, Diary. Thanks for only getting a little bit crumpled in my rucksack. You're holding out considerably better than me. x

Inca Trail. Day Four.

All right, Diary?

I'm back in the Leonard Hotel now, tucked up in a bed with blankets so tight that reception might need to come see why I haven't checked out in the morning. I'm still writing in you, Diary, a) because we've become so close, and b) because my laptop is still in the safe downstairs and whoever has the key appears to have gone home.

We got back to Cuzco late after taking the train from the town of Aguas Calientes and then a rattling minivan along a highway lit only by a star-scattered sky. The AFL guys passed out with their heads against their duffel bags. It's been a looooooooong four days.

But Machu Picchu. Wow. We had to pack up camp and wait in line in the dark in order to get through security early this morning, but once that was done we were all propelled by an extra burst of adrenaline on the hour and a half march towards Inti Punku (also known as the Sun Gate).

Getting there involved a lot more walking uphill on nothing more than a few crackers and an apple. The porters, including the fabulous Octavio, all raced off early to catch a 6 a.m. train back to Cuzco, so there was no proper breakfast. Elias told us most of the porters have never even seen Machu Picchu. Can you believe that? They just do their job on the trail and then go home. I guess it's like living in New York and never bothering to go up the Empire State Building. What is the prize to us, the pay cheque at the end of all that hard work, is just another thing they can see any time ... preferably when they're less tired.

It's funny. When you start to get close to the Sun Gate, you can hear the excited shrieks of all the people seeing Machu Picchu from up high. You get a tiny bit jealous that they got there before you, and resentful that you've still got about 300 more steps to climb. But onwards you must go. I marched ahead with Emma and Elias just in front and I almost cried when I got my own first glimpse of the ancient city below, all twinkly in the morning light and then streaked by wispy clouds moving across the mountains.

Elias offered me a huge hug and a high five as I took my final steps onto the viewing platform. The AFL boys all whooped and I shrugged my rucksack onto the ground, ditched my hiking poles and just stood there on the grassy terrace, hot, sweaty and soaking in the magnificence of Machu Picchu. Finally.

It was an emotional moment, Diary. Suddenly, all the pain and exhaustion was worth it. Suddenly, as the sun's rays reached through the gate, illuminating the city as they've done for hundreds of years at the same time each morning, not showering for four days didn't matter. Running out of Toblerone didn't matter. Having to sleep on a precarious slope for three nights on Autumn's travel pillow didn't matter. I had made it to one of the world's greatest wonders. I had climbed a mountain on my own two feet.

From the Sun Gate, it was another hour and a half to the site of Machu Picchu itself. On the hike down, we started to pass the day trippers all making their way up and, I have to tell you, Diary, I have never loathed the sight of tourists so much in my life.

'You look like you're going skiing!' drawled one American woman at the sight of my hiking poles. I wanted to stab her in the eye with one. 'Skiing?!?!' I wanted to yell. 'Lady, I have just been HIKING for the past four days. I have WALKED here, whereas YOU just plonked your arse in a train seat two hours ago! I'll show you skiing ...'

To make matters worse, Elias had to tell these tourists to form a single line on the trail, as most of them were so eager to reach the Sun Gate that they threatened to knock our knackered bodies off the path and down the cliffs in their haste to get past us.

Having made it safely to Machu Picchu, we took the obligatory smug photos and, luckily, no V-toting Asian tourists got in the way. Strangely, I saw a girl I know from the UK, someone I went to uni with, in the middle of the ruins. I never even knew she was in Peru. As I pondered the chances of that and this weird, small world, Elias gave us a tour of the mighty Lost City itself. It's even more amazing up close. Seventy per cent of it is pre-sixteenth-century original, apparently, and excavations are still going on in the surrounding valleys. Elias told us that just two months ago they discovered a stone wall running up the side of a nearby mountain, but as yet no one knows what it was for.

My own smug 'look at me at Machu Picchu' shot,
with Elias.

As I mentioned before, no one really knows what Machu Picchu
was for, either. There are a few theories. One is that the area was a
retreat for Inca aristocracy. This might explain why no Peruvians
knew of its existence and also why the majority of it is built to such
an impressive standard. Another theory is that Machu Picchu
was actually a university of sorts, as it seems to offer unparalleled
opportunities for studying astronomy and agriculture. Either way,
it's monstrous when you're standing in it, and it was built to house at
least 1000 people, all of whom obeyed the Incan moral code — *ama
suwa, ama llulla, ama quella* (do not steal, do not lie, do not be lazy).

Not being lazy at all, the AFL boys wanted to climb to the peak
of Huayna Picchu, the mountain that overlooks the spectacular city

and features prominently in so many stone sculptures around Machu Picchu. But they couldn't because they didn't book it in advance. Personally, I was so hot and exhausted that, after a couple of hours' wandering around and sweating profusely through my shirt into my rucksack, I took myself to the bus stop and hightailed it to Aguas Calientes — just a twenty-minute zigzag away — where I holed up in a cafe with an overpriced coffee and rested my weary limbs. Eventually the others joined me for lunch, after which we made the hike uphill to the hot springs.

These were average, as far as hot springs go. To be honest, I had the distinct feeling I was bathing in a square tub of warm sweat and dirt, seeing as most of the people in it had, like me, come straight off the four-day hike and hadn't showered in as long. I spent perhaps an hour in there, washed my hair under a hot fountain, put my grim and bedraggled clothes back on and went with the boys to a nearby bar for a well-deserved drink.

Here in my super tight-sheeted bed back in Cuzco, I can barely believe the journey I've just been on, Diary. The Inca Trail is probably the most exhausting, yet rewarding, thing I've ever done … a thrilling and simultaneously shattering experience that I'm sure won't be matched until I give birth to a child. Machu Picchu is everything people say it is, and more, and I'm so glad I didn't wimp out like those other tourists and take the train on a day trip. To really feel what the Incas must have felt, except maybe the Coneheads who were flown in on the spaceships, you have to live it for yourself.

Thanks for coming with me, Diary. I'm sorry we have to end this thing here, but you know how it is. See you next time my laptop gets locked in a safe. x

Cult happenings and coffee in Cuzco ...

So, I'm having to stop what I'm doing and write things as they happen because what I'm witnessing right now is a rare gem. I'm sitting in Starbucks in Cuzco's Plaza del Armas catching up on some Facebook admin after abandoning civilisation for four days, and a group of hippies appear to have taken up residence at the table next to me. There are twelve of them, all sipping Grande Lattes in Christmas cups, sporting those terrible stripy trousers that look like pajamas. I didn't notice them until the wailing started. Now it's getting interesting.

One woman, I think she's the cult leader, is currently chanting in an indecipherable language in a considerably manly baritone. Another guy is rolling around in his chair with his head back, as though in a trance, and a man with a yellow long-sleeved T-shirt and cropped greying hair is holding his hands to his heart, rocking like he's possessed and muttering under his breath. His eyes appear to be rolled back in their sockets.

Oh my God. You can't make this stuff up.

Oh ... wait ... they're all wailing now. In harmony. And their leader, the woman, appears to be speaking in a voice from another dimension. I can't hear exactly what she's saying, dammit. But I swear I just caught the word 'chihuahua'.

Five minutes later ...

The trance guy is swaying in his chair again, even harder this time, and another lady in a purple V-neck cotton top, who seems quite sane, is looking between them all with some confusion on her face, as though she's not entirely sure what she's doing here. I think her son is with her. He looks about fifteen and keeps catching my eye when I glance over. I feel so sorry for him. His mum probably thought bringing him on some spiritual tour of Peru would stop him shoplifting or spending all day on Facebook, but what she's actually done is ruin his street cred permanently and made him believe in aliens.

Oh, wow … the woman leader is at it again. She's now got her hands out in front of her over the table and she's moving them in a stirring motion, muttering things in changing octaves. I can hear her words now, but they make no sense. I don't even know if they're English. Or from this earth. I feel like I'm in *Doctor Who*; some sort of parallel universe.

How do people do this? It's Starbucks, for goodness' sake. Don't they have some kind of commune to do this in, where no one can judge them? Since when is the world's largest coffee chain the place to sit and channel Peruvian mountain spirits? I mean, don't get me wrong, it's intriguing but …

Oh my Lord, now they are *all* wailing. Wait, the leader is muttering in English. And … is she … crying? Yes, she's crying.

'Tell us who you are. For life and pure love. We love you.'

She is seriously weeping now, guttural bursts, like someone's died.

'For life and pure love, welcome, friend.'

Now she appears to be seizing up. No … hang on. She's scattering imaginary grain around the table with her hands. The man in the yellow T-shirt is gasping, like some of it's got wedged in his throat and he can't breathe. She's still throwing it anyway. If it were real, she'd be making quite a mess. Perhaps she's actually distributing the life and pure love, which we can't see, which we can only feel? I can't feel it from here, mind you, two metres away. I just feel awkward. I keep looking around for the Tardis.

She's singing now. Most of the other people have their hands in a prayer-like position. The trance guy has his head on the table, as though it now weighs too much for his body to hold up. The teenager is concentrating very hard on something with his eyes closed, as is his mum. Perhaps she's decided this is where she belongs after all. No one apart from me is laughing, but then the other customers are round the corner in a separate section, missing out.

It's getting better. I should be paying for this.

The female initiator is now nodding her head, waving her arms about in short, sharp, dramatic movements like a conductor. She's done with the grain but she's still crying. She's so choked up she's struggling to sing.

A cleaner has started vacuuming round the corner — maybe someone spilled their coffee? Remember, we are still in Starbucks. God, this vacuum is loud.

The waitress is approaching. Oh, this will be gold …

'Can I take your empty cups, please,' she asks them over her tub of empties. And everyone, and I mean everyone, stops being weird and hands over their cups. For God's *sake*.

Oh, wait … now they're getting ready to leave. Seems the show's over.

'Thank you so much for that love. It just came to me,' one guy is saying, as he mops his brow with a Starbucks napkin. Everyone else is nodding.

'I felt the energy in my shoulder,' says the guy in the yellow T-shirt.

'I felt it all through my legs,' says a pensioner with copper-dyed hair.

'He was definitely here,' says the trance man.

'My legs have been hurting but I felt this, like, hot energy in my ankles and it's still there!' says the teen, who's going to be laughed out of every friendship circle as soon as he gets home. Poor thing.

OK, chairs are scraping back. They're all off now. The vacuuming cleaner is approaching. Oh, wait, no.

They're hugging.

The leader is wiping her eyes on another Starbucks napkin, as the mum in the purple top presses hers against her bosom, muttering, 'Thank you.'

Still hugging.

OK ... now they're really going.

Wow. And to think I only came in for a Caramel Frappuccino.

A birthday of deathly proportion ...

Being one of only three people staying in the catchily named Casa Hacienda Nazca Oasis Hotel here in Nazca, I had a lovely birthday eve chatting to the other two guests last night — a retired couple called Janice and Bill from Massachusetts. Janice and Bill love travelling. They've been everywhere you can imagine.

Bill works for his own small town's local council and his boss is the mayor. He regaled me with an excellent tale, over our decidedly un-Peruvian chicken *cordon bleu* dinners (we refused the roasted local guinea-pig special, for now, much to the chef's disappointment), about how one day, he was called to remove a severed goat's head from a local bench. Another time, he called the shots on what to do about a severed Asian man's head seen floating down a river.

It was an amicable evening discussing life's little sidetracks, our voices echoing around the empty dining room as the chef looked on in boredom, wondering when we'd piss off to bed. I don't know why there's no one else staying here. It's quite a nice resort overlooking the dimpled mountains of southern Peru's Nazca region. There's even a refreshing swimming pool with a massive rocky water feature in it, which an eager little man rushes to turn on with a remote control every time I step outside. It's a shame there's no one else to appreciate it. Mind you, Nazca doesn't seem to be a very endearing town in which one might stay very long. I have a feeling it wasn't particularly endearing before the earthquake helped demolish most of it in 1996, either.

It's since been rebuilt, but the majority of people who come to this scorched little pocket of Peru, come purely to either sand-board on the world's biggest sand dune, Cerro Blanco, or to see the ancient Nazca Lines from a small plane, which is exactly what I did first thing yesterday morning, having caught an overnight Cruz del Sur bus from Cuzco.

The bus was actually pretty good, as far as these things go, although when I boarded I was asked to pay extra for something. I wasn't exactly sure what it was that the woman was selling but it was cheap, so to save any hassle I handed over some money and took the ticket I was given. Some three hours later, the bus stopped and everyone got off. I wasn't sure why but I figured I didn't need a wee so I stayed put, and then I realised that my fellow passengers were actually all exchanging the tickets they'd bought for some kind of all-you-can-eat buffet in a roadside restaurant. So I missed out on dinner, even though I'd paid for it. I tried to sleep again, but the road after that had more ridiculous twists in it than a South American soap opera and every time I came close to nodding off I would slide on my slippery leather seat, or start to suffocate in the window curtain.

Anyway, the Nazca Lines. They were a bit smaller than I'd imagined, for some reason. I guess the perspective was a bit off from so high up. They're actually spread over 500 kilometres and the largest figures stretch almost 270 metres. I didn't get any good photos 'cause I wanted to puke every time we circled, but either way, paying $95 for the twenty-one minute experience was worth it.

Soaring over these mysterious lines took my breath away. This was only really because the plane kept jostling up and down and doing loops round each pattern, so all four of us passengers could see them. At one point the plane's sick bag wouldn't stop taunting me:

'You're gonna have to use me.'

'No I'm not.'

'Yes you are. You're feeling it. Did you feel that bump? You're gonna have to use me.'

'No I'm NOT. Fuck off.'

I didn't have to use it in the end. But it was a close call.

I'd first seen the Nazca Lines in a documentary when I was a kid and I've been fascinated ever since. They were, after all, like Machu Picchu, created with the assistance of extraterrestrials.

Of course, there are other theories, too. If you haven't ever seen the Nazca Lines, have a little Google, but basically, set quite clearly into the sands and preserved almost completely by the flat, dry, windless desert plateaus are a series of ancient geoglyphs supposedly created between 400 and 650 A.D. They were discovered by a hiker in 1927, although it was an historian studying ancient irrigation systems in the 1940s who flew over them in a plane and realised that the strange lines and symbols converged at the winter solstice (when the sun is at its lowest altitude above the horizon). I can't even imagine the concentration and *time* it must have taken for the Nazcas to get that positioning right. Did they move stuff about on every solstice?

'Not there … not there … nope, not there … not there … nope, not there, not there … nope, not there. Forget it, let's try next time.' Until one year, 'THERE! Yes, there. That's the ticket, guys! Lovely work. Only took 200 years. Shall we grab some corn and potatoes and celebrate by painting some pots?'

It's crazy when you think that these people had none of the measuring tools we have today. Wooden stakes have been found in the region, which may have been the tools used to create the shallow trenches in the ground that constitute the lines, yet the accuracy and intricacy of hummingbirds, a giant spider, a monkey with a spiraled tail, a cartoon-like whale, a flower and a tree — even what looks like an astronaut on the side of a hill — is unbelievable when you see the scale of them.

Some people believe the lines have a religious purpose, although I stand by the alien visitation theory. It's the only one that makes sense to me. Erich von Däniken, a popular Swiss author, maintains that all the Nazca Lines are actually runways in an ancient airfield once populated by extraterrestrials, who the Nazcas mistook for their gods. Several patterns, I swear, really do look just like the outline of a small airfield. You can almost make out a landing strip and spirals shaped suspiciously like landing pads, all etched into the dirt like a blueprint among the pictures of animals. It's creepy. The officials don't agree and don't encourage von Däniken's ramblings but we'll never know anything for certain, so personally I say why not make the sci-fi nerds among us happy and just go with it? Some people are so boring.

Anyway, I'm glad I got to see them after all this time, even if they were more exciting in the documentary.

Seeing as Janice and Bill left for Lima this morning and I was faced with a day alone, I booked a tour to the Chauchilla Cemetery, just out of town. It wasn't the ideal birthday outing, turning thirty-three surrounded by withering corpses, but it was better than sitting around in the empty resort with no friends, waiting for the bored pool man to turn the water feature on.

Chauchilla Cemetery is the only archaeological site in Peru where ancient mummies can be seen in their original graves. The site, dating back to 200 A.D but only discovered in the 1920s, was looted by treasure hunters who took the valuable stuff and left behind the bones of those long dead. They left a lot of pots, too, of course. And bits of pots. I suppose there are only so many pots one knows what to do with, really. Even the tomb raiders were probably sick of them: 'Not another fucking POT. I don't care what it's worth. Leave it there.'

It was pretty cool to see the place in its lonely stretch of desert nothingness, with the mummies returned to their original tombs, exposed to the air, no glass covering over them or anything. These thousand-year-old bodies have been preserved so well by the natural climate that they still have hair on their heads — huge Rasta-like dreadlocks curling around their skeletons, which are a sign apparently that the Nazcas were probably a nation of highly respected priests. Some even have the remains of soft skin tissue in places (mostly on their feet) and coloured clothing still wrapped around them. These people were dyeing clothes, creating some sort of 'fashion' 400 years before Christ; they were priests, warriors, architects (they built some nifty aqueducts, which you can also go and see), and excellent metalsmiths who worked with gold from the surrounding hills. They did heaps of cool stuff with next to no tools, those Nazcas.

Sometimes I think we should change the meaning of BC from Before Christ to Before Computers because, seriously, people got a lot more done before they came along ...

Anyway, so here I am, still alone on my birthday with nothing much else to do in Nazca. At first it was quite thrilling being queen of the hotel but now, having read some more of my ayahuasca book collection, stared at the sky and failed to spot any aliens (again), I'm a bit bored, really. I feel all fidgety and friendless and I'm even considering ordering and eating some guinea-pig, just for something different ... although my brother had a guinea-pig when we were kids and every time I almost order some here in Peru I think of skewering and eating poor, trusting Rumpelstiltskin and I feel like a bad person. Plus, they look like boiled squirrels on sticks. I'll probably just have the chicken *cordon-bleu* again.

Had Janice and Bill still been here, of course, we would have swigged some birthday Fanta and talked some more about the severed heads that Bill's had to evict from various Massachusetts landmarks. That would have been a fun birthday. But as it is, I think I might leave early and take another overnight bus — to Arequipa.

21/11

Canyon cock-ups and Arequipa ...

I thought seeing as I'd had rather a lonely birthday I would book myself into the rowdiest hostel I could find as soon as I arrived in Arequipa, the sort frequented by anatomy-exposing Brits and Australians of the calibre I met on the Death Road. I thought we could all get drunk together and maybe a little bit stupid and I would feel young and rejuvenated and alive.

But on the way to the Wild Rover Arequipa (yes, the place in which the Irish lad soiled his mattress in a drunken stupor is a *chain*), I gave a taxi driver 100 soles, only for him to ditch me and speed off with my 90 soles change.

It's my fault, I suppose, for breaking the traveller's rule and handing him such a huge bill, but I was tired after eight hours on a bus and didn't have anything smaller. So that was the equivalent of $40 down the drain — money I was going to use to pay for the hostel, buy drinks and act like a fool with pissed-up backpackers.

Maybe the universe was trying to tell me something.

I went to the bar anyway, waited about ten minutes for a drunk bartender in a leopard print coat and sunglasses to break away from the girl he was chatting up and begrudgingly serve me a bottle of water, then went to bed in the dorm, where I lay awake waiting for the pulsating throb of house and trance music to stop echoing through the corridors and into my ears.

Not to be deterred, the next day I took myself on a walking tour of beautiful Arequipa and signed myself up for the requisite trip to Colca Canyon, a two-day 'moderate' hike to the world's second biggest canyon (and Peru's third most-visited tourist destination). The brochure made it all look so lovely. It included an overnight stop in an oasis with a swimming pool, all my meals would be included and the tour company would pick me up at three the next day. Excellent.

'That's 3 a.m.,' the young booking agent at the hostel informed me, printing out my voucher dot-by-agonising-dot on the planet's oldest printer.

'Sorry, what?'

'3 a.m. They will collect you here.'

'3 a.m.? That's not still a real time, is it?' I stared at her in horror. I've not seen 3 a.m., I don't think, since I was in Buenos

Aires, probably because I've not really been drinking much, thanks to all these high-altitude pit stops. Funny what a bit of altitude's done for me, come to think of it. Maybe I should move to a mountaintop permanently. My lungs would struggle but my liver would thrive.

Anyway, 3 a.m. rolled around and I rolled myself sleepily out of bed just as everyone else in the Wild Rover was rolling into theirs, whereupon I and roughly twelve other people were driven three hours into daylight in a bumpy van. Then, in a dusty village, in what appeared to be someone's living room, we were fed a 'buffet' breakfast of the obligatory tour-sponsored stale bread, some sort of neon pink ham product and some delicious olives.

The olives in Peru are all delicious, I should say. You can't get a decent cup of coffee anywhere (where do they send it all!?), but the olives are first rate. In Arequipa I discovered an outstanding restaurant that serves the best olives I've ever had. Its main offering is a variety of gourmet crepes filled with yummy stuff (think juicy steak and mushroom, chicken and Roquefort, chicken curry with pineapple, etc), which are all exceptional, but the olives are worth the detour alone. It's called Crepisimo. Look it up.

I like Arequipa, by the way. Apart from their thieving taxi drivers, it's probably my favourite place so far in Peru. It's dubbed the White City because, unlike the grubby London tube stop of the same name, Arequipa is full of pristinely maintained Spanish colonial architecture, built of sillar, a white stone which was quarried from the surrounding volcanoes. A short walk over the bridge towards a Western-style shopping mall provided humbling views of the towering El Misti volcano, sprinkled with a dusting of snow.

Arequipa seems spotlessly clean. There are some lovely churches and monasteries to idle around. The shops are modern, including an unsettlingly large array of optical stores, which most Bolivian and Peruvian cities seem to have an abundance of, I've noticed; are more people blind or partially sighted here than anywhere else? People seem to obey traffic lights, at any rate, a rarity in these parts and their crepes are magnificent. What's not to love? It's the most Westernised city I've found myself in for several months, which I'm not ashamed to say makes me deliriously happy.

What doesn't make me happy, however, is thinking back to the tour I just took. So, where were we? Oh yes, the trip to Colca Canyon. After breakfast and paying an additional 70 soles each to enter the park, we were driven to see some condors at a lookout point. I'm quite sure the condors weren't there, although our tour guide, having promised we'd see them, seemed to think we'd think him a great man if he pointed at distant dots in the sky, which were probably finches, and exclaimed, 'Look, look! Condor!'

Then, off we set on foot down the canyon, along a winding path with even more terrifying vertical drops from it than the Death Road. It was slippery, too. Everyone's feet were skidding on the dusty rocks, even in the sturdiest of hiking shoes. I fell over, as did the girl I was walking with, Charlotte. We bonded as we trekked (she was alone, too, as her boyfriend had to leave their three-month trip early because of severe altitude sickness in Bolivia), and both being British we had a good moan about everything. But rightly so, because our knees were in pain — a pain that steadily became more severe the more we walked downhill. It got to the point, after three more hours or so, where neither of us could walk ten metres without stumbling over in sheer agony and exhaustion.

Just to paint a clearer picture, Colca Canyon is more than twice as deep as the Grand Canyon. It's promoted as the world's deepest canyon at 4160 metres, which you must drop and then ascend. It might sound like a moderate hike when coming from the mouth of a booking agent who wants your money, but in actual fact, when your quads are about to crack, it becomes clear that it's not for the weak-of-leg or wimp. Personally, I found it infinitely more difficult than the Inca Trail, perhaps because I wasn't warned or given any hiking poles.

I will say, though, that although brown and dry, streaked only occasionally with shrubbery or a waterfall — at least until you get to the lush, tropical bottom — Colca Canyon is definitely worth seeing. The perspective it offers to the tiny, insignificant human as the earth gives way to tumbling cliff face is one you know you'll never forget when you're standing at the top, listening to an idiot pointing to a finch and shouting, 'Condor!'

Most of the time, however, you're just looking at the ground, trying not to fall over the edge.

We quickly realised we were also expected to pay for all of our own drinks along the route. This might sound like a silly complaint to you, but these bottles of water we all found ourselves gasping for were *four* times the price of what they cost in shops, and neither Charlotte's nor my own booking agent had told us water wasn't included. On the Inca Trail, they boil water for you as you go, which is free and also helps prevent the trail becoming littered with thousands of plastic bottles.

In Colca Canyon, there are empty plastic bottles scattered everywhere, along with women in those ubiquitous voluminous skirts all trying their best to sell you overpriced beverages at various pre-arranged stops.

When it came to lunch, a stop in a surprisingly green and flowery Garden of Eden halfway down, we were fed a meal of typical Peruvian salted beef and rice and still not given a drink.

Apparently, boiling a kettle was out of the question, even though there were hosepipes coiling and spitting their abundant natural water supply all over the place. There was also an overflowing bucket of 'recyclable' plastic bottles, no doubt waiting to be plodded back up the canyon on the back of a mule, but which, with a bit of planning, could easily be refilled on-site. It was actually depressing.

Once we finally reached the bottom of the canyon at roughly 5 p.m., weary, aching like never before and dehydrated, we were led to our ramshackle rooms in the equally lush, green Oasis resort, but again, offered no drinks. Nada. Dinner was cheap pasta with chopped tomatoes on top, during which it was explained that we'd have to leave again at 4 a.m. for the three-hour ascent back up to the top.

'Do we have to get up even earlier for breakfast then?' I asked.

'No, there is no breakfast.'

'Sorry, what?'

'No breakfast until we reach the top of the canyon, then we will walk to the restaurant.'

'No breakfast before a three-hour uphill climb?' I was stunned.

'You can take a mule, if you like. They are 60 soles.'

'Can we not even have, like, a biscuit or something first?'

'No, sorry. But you can take a mule up, if you like. They are 60 soles.'

'It sounds like you want me to take a mule.'

'Do you want a mule?'

'Do we get coffee first, at least, before the three-hour uphill climb?'

'No, sorry.'

'Then yes, I'll need a fucking mule, won't I!'

Well, Jesus. Honestly.

When we finally got to the top, my bare legs were all chaffed on the insides from rubbing on the mule's stirrup straps. I hoped they might surprise us with a buffet breakfast like no other, a veritable banquet of eggs a thousand ways, coffee of the finest Peruvian bean and semi-naked supermodels in diamante g-strings pouring fruit juice from golden flasks. I mean, you'd expect that, right? But what did we get?

That's right, more stale bread rolls. Only one each, mind you. When we'd devoured them and asked for more, the grumpy server in the restaurant, bedecked in a grotty, stained jumper, said she didn't have any. Oh, and could we please stop asking for coffee sachets too, because we'd used our allocated lot.

I should say that even my mule had a bit of trouble getting up that canyon, and he had four legs. I don't know how I would have done it on two, never mind with no caffeine inside me. Had there been no mule, I'd probably still be sitting there, halfway up, motioning people past me with a pathetic wave until someone three weeks later thought to drop a winch from a helicopter. I can barely walk out of a hostel in the morning without a coffee, and they expected me to scrape my way out of a canyon? We were given coffee on the Inca Trail — why not here? I've never heard of anything so ridiculous in my life.

I guess the moral of this story is, do a bit of reading before you sign yourself up for something silly, which is something I never seem to do enough of before these trips. It's my fault for underestimating the steepness of the canyon, of course, and for thinking myself somewhat of an experienced hiker after conquering the Inca Trail (ahem). But it's also the tour company's fault for not telling us to bring extra supplies, or even providing hiking poles, which would have taken some of the pressure off our knees and stopped us skidding next to perilous cliff edges.

Robbing us every hour for drinks that we'd perish if we didn't buy didn't help either.

When I got back to the Wild Rover, I dragged my aching limbs round the corner to Crepisimo and, over a fine glass of hard-earned Malbec and some more olives, I Googled the hell out of my next stop-but-one, Iquitos. I was determined to do even *more* research into my upcoming jungle adventures with ayahuasca.

I came across a blog on the dangers of dodgy plant dealers and, as a result, exchanged a few emails with a lovely British expat called Andy, who regularly takes tourists to see a trusted shaman called Don Lucho. I'm getting the feeling I've met my guides for this impending spiritual journey, but, as you can imagine, I'm still reading carefully on the subject. After what just went down, the last thing I need is to under-prepare and end up stranded in the Amazon, being eaten alive, while losing my mind to the 'spirit of the vine'.

Not even a mule could help me out of that one.

28/11

Mother Ayahuasca and the three-day itch ...

From the sky, the Amazon rainforest is an incomprehensible mass of green. You can't imagine the sheer size or scale of it until you see it from the window of a plane. I flew into Iquitos after two quite low-key and short days in Lima, and shadows of clouds cast patterns over patches of the formidable forest like darker, deeper sections of a mysterious sea. It was impossible not to wonder at all the life down there, what's been discovered and what's still waiting to be found … and what it had in store for me.

My former brush with the jungle in Ecuador gave me hairy, ceiling-dwelling tarantulas, pink dolphins and a surprise snog in a canoe, but this time I'm getting up close and very personal with the mind and spirit-altering plant medicine, ayahuasca. I'm not going to lie to you, I was pretty nervous on the way here. As soon as I took my first breath of jungle humidity, however, filling my lungs to capacity for the first time in what felt like forever, I had the strangest feeling that only good things would come from this adventure. And it *is* an adventure, isn't it, heading into the Amazon rainforest to drink the sap of trees with people you've never met before in your life? I've still not told my mum.

The Kapitari Centre, my spiritual station for the week, is located a few kilometres outside of Iquitos on the opposite side of the Nanay River. It was founded in 1980 by the shaman Don Lucho. Now in his sixties (although he doesn't look a day over forty-five), this sweet, smiley man spends his days training local communities and farmers in land management techniques, thus preventing further deforestation in the area and creating new opportunities for permaculture around Iquitos. By night he is a full-on demon-banishing, icaro-chanting, healing shaman, of course, who I've since discovered has learned every ounce of valuable information on permaculture he knows by drinking ayahuasca and taking the advice of various plant spirits summoned via his shamanic ways.

No shit. This is serious business.

I met Andy, my email guru, in the popular Iquitos traveller's haunt, Karma Cafe. I've got to say, while my falafel sandwich was exceptional, it wasn't very karmic when I was in there, really. The guy behind the bar was shit-faced, pouring himself large glasses of wine and serving all the hippies their alcohol-free smoothies with the kind of violent swagger that could dent even the most perfectly aligned aura.

Anyway, with rucksacks containing insect repellant, sunscreen, swimwear and not much else, Andy and I headed to Iquitos's little port (in a market, by the river) on bouncy, loud *motocarros*. Here we hopped on a boat and headed out into the thick and sweaty green with a gaggle of soul-searchers, all of us hoping for the kind of head-spinning spiritual enlightenment that would turn our lives around.

I'm currently typing from a netted-in dining room at the Kapitari Centre, doing my best to prevent even more vicious sand flies from feasting on my flesh. I'm wearing a feathered earring, which I bought from a teenage vendor in Iquitos because it felt quite appropriate. I drew the line at fisherman pants and put some deodorant on, but even so, in spite of all this, three days in I'm finding it increasingly difficult to concentrate on anything other than the outrageous itchiness of my skin. Every time I step outside to become one with nature, nature attacks me and tries to eat me.

Luckily there are no tarantulas. We're not as deep into the jungle as I was before and the only wildlife I've seen so far are the numerous cats and kittens who live at Kapitari, and four squawking, Spanish-talking green parrots. These parrots are free to fly around the entire jungle, but choose to spend their days perched in the rafters, shitting on the kitchen cooker or diving at people's heads. They have an eerie habit of mimicking the laughter of the resident children when you walk past, or screeching 'Ola!' at full volume in your ear when they land next to you, eyeing up your pineapple chunks.

Kapitari is located five minutes by boat up the river and then a forty-five minute hot and sweaty stagger through lashings of mud (wellies are a must for this). My group and I arrived at roughly midday three days ago in dire need of a shower, only to learn we wouldn't get one for six days. The only water available for washing in at Kapitari is a lake the colour of miso soup ... oh, and the nightly 'flower bath' behind a wooden screen, which is an essential part of each ayahuasca ceremony, intended to cleanse your body and soul beforehand. You can't use soap in this bath, though, because soap would make the water impure.

We each have our own tiny, netted cabins to sleep in, complete with toilets that have no seats, which is great, but aside from that it's basic at best. There are tons of these retreats around Iquitos but, as I've mentioned before, you have to be extremely careful where you choose to undertake these experiments with ayahuasca in South America, as sometimes, the more expensive, more luxurious options are operated by Westerners with no idea how to hold a proper ceremony.

Or worse. Just a few days before our visit, an eighteen-year-old traveller was found dead and buried in the jungle by a dodgy 'shaman' after an ayahuasca session that went wrong. Ayahuasca itself is not dangerous. There are no known long-term negative effects whatsoever. You don't even get a comedown or a hangover the next day ... in fact, you feel reborn. But if you're allowed to wander off into the anaconda-infested Amazon rainforest tripping on DMT (dimethyltryptamine, a natural component in the brew) you're probably not at the right retreat.

Go with a reputable shaman, like Don Lucho, who not only knows what he's doing with ayahuasca but practises animism — nature-worship and the belief that every living thing has a spirit and soul. I learned a bit about this last year in Bali, where they worship the good spirits as well as the bad to keep everything in harmony, but I'm learning even more in South America. There was a time when much of the world practised animism, but the introduction of structured religions, the concept and personification of a God and the belief that He blessed humans as superiors in the natural world, changed things in Western civilisations, where the natural environment has become secondary to manmade creation. This is probably why so many people are miserable and lost, when you think about it. Our roots are no longer planted in Mother Earth. We look for satisfaction in all the wrong places.

Don Lucho undertook his first plant diet at age twelve. He knows the forest and its fruits like the back of his weathered hand and spends all of the money earned from tourists on his permaculture projects (I paid roughly $500 for this experience). If someone charges next to nothing for an ayahuasca retreat, or similarly way too much, take their promises with a pinch of salt and look elsewhere.

Speaking of salt, we're all on a strict jungle diet while we're here, which is also known as the 'ayahuasca diet'. Lots of cafes in Iquitos offer the same thing and it's basically the most boring diet you can imagine. No salt, sugar, oil, spicy food or sex is allowed. Abstaining from sex is an important part of any ayahuasca retreat because, during the medicinal process of ayahuasca's healing, you're becoming at one with yourself. This is essential, of course, if you're to truly ever let anyone else inside.

I've also been drinking a special concoction in the mornings, consisting of boiled plant juices, which was recommended to me by Jeannie, an Australian and our resident healer. This juice is meant to help open me up to the plant spirits, because in my very first ayahuasca session, I got absolutely nothing from it. *Nothing.*

That's right. After all my weeks of reading and psyching myself up for one of the most intense experiences of my life, I had no experience at all.

'It doesn't always affect you at first. It depends on whether she thinks you're ready,' Andy told me when I expressed my disappointment at the next day's essential group meeting. They always call ayahuasca 'she'. The 'spirit of the vine' is most definitely female, according to those who've seen and heard her.

I was even more disappointed when Gary, an ex-army lad from Britain who's here with his Ukrainian girlfriend, spoke at length on his new understanding of the meaning of life, thanks to the visitation of some remarkably forthcoming aliens. Aliens appear to lots of people during ayahuasca ceremonies, in various forms. Gary seemed totally blown away by what he'd seen.

'I was shown that we're all just energy in human cases, living out these lives, learning our lessons until it's time to go home. But this isn't it. This isn't all there is,' he said assuredly. 'Where we come from and where we'll all go when our human time is up is an infinite space. It exists and it doesn't. But here, where time matters, all we have to do is love each other. She told me. She *showed* me!'

I listened to him go on with my mouth open. At one point, he was almost in tears. I felt so cheated in comparison. I'd been trying so hard. I was even wearing a feathered earring. Yet, while Gary had drifted away from earth with light-beings, I'd just lain there for four hours on my bed-bug-riddled mattress, listening to Don Lucho's chanting, thinking it was the most boring sleepover I'd ever attended. I did vomit in my bucket, though, which made me feel as though I'd participated, at least.

'If you purged, it means the ayahuasca was working on you, even if you didn't get any visions,' Andy told me, sitting cross-legged on the floor of the *maloca* — the circular room on stilts in which all ceremonies are conducted at Kapitari. He was wearing an ayahuasca fan shirt featuring crisscrossing vines, which read, 'Drink a tree. Hug a bucket.'

I already knew from my books that ayahuasca works in mysterious ways and every person at every session, which always takes place in total darkness, gets given a bucket in which to expel their demons when the need arises. The cynic in me still says that in reality I'm downing poisonous tree sap so naturally my body will kick it out, but purging is considered by many shamans to represent the dramatic release of pent-up emotions and negative energy, which tends to build up over your lifetime if left unaddressed.

I felt the sacred medicine swirling around my stomach pretty much straight after I drank it. Ayahuasca, I should tell you, is one of the most hideous things you will ever put in your mouth. It's a rich, thick, brownish-orange substance that tastes like … God, I can't even describe it. Even thinking about it makes me want to puke again. I guess it's a bit smoky and at first I thought I detected a hint of cinnamon and maybe chocolate, but once it's down it's so potent, bitter and vulgar as it burns the back of your throat that your body wants it out, instantly. Some people shit themselves, another form of purging and nothing to be ashamed of.

When you take ayahuasca, you have to kneel before the shaman, who blows some sacred tobacco, known as *mapacho*, over a little bowl of the brew before handing it to you. You down the mixture like a shot, and then try not to hurl on yourself as you walk back to your mattress. You can't chase it with water because it's important not to have anything else in your stomach as the spirit gets to work.

While I said I experienced nothing that first night, I did get a dizzy feeling akin to being strapped onto one of those fairground gravity wheels … which eventually caused me to throw the ayahuasca up, roughly half an hour in. Before my eyes shot open I heard my inner-voice chanting, *faster, faster, faster,* which appeared to be a response to both the spinning sensation and the fluttering sound of Don Lucho's *chapada*, a bunch of leaves, basically, which to me, sounded like a flock of birds taking flight.

After *that* I lay there waiting for aliens to land, until the potion wore off without consequence.

Well, actually, I did find myself crying at one point. It was over something stupid, like being horrible to an ex-boyfriend over four years ago.

'You were crying?' Jeannie said. 'Well, you were releasing your emotions then. And you heard your inner voice, your Higher Self! The ayahuasca was definitely working! You purged, too. How can you say you didn't experience anything?'

'I didn't see heaven or hell! Or aliens,' I replied.

'Then that's not what you need to see. She'll only show you what you need to know.'

'I need to see aliens!' I wailed at the whole room. Well. I've failed at this alien business in both Capilla del Monte and Nazca now, and quite frankly I'm starting to doubt they exist, which is sad.

'She's got other things in store for you,' Jeannie said then, smiling knowingly. And I had to believe her because, since we arrived, this fascinating lady from Sydney, who's been seeing spirits since the age of five, has been startlingly accurate in all sorts of psychic matters. I'll have to tell you more of her extraordinary story later.

I also saw my own aura by torchlight when I staggered back to my cabin after that first session. Waves of energy surrounded me as I did normal things, like brush my teeth and crouch over my toilet with no seat. I seized the opportunity to act out a scene from *The Matrix* in the middle of the floor. Well, you would, wouldn't you? I amused myself for at least an hour, crouching and kicking in slow motion, making whooshing sounds like Trinity dodging killer laser beams.

I put it down to the lingering effects of the DMT but, strangely, no one else saw anything like that, that night. That's the weirdest thing about all of this, I think. Normally, with any other drug, people tend to experience more or less the same things, but not with ayahuasca. So yes … while I said I had no experience that first time, I *did* have an experience, I suppose. It just wasn't like anyone else's.

After a long day in the jungle with not much to do except read, swim in the lake and get eaten by more sand flies, I entered the *maloca* for my second ceremony, expecting much of the same last night. But perhaps something in the plant juice Jeannie had me drink really did open me up because, shortly after I downed the brew, I had a flurry of thoughts and flashbacks to my childhood, stuff I haven't thought about in years.

I experienced strong emotions along with these visions that had me laughing and falling internally to my knees. I heard a voice … whether that was Mother Ayahuasca or my Higher Self, I don't know … telling me to relax. Then, 'Listen,' something told me. 'Listen.'

So I did. And once I'd vomited again into my bucket, I flew. A powerful energy seemed to be coursing through me. I felt calm and blissfully happy and, while I was always very aware of my own body, I was able to flow with wherever the ayahuasca sent me. It occurred to me at one point that maybe if I let my ego go, stopped trying to understand that which is simply not in our realm of understanding, I might reach an even higher level … but even though I heard a resounding 'Yes!' from somewhere, I still couldn't see what that might be. And as the world got stranger I felt myself holding back.

Visions were colliding behind my eyes. I saw green and felt red and heard yellow as my senses warped and tricked me. The enormity of space between each life-affirming thought was so wide and deep I was almost a bit scared of falling into the abyss and never coming back.

I stopped trying to think so much and almost instantly understood, somehow, that people who experience God are simply experiencing their own true selves, minus the ego and social conditioning that's always done nothing but mislead them. I tried to keep a hold of this thought but felt it slipping away with other revelations. Thought after thought after thought crashed in from the stratosphere and split, like someone driving a truck through the fragile strands of a spider's web. I was pure energy. I was the girl travelling the world, and the world, travelling through the girl. I was in a magical, metaphysical paradise, knowing I was God, that *everything* was God, but I was also in hell knowing I've lived so much of my life without really knowing anything at all. (Is this what it was like to live in the acid-riddled 60s?!)

For a moment, it all felt like a colossal waste of time — this constant struggle to *know* everything. And then I saw what Gary had meant when he said, 'Here, where time matters, all we have to do is love each other', because nothing else *does* matter. I saw it then. I felt it, too. Nothing else matters. Not even time. When we die, we live on. We simply float off into the cosmos and become part of it all again, this beautiful, infinite, timeless swirl of energy, and nothing we can do in our human forms will ever compare to the bliss we will feel when we finally let go.

'Listen,' the voice said again. And the world as I knew it exploded into stars.

The hum of the cicadas and crickets outside blended into a monotonous, high-pitched frequency as I buzzed; it was like a dentist's drill driving to my skull, setting every nerve ending alight. This was really intense for the first hour or so. I wonder now, as memories from the trip weave back together in my mind, whether this sound could be the reason for so many people seeing and feeling aliens and alien technology working on their brains during ayahuasca sessions in the jungle. Or are these aliens simply our own selves appearing in a form that has long gone unacknowledged?

After a while, things got weirder. I swear I saw three tribesmen towering over me when I opened my eyes, all with long hair, all carrying spears and wearing those over the shoulder warrior vest-things, like shields strapped on, if that makes sense? I know that sounds bizarre, but that's what I saw. They didn't worry me; I felt a calming energy around them as they studied me. But there were a few other creepy shadows in the *maloca* that didn't feel very nice.

At one point, I saw Don Lucho heading for the door, along with someone else. In spite of my trippy state (although I was coming down a bit by then), I did think it was odd that they were leaving so quickly mid-ceremony, but at the meeting this morning Jeannie explained that Don Lucho had ordered a demon outside, a pretty nasty one apparently, that was threatening to attach itself to his wife. Our shaman had actually left alone, but I wasn't the only one who saw two figures moving through the *maloca* and out the door. I also wasn't the only one who saw and felt some pretty dark energies around us as we all slowly returned from another realm.

Also, last night, the people who came here with the most issues (drug abuse and physical abuse from their childhoods) were the ones who purged the loudest and the most into their buckets. They're also the ones displaying decidedly brighter energies around the retreat today.

There's definitely some magic at work around here. I can't deny that any more than I can deny the stench wafting out from some of my new friends' armpits. It's just a shame that shamans and ayahuasca can't banish the sand flies like they can the evil demons in people. I'm itching so badly right now I'm in danger of scratching my own limbs off.

3/12

A demonic rumble in the jungle...

On the third night at Kapitari there was no ayahuasca ceremony, but weird things were happening all over the place. After the dark energy force that tried to attach itself to Don Lucho's wife, Jeannie saw clearly what most of us were feeling: a number of spirits hanging around, both good and bad, which apparently is quite typical when people are healing. All the negativity comes out and it's the shaman's job to get rid of it once and for all ... another reason why you should never do ayahuasca with a phoney shaman!

Still, it really threw the balance off at 'ayahuasca camp', as did the bizarre behaviour of one guy I'll call Ryan.

Ryan's the kind of guy who always has to be centre of attention, the kind who talks over everyone else and, more often than not, talks for the sake of making a noise. He's in his thirties but has this macho, bad-boy arrogance about him that, in a close environment like this, can tend to do your head in. Most people, including myself, have been trying to stay away from him, and Don Lucho, sensing without being told that Ryan has had some, shall we say, issues with addictive substances in the past, put him on a strict plant diet, including tobacco.

To accelerate the expulsion of his demons, Ryan's been having to drink a jug of tobacco every day, which is basically like drinking the contents of a giant ashtray mixed with water. It's highly toxic. The sound of his vomiting can probably be heard for miles. It hasn't stopped him smoking, however. Most people at Kapitari have been chain smoking since they arrived. I find it quite bizarre that such spiritual, health-conscious people insist on inhaling such repugnant filth. I've spent more time passive smoking on this jungle retreat than breathing fresh air.

On the fourth afternoon, Ryan got a few harsh words from those he's been pissing off. Things were weird, tension was high. Everyone was hot, bothered, bitten to shreds and hungry. I felt like I was trapped in an episode of *Survivor* and there was no way I was going into the *maloca* feeling so negative, so I passed on the ceremony. But while I was reading my Kindle in my cabin, I had the strongest urge to sleep, and some five minutes later — I swear I'm not making this up — I felt myself about to be dragged off my mattress!

You might call it sleep paralysis — you know, when your mind wakes up before your body and you can't move? But it felt so real and when I flung open my eyes I'm a hundred per cent positive I saw a dark shadow over me subside and then disappear. I freaked out, as you can imagine. But there was nowhere I could go, because literally everyone else was in the *maloca*, tripping.

Weirdly, the next morning at the meeting, Jeannie said she'd felt the exact same thing happen to her as she lay on her mattress in the *maloca*, and she'd felt it at the same time as I had. Another dark spirit was apparently trying to make its mark.

Jeannie, as I've mentioned, has been seeing spirits since she was five years old. She's also been able to detect illnesses in other people and, sometimes, cure them. As a teenager in Sydney, Jeannie detected terminal cancer in a woman and later healed her but, not knowing back then how to dispel it afterwards, she contracted it herself. Given months to live, with an untreatable type of lymphatic cancer known as lymphangioma sarcoma growing up her arm, Jeannie asked her dad to take her camping so she could finally see her favourite animals, crocodiles.

Ever since she was small, Jeannie has been visited in her dreams by a middle-aged Indian man in a feathered headdress who would often show her crocodiles and tell her never to fear them. As her dad slept in their tent just outside of Kakadu National Park, the teenage Jeannie wandered off into the lake, where logic went out the window and she decided to go swimming. She touched several crocs before anything happened, but finally one grabbed her, performed the death roll and promptly chomped off her right arm.

When she awoke four days later in the hospital, having lost over two pints of blood, Jeannie's dad told her she'd shown up back at the tent, bloodied and bewildered, asking where the Indian man who'd saved her had gone. He'd appeared to her once again at the bottom of the lake and, once again, told her not to be afraid of crocodiles.

Amazingly, with the disappearance of her arm, the terminal cancer completely vanished, leaving no trace. Could it be that the crocodiles were supposed to save her all along? And isn't that the

231

most extraordinary story you've ever heard? Seriously, someone should make a movie of this lady's life.

Jeannie finally made it to the Amazon years later and knew instantly that this was her home. She now lives in a small village near Iquitos called Padre Coche and, while she hasn't formally followed the shamanic path, she does use her gifts to help people and does a whole lot of great stuff for the local community, including paying for all the kids to get hot chocolate and cookies at Christmas. I've loved getting to know her, actually.

Anyway, with my time at Camp Crazy coming to an end, I decided to participate in the fourth ayahuasca ceremony. Ryan puked more than anyone, which didn't surprise any of us, but as far as my own 'healing' is concerned, Mother Ayahuasca decided to make an award-winning appearance, perhaps even better than the last time.

To begin with, I saw the face of a jaguar right up close, practically stamped on the back of my eyelids. I later recalled that the jaguar is considered a protective animal, as are crickets and praying mantises when they appear in your visions, apparently. Snakes are a symbol of rebirth, and I saw many, many snakes this time, too.

I felt a buzzing current through my body like before, but this time the visions were intense and much clearer, sometimes almost cartoon-like. I saw animals I can't describe and creatures you'd usually only see in fantasy films running through the jungle, leading me to distant shores. But every vision was ephemeral and catapulted into the next. It was almost as though the ayahuasca knew she only had me for a limited time and wanted me to see as much as possible.

I saw people from my past, and people who I've never seen before in my life, including a dark-haired man who I can't picture now, but I remember he had the most beautiful smile. I saw Ryan across the room floating in mid-air with his legs crossed as though he was praying in a monastery (and later learned he used to do just that all the time, in Japan). And *then* I was shown the entire plot of a book. I even saw the cover being waved in front of me by a pair of invisible hands, which were actually more like beams of light. I'm not going to tell you what it was about, but it sounds quite exciting. If I ever get round to writing it, I'll probably have to lie a bit about how I got the inspiration. 'I was lying on a mattress in the Amazon rainforest, tripping my tits off when it struck me,' probably wouldn't make the most satisfactory explanation for some.

I still didn't see any aliens as such, but again I felt the sense of being everything and nothing, at one with nature and the world. At one point, I became aware of an almost uncomfortable heat in my right ear. I vaguely remember shifting positions and 'seeing' a glow around it. And you know what? Afterwards, I wasn't deaf in that ear anymore. I swear to God, the ear that's been troubling me on and off since the salt flats tour in Bolivia was suddenly completely fixed.

I think it was the most powerful ceremony yet for all of us, actually. Another guy here said he's been walking with a slightly twisted foot for years and, during *his* fourth session, he saw a giant lotus flower open up above his head and two alien beings emerge, one of which emitted a beam of light that lifted his leg into the air and sent a high frequency pulsing through it. The next morning, his foot, just like my ear, was absolutely fine. He literally walked out of the jungle with zero trouble. It can't just have been the high-pitched hum of the cicadas in the trees and our DMT influenced minds that did all that, can it?

I'm aware now that I may have lost you several paragraphs ago. Do I sound crazy? Do I sound like a hippy who's about to say, 'Sod the world, I'm going to grow my armpit hair really long and move to Peru, where I will live in a hut and practise astral travel with my new invisible jaguar?'

Well, I'm not going to do that, and I'm not crazy. I don't think. But wow, that was a weird, weird, weeeeeeird experience. Way weirder than anything I ever did in Bali. I can't deny the things I saw and felt any more than I can explain them without sounding like a looney. Some things just *are*, I suppose.

Back to Ryan. We knew from the start he had a troubled and disruptive spirit but now that I'm back in Iquitos I've since learned he went a bit mad at Jeannie's house last night and ran off into the jungle. He must have got hold of some drugs somehow and slipped back into his old ways, which is sad. I guess for ayahuasca to help you heal, a part of you has to want to change.

You're supposed to go into every session with an intention, or a question, and pretty much everyone else who went to Kapitari has come away with the answers they were looking for. Gary, the ex-army guy who saw the aliens on the first night, labelled it as the most profound and life-changing experience he's ever had. For someone who's been in the army, that's pretty huge, and he had come wanting something to make him 'feel' again. Another girl, a beautiful, bubbly Southern girl called Jennifer, also admitted she'll view things differently after vomiting up negative thoughts about broken friendships and people from her past. She felt a lot of love from the people who've stayed in her life, which has reassured her that it's OK to let the others go.

I personally asked for direction, seeing as I never bloody know where I'm going next. I feel as though I was told that I'm doing the right thing just living in the moment. The here and now is all that exists. Tomorrow isn't even real.

When you switch off the mobile phones, laptops, thoughts of money, shopping, work, cars, all the other stuff that clouds and crowds our heads and hearts, this *is* all we have, I guess. The earth. The trees, the sky, each other. At the end of the day, when you consider everything we still don't know about this universe, it isn't really so hard to believe that plant spirits exist and can actually help us channel our higher, better selves; or that they've actually been talking to those who care to listen for centuries in the world's most incomprehensible yet open pharmacy.

Sitting back in the Karma Cafe tonight, reflecting on what has surely been the most bizarre, enlightening experience of my life, I looked down and saw a giant green cricket perching on the arm of my chair, just watching me, like Jiminy about to break into song. There were no plants for miles, nothing but madness and *motocarros* outside. I have no idea where he came from. Perhaps he was a final gift from Mother Ayahuasca, seeing as a jaguar wouldn't have been appropriate for a busy cafe?

I'll never forget my ayahuasca experience, or Don Lucho and his tireless work at Kapitari. Or Andy, or Gary, or Ryan, or the others who've all shared their incredible experiences and time this week. Oh, and if you want to go and stay in the wonderful Jeannie's house in the jungle when *your* turn comes for enlightenment in Iquitos, you are also more than welcome. She opens her home to open-hearted people and, who knows, she might even be able to help you heal, along with your shaman. Get in touch, get some mozzie repellant (for God's sake, get a ton of the stuff, I look like a leper right now) and get ready to go a little bit hippy on the world.

Pirates, the Caribbean and some crepes and waffles ...

I love Cartagena! I can't say this loudly or enthusiastically enough in written form, but picture me jumping on a sofa Tom Cruise style in front of Oprah shouting, 'I love Cartagena!' and you've got the right idea. I think I've been looking forward to Colombia the most, ever since Farzana told me how hot the boys were, how sunny the coast was, how much everyone welcomed her in wherever she went.

Of course, it wasn't so long ago that Colombia was one of the planet's black holes as far as travelling was concerned: a lawless country full of drugs and crime, torn to shreds by civil war, the kind of place that, should you tell your parents you were about to visit, would induce a shaking of the head and a stern talking to about safety. Buses were, and occasionally still are, hijacked.

Drug cartels continue to control small towns, and the country is still the world's largest producer of cocaine (although some might argue that Bolivia still produces more) in spite of 'Plan Colombia' — a US policy aimed at drug smuggling and left-wing guerrillas — driving the violence off the main tourist trail. Most people I've met so far who've been mugged in South America have had it happen in Colombia, but even still it remains most people's favourite country on the well-worn Gringo Trail and tourism is booming year-by-year.

To get to Cartagena I took the ten-hour speedboat from Iquitos to Leticia, where I had to stay overnight, and then an afternoon flight to Bogota, which was cold, dark and depressingly rainy when I arrived. The next morning I flew Copa Airlines to

Cartagena and as soon as I stepped off the plane into the muggy sunshine I knew I'd made the right decision. I made my way in a yellow cab to a hostel called Casa Nativa in the walled city, where I was shown to my bed in an air-conditioned dorm by a cute, ponytailed guy called Carlos. My bed, a bottom bunk, had a curtain around it for privacy, as did all the others, which I haven't seen in any other hostels on my travels. It's such a great idea, right? Sleeping in bunk beds in shared dorms does tend to make you feel a little cheap, not to mention exposed. Why don't all hostels put curtains around them?

The bunks here at Casa Nativa are all custom built and bolted to the walls, like someone's dad's been in with a measuring stick and some chunks of wood and power tools, which only adds to the charm.

After ditching Winnie in the dorm and playing with my private, sliding curtain in my bunk like a kid who'd just been built a tree house, I met a Canadian called Michelle and an Aussie called Naomi sitting in the common area, sweating under a fan with their laptops. Upon learning of my hunger, they marched me out through the maze of narrow streets to a soundtrack of salsa, horse hooves and carriages on cobblestones and pearly-toothed black men shouting, '*Dulce de coco para los locos!*' and on to a place called Crepes & Waffles. My God. Where has this been all my life?

It occurred to me, sitting in air-conditioned bliss, feeding my face with an artery-clogging whipped cream and almond concoction, that even if I never saw anything else in Cartagena, I could leave happy for having discovered my bunk bed and Crepes & Waffles. Granted, Crepes & Waffles is not the most authentic choice for dining in a uniquely preserved UNESCO World Heritage site but when you've been subsisting on unsalted rice and hallucinogenic tree sap in the Amazon rainforest for the past six days you tend to think, 'Screw it.' I was instantly grateful.

With full bellies, Michelle, Naomi and I set off back to the hostel, but it took us literally two hours to make it. The streets were even more alive as dusk crept in and, after taking in a streaky pink sunset from the wall overlooking the crashing Caribbean Sea, I swear, we stopped at least nine times to talk to various people, all of whom wanted to sell us stuff, but who also just wanted a nice chat.

I was introduced to the *arepa* — a delicious and addictive grilled corn patty stuffed with butter and cheese that may just be the greatest food item on earth. We bought beers for 4000 COP ($2) from a vendor and walked along, chatting with others selling coconuts and mango chunks sprinkled with salt, as well as other tourists, butlers outside hotels beckoning potential customers inside, and buxom black ladies with cleavages spilling out of frilled red dresses ... we even got our tarot cards read by a hilarious guy called Ricky, who pulled out one card for each of us and then proceeded to read the meaning word-for-word from a tatty book, in bad English.

We tipped Ricky extra because, after informing us of our decidedly generic destinies, he went on to tell us about some great places to visit in the vicinity and we all sat round on the street together drinking wine from a box. In a city that looks as though a secret gem could be sparkling behind each humongous, colonial bolted door, you definitely need a few tips from the locals. You can do without the wine in a box here, though, to be honest. It's not great. Stick with the $2 beer.

Cartagena's history has inspired many an artist, author and movie-maker over the years. Walking through the Plaza de los Coches, I was reminded that this was the spot in which more than a million Africans were once sold into slavery. I also thought how, unless you read up on the topic, or made an extra special effort to read every plaque in this tantalising tourist trap, positively bursting at the seams with five-star dining opportunities, boutique hotels and bougainvillea, you'd never know it now.

This Spanish colonial town was a major maritime hub for ships that would offload African slaves to work in gold mines and on cattle ranches, sugarcane plantations and large haciendas. The Spaniards would then sail back to Spain, full of exciting stories of pirates and pillage, dripping with the glorious riches of the New World.

Such riches created a land that was rife with violence, of course. Long before cocaine production came into play, Colombia's wealth of gold, silver, exotic birds and tropical fruits caused pirates to loiter with intent around the neighbouring Caribbean islands, attacking at random and trying their best to take what they could from the Spanish, who, poor things, had tried *their* best to take what *they* could from the natives already (karma, anyone?).

When England's Sir Francis Drake came onto the scene with a ho ho ho and a bottle of rum and possibly a talking parrot, the Spanish kings, sick to the back teeth of his antics, ordered the construction of the city walls and fortifications, which cost a fortune and took more than two hundred years to complete. Imagine! King Charles III, when informed of the ridiculous costs for this project halfway through, whipped out a telescope and proclaimed, 'This is outrageous! For this price, the castles should be seen from Madrid!'

He didn't get his way. You can barely see them from Bocagrande, the gentrified strip up the road with high-rise buildings so tall they make the place look not too unlike Miami. But the walls did create the most scenic, jaw-droppingly awesome maze of old colonial splendour inside. Back in the day, the rich lived within these walls, all the viscounts and snooty governors, while the poor crossed over the drawbridge every day to work for them. They were promptly ejected after dark — a bit like most of the tourists are now, when they're ushered back onto their cruise ships.

The next morning I woke up late feeling ill in my curtained bunk, thanks to sitting up most of the night drinking rum shots and listening to a famous Colombian guitarist who, as a friend to the ponytailed Carlos, played an impromptu acoustic gig in the common area. With an aching head and still feeling tipsy, I stumbled back onto the streets for a coconut (because they always cured my hangovers in Bali) and found myself lost until I was found again in the rabbit warren of the walled city, taking in the Christmas trees and flickering, swaying decorations, even more colourful street art, hat stalls, vendors with plastic cups full of watermelon slices … and dodging cruise passengers in their hundreds.

These gaggles of lost-looking crinkly folk are dumped in Cartagena while their captains run off and seduce hot young Colombian girls with salsa moves and sweet-nothings in darkened corners, probably. It appears to be the unwritten rule that, while on land, these passengers must run around spending as much of their money as possible in extortionately priced gift and clothes stores, before heading back to their ships, drooping with perspiration and shopping bags. Judging by what I've seen, most do play by this rule. The rest sit in Crepes & Waffles and moan that they're too hot and that there's not enough whipped cream on their super-sized, calorie-laden sundaes. Like me.

With a fading rum-over, I eventually found myself at the home of what my free, downloaded audio iPod tour told me was the home of Gabriel José de la Concordia García Márquez, the Colombian novelist, screenwriter and journalist. 'Gabo', as he's known here, won the Nobel Prize for Literature in 1982. His most famous books perhaps are *One Hundred Years of Solitude* (1967) and *Love in the Time of Cholera* (1985), which was also, if you remember, a great but ultimately depressing movie. I'm told that this tale of brooding love and suffering in the time of a cholera epidemic was in fact a slightly exaggerated version of his mother's life story.

As a writer with no home, I was quite excited to see this famous writer's house, which stands in full ochre-coloured glory just beyond the seafront. I could almost imagine a writing room inside, with one of those old clunky typewriters and a window looking out over the ocean, and all those romantic couples, pecking at each other's cheeks and lips like lovebirds from their perches on the wall.

Gabo penned stories of the endlessness of death, of loneliness, the beauty in solitude and the search for peace and truth. And as I sat with my coconut, as close to his house as possible, I imagined him gazing at the same sights and felt inspired by the thought of him feeling inspired. Gabo has a very impressive home, it can't be denied, but I bet he doesn't have a bunk with a personal sliding curtain around it. I love Cartagena!

11/12

Candles, muggings and machetes ...

I keep forgetting how hot it is in Cartagena. Today, in my bedraggled, slightly deluded state, I decided to take the tour bus. The first stop was within staggering distance of the wall on the outskirts of the historic centre, about a five-minute walk from the hostel, so all I had to do was hand over my money to the nearest ticket tout and cross the road. It didn't require any thought or brain power whatsoever, which was perfect.

The tour bus is one of those big, red, double-decker embarrassments that you instantly hate yourself for boarding. As I climbed the steps clutching my ticket, I saw the Japanese couple with their huge Nikon camera, and the American ladies with their bleached knee-length shorts and varicose veins, and their husbands with T-shirts too bright for their fading skin tones and I thought, Jesus, Becky, has it come to this? Can you not even think for yourself anymore? Is it really so hot that you can't plan beyond getting off a bus and then onto it again, two hours later, shuttled about on a pre-arranged schedule like a sheep with *tourists*?

And then I thought, *yes*, yes it *is* that hot! It is that bad! And I am a *tourist*! I plugged myself into the American man talking history through my headphones in the air-con and off we rolled around Cartagena. I actually learned quite a lot.

I have fallen in love with Cartagena in a way I never expected to. I feel like I've embarked on a beautiful relationship, one of colour and music and romance … just minus the man. I decided to extend my stay at Casa Nativa because I know everyone there now and, even though it's a bit more expensive than some other hostels (AU$15 a night), I'm loving the privacy curtain, and you always need to pay more for air-con anyway. And also, ponytailed Carlos and Juan Carlos, the manager (you can never meet too many men called Carlos in South America), were both really nice to me after 'the incident'.

It's kind of hard to talk about 'the incident'. I guess I should start by telling you that a few days ago, on 7 December, it was Día de las Velitas, or Candle Lighting Day. It's one of the most observed traditional holidays of Colombia and is celebrated every year on the same date on the eve of the Immaculate Conception.

Día de las Velitas is a country-wide public holiday and the unofficial start of the Christmas season. It's the time when people place candles and paper lanterns on their porches, on the pavements, on their windows, balconies, in parks, streets and squares late at night and let them burn for twenty-four hours.

Looking forward to the event, Naomi and I, and another girl we met at the hostel called Jen, went out to see the sunset, as I've done every day since I've been here. This time we watched it from a table at the famous Cafe del Mar, which is an overpriced tourist trap on the wall overlooking the sea and the Bocagrande skyline. When we arrived, the serving staff seemed to be having a competition among themselves called 'Who can look the most uninterested in customers?' A group of corpses would have done a better job.

Here's a tip. If you're going to watch the sunset in Cartagena, go down to the marina at Manga, which is much less touristy, or settle yourself on the sand close by, in front of some seriously luxurious holiday apartments. Alternatively, if you want to stay in the walled city, buy yourself a cheap bottle of rum and a couple of coconuts and go grab yourself a cannon to sit beside, up the way from Cafe del Mar a little bit. If you're lucky you'll be able to bag yourself one of the arched windows in the wall, which are big enough for two to sit in. These are frequented by snogging teenagers. I always get slightly envious when I see them, because I can't help but think back to when I was their age and how the most romantic place to snog a boy in my town was on the window ledge of Woolworths, or in a phone booth.

After Cafe del Mar we drank some more beers on the streets, chatted to a million more people and discovered that, contrary to what we'd been told, they weren't going to celebrate Día de las Velitas in the historic centre, and if really we wanted to see people lighting up thousands of candles between 3 and 4 a.m., we would have to go out of the city in a cab. Feeling a bit deflated, we started walking back to the hostel. It was, after all, after midnight at this point. And then we met Jonny.

Jonny told us all about his nightclub and how he would love it if we went inside so he could get his commission (not in those words exactly). A lot of the guys in the historic centre are employed to be nice to tourists on the streets, in order that they visit their various shops and restaurants. When we told Jonny that we really just wanted to experience the Día de las Velitas celebrations, he beamed and said, 'Well, I'm finishing up now, why don't you come to my neighbourhood? We're having a party and we're all gonna be lighting candles!'

Of course, the last thing you should do as a trio of slightly drunk girls is get into a cab with a guy going to a distant neighbourhood, in Colombia, at midnight but, like I said, we were a trio of slightly drunk girls and … well … Jonny seemed nice, and we really wanted to see the candles! So we hailed a cab and drove roughly fifteen minutes out of the city, with Jonny in the front seat telling us how his girlfriend's mum was going to be so glad we could come.

At one point, the driver stopped and put some black, mesh screens up over our windows, which I thought was a little odd because it meant we couldn't see out, but pretty soon we pulled up outside a house, where we were promptly thrown into a scene from the movie *Step Up*.

People were dancing on every balcony and front porch, music was blaring from a host of different speakers, and groups of people drinking from bottles and plastic cups were sitting around what looked like open sewers, running like concrete-walled rivers through the streets. It smelled a bit iffy. A few small fires were burning on the sidelines but Jonny ushered us along (after making sure *we* had paid for the taxi) to a little shop, where he made sure *we* paid for the bottles of rum he said were essential.

Then, gradually gathering more and more people behind us as we all walked through the streets, Jonny led us to his girlfriend's house. A large lady called Mama Maria (her mum, we assumed) welcomed us in, took one bottle of rum, which we never saw again, and started pouring shots with the other. We started dancing. We spoke to everybody, although no one spoke any English. We were clearly the stars; the only white people for miles.

I was dancing with a guy on the porch, with my back to the railings and a giant pillar, when suddenly the side of my head was yanked into the pillar at full force at least three times. It took me a second to realise that someone was grabbing the strap of my bag from behind the railings and, seeing as the strap was around both shoulders, they couldn't get it over my head, so they just kept pulling me instead. Naomi tried to get the bag over my head so that whoever it was could just take it and stop whacking my head against concrete, but after a couple more attempts the mugger ran off and I never even saw who did it. I reached up and felt the giant golf-ball-sized lump forming on my head and realised I had gashes on my arm and neck from the strap, too.

All hell broke loose in the neighbourhood. It was *Step Up* mixed with *City of God* all of a sudden. Mama Maria ushered me into the house, followed by Naomi and Jen, and we were instructed to climb a ladder up to the attic. We crouched on the floor while a man with a towel around his waist— I'm assuming Papa Maria — ran outside with a machete. People were shouting. Jonny's girlfriend, who I'd been dancing with, too, was trying to touch my head, sobbing hysterically like she thought I was going to die in her house, while I just thanked my lucky stars it wasn't my actual face he'd smashed against the pillar. He could have broken my nose!

He was also a shit mugger because he didn't actually get my bag. After all that, he didn't even break it and it was only a cheap, shitty thing from H&M. You'd think he would have been a bit smarter and brought some scissors to at least cut the strap but, as it was, he completely failed in his mission *and* got chased with a machete. I dread to think what happened to him, but I'll never underestimate H&M again.

Just as we were wondering how to make our escape, one of Jonny's mates pulled up in yet another car with blacked out windows (which now made sense) and sped us off through the streets like we'd robbed a bank or something. On the way back to Cartagena we saw a lot of candles being lit along the streets, which is what we went out in search of anyway, so it wasn't a total disaster. Mind you, it could have just been that I was seeing stars.

We thanked Jonny as he made sure we got back to our hostel safely. He also made sure we paid his mate 25,000 COP for driving us 'the scenic candlelit route', and him 10,000 COP extra for escorting us home. He also kept our rum. Thanks, Jonny.

So, hmm, it wasn't a very nice ending to the night, but it hasn't stopped me falling in love with Cartagena. We shouldn't have been in that neighbourhood but you can't just sit in air-conditioned tour buses and Cafe del Mar when you're trying to explore a new city, can you? Besides, everyone else, apart from the shit mugger, was really nice.

I just emailed my friend Charlotte (the girl I met on the dreaded Colca Canyon trip back in Peru) and she's decided to travel up this way to spend a 'British' Christmas with me, purely because I've been going on about how awesome Cartagena is since I got here. We can't let one guy ruin things now, can we? I was having one of the most exciting and fun nights of my entire trip so far, before that happened. It's not every day you get to be in a street scene from *Step Up*.

If he'd managed to nick my iPhone and credit card, however, well, that would have been different.

16/12

Playa Blanca and a bit of blubbering ...

I only went on today's excursion to Cartagena's most popular beach destination, Playa Blanca, because I'd already bought the boat ticket. Plus I had a red wine hangover the size of Colombia, having spent most of last night chatting to random guys in a bar in the walled city I've come to frequent called La Bistro. I thought a day ogling hot Colombian boys with no shirts on might ease the pain.

Farzana was right, by the way — the men are delicious here. They all seem to have very white teeth, the gift of the gab, and rhythm.

The guy behind the bar at La Bistro, Klaas, regaled us all with tales of his woebegone yet ongoing relationship with a Colombian girl, which involves a lot of dramatics, by the sounds of it. In spite of the bar being very busy, Klaas took a lot of time out to do things like lean forward on his elbows and bury his face in his hands and make a sort of muffled scream before checking his Facebook page again on his phone.

'This morning I found out she's single,' he said incredulously. 'Can you believe that? We've been living together for two months and she changed her relationship status to single this morning without telling me!'

The poor guy was more perplexed than distraught. I didn't want to say it but by now I've heard plenty of stories involving men who've embarked on relationships with South American girls on their travels. While I don't think any continent's population of females deserves to be stereotyped, it does sound like the girls here are a lot more … shall we say, demanding. And passionate. One guy I met suggested that the females in these countries spend a lot of time sitting around watching the terrible *novelas* — South America's infamous soap operas.

These badly acted shows, bursting with botoxed, trout-lipped, large breasted ladies and long-haired lotharios sleeping their way through well-respected family circles, can be seen crackling from a screen in the corner of pretty much every family shop or restaurant. Each episode is filled with such blubbering angst it's a wonder they don't issue Prozac with the sale of every TV set.

They're very low budget, these soaps, usually. I mean, we're definitely not talking *EastEnders* here, although I suspect much of the budget is spent on tubs of Vaseline, or whatever it is the actors have to rub into their eyes to make them cry.

The theory goes that women are subjected to this nauseating melodrama from the word go and, therefore, they grow up making similar scenes in front of men who don't turn out to be perfect.

'I think she's mad at me because the other night, when she asked if I would cry if she died, I didn't say anything,' Klaas said, shaking his head as though this grave mistake was going to haunt him his whole life. 'I mean, who asks that?' he continued. 'I've been living with her for two months. Is that not letting her know I care? Does she really need to ask if I would cry if she died?'

Later that night, Klaas's girlfriend strolled into the bar after totally erasing their relationship from cyberspace, dressed in the standard Colombian female uniform for a casual evening out — tight white jeans and a halter top with glittering platform heels — and announced that she had terminated their unborn baby (of which he had no idea). She said that when she'd changed her status to single she had actually meant to announce that she was one person again instead of two. Then she kissed his cheek and ordered a drink and went on as though nothing had happened.

Back to the beach trip. Playa Blanca is, as the name states, a white sand beach. It lies on Isla Baru, one of the largest islands in the Islas del Rosario cluster, which is in turn one of the forty-six national parks of Colombia. I'd bought a 'direct' ticket and was hurried onto a boat at 7.30 a.m., where I was instantly perturbed by the ear-bangingly loud Caribbean salsa music blaring from a large set of nightclub-worthy speakers.

A Colombian family, two of whom were respectable-looking women in flowery dresses and sun hats, were drinking Aguila beer from bright yellow cans and screeching. Another guy was falling over the seats, singing a song of undying love at high drunken volume, and a child with beaded dreadlocks was running between them all, begging for attention. The rest of the boat passengers were eating orange-coloured fried goods from folds of tissue, which I'm told are yummy pasties filled with meat and plantain. One day I'll try one, but they always look so dangerously carcinogenic to me, even with a hangover.

We sat there for about forty minutes, ears bleeding in this heinous acoustic mess, while more people piled on, along with vendors trying to sell us cigarettes and bananas and overly sweetened coffee in tiny cups. The music never stopped but occasionally a woman on a megaphone, or at least it sounded like a megaphone, would yell something into the mix that was so muffled it sounded like she was chewing on socks.

One such announcement made the drunk man cheer, crack open another Aguila and dance around everyone, stopping midway to straddle his wife and grind his crotch in her face like a horny monkey. This made the other tourists on the boat, like me, who'd come for a peaceful morning boat ride to a lovely island, want to slit our wrists. I could tell the lady to my left, a sweet oldie who looked American, wished she'd just gone to Crepes & Waffles instead.

My hangover rose a level and, as the boat took off to another round of cheers, I took myself out to the deck, in case I hurled. This was when I realised another giant speaker was poking out of the window towards me in the event that I might miss a beat of what had now switched to some sort of reggae/trance mix. It was like being forced into a party when I'd just crawled out of bed.

I tried to drown it out with my iPod but then the lady with the megaphone/sock came back on and yelled something periodically in Spanish, which I couldn't decipher at all. After roughly fifty horrible minutes, being stepped on by children and danced around by the beer-swilling monkey man, we stopped in Caribbean paradise.

Two guys with caramel skin in yellow board shorts straddled surfboards in the crystal clear blue waters, cormorants swirled, pelicans dived and swooped. And we all piled off, pushing and shoving into the hollers of about a hundred more vendors trying to sell us hats and water.

Because I didn't understand the muffled sock lady, I was a bit confused as to what was going on. I walked around and failed to spot a beach, but people were queuing up for some sort of attraction surrounded by fish tanks. Where the hell was Playa Blanca?

Eventually I was told by a nice Argentinean lady that we weren't on Playa Blanca yet and we were stopping here on this tiny beach-less island for an hour so that people could visit the aquarium. I can't think of anything more depressing than watching fish swim in tanks on a tropical island, can you? It's cruel. Why don't they just leave them alone and sell you a snorkel instead?!

Realising I'd been duped with my ticket and had somehow found myself on the Colombian sailing equivalent of a round-the-houses bus ride that takes four times as long as it should to get anywhere, I sucked it up and plonked myself on a bench by the rocks. Here I watched about 300 people try their best to find a personal piece of paradise in front of five giant passenger boats and even more hassling vendors.

Then, when my time was up I made my way back to the harbour, only to find my party boat chugging off without me. The deck hands even waved back cheerily when I gestured frantically in my bikini to get them to come back. I'd missed the boat by two minutes. I was marooned in tourist hell and, what with my hangover and the hassling men and the serious heat and being abandoned by a boat I hated anyway, I started to cry. I stood there waving and crying like some tortured wife saying goodbye to her sailor husband until a nice man in a uniform came to usher me onto another boat going the same way.

Luckily, this new boat didn't play devastatingly loud reggae/trance the whole way to our next stop. It played brain-numbingly loud Spanish pop instead. And the open bar graciously provided even more opportunity for obnoxious, swaying drunks. I was not having a good day.

After a while, I realised that this second boat was actually going much slower than the first one. It wasn't a speed boat like the other one had been. For about an hour I sat in the middle of shrieking teens and boozing adults and, when we finally reached Playa Blanca, I had about forty minutes before I was expected to join my first boatload again and head back to Cartagena. Turned out my original boat got there in about ten minutes and they'd already eaten their included lunch. Some were even riding on banana boats and lounging around drinking more beers. Fuckers.

I was faced with a choice. I could either eat my included lunch with the new boatload, then relax on the beach and get the slow boat back with them, which at that speed would probably have taken three hours. Or I could skip the food, enjoy the beach for forty precious minutes and only have to endure *one* horrible hour back to Cartagena on the original musical speedboat from hell.

In the end, I decided I couldn't be bothered to eat, so instead I just walked up and down on the sand for a bit, dodging people. Which was quite difficult. I sat down for a moment and watched the kids swimming in the turquoise waves and I was just starting to relax when I felt someone grab my shoulder. I spun around to the freakish site of a lady, who must have been in her sixties, wearing hot-pants and a child's T-shirt with a teddy bear on it.

'Massage,' she said as I did my best not to recoil in terror, and it wasn't even a question, really, because by then she'd taken both my shoulders and was working her bony fingers into my flesh, right where the shit mugger had tried to yank the strap of my bag and where the gashes still hadn't healed. I pulled away sharply, at which she looked highly offended and remained towering over me, right next to me, until I was forced to stand up and walk away. I bought some water from a kid, who went off to look for some change and never came back.

There were hundreds of people in the water. And, unnervingly, loads of jet skis were zooming about within inches of the swimmers and snorkellers. In fact, Playa Blanca, while unquestionably beautiful, was barely visible thanks to the people and touts running all over it.

I'm sure if you stayed the night in one of the tree-house type structures and waited for all the boats to sod off, it would be an entirely different experience (in fact, it is, because I've met people who've hired a hammock for the night and loved it) but I couldn't help thinking how the beach has been quite spoilt and how there are probably going to be better beaches when I get up to Parque Nacional Tayrona, further north (Charlotte's coming now, too, yay!), and how I should have waited for those.

When I walked into La Bistro tonight, Klaas waved and asked if I'd had a good day.

'Compared to you with your girlfriend problems, yes, but actually, not really,' I told him.

'Oh yeah, it's a Sunday,' he said. 'Should have warned you it would be packed. It's always worse on Sundays. Sorry, last night was a bit … well, you know …' He looked at me sheepishly.

'That's OK,' I told him as my wine was placed in front of me.

'You survived!' he said, raising a glass to mine.

'That's true, Klaas, I did. But would you have cried if I'd died?'

29/12

A Colombian quest for paradise …

Not too long ago, Taganga was nothing but a sleepy fishing village, lightly marked on the Gringo Trail thanks to its

Always fun to stand in the location of a Lonely Planet
guidebook cover!

proximity to Parque Nacional Tayrona. This picture perfect paradise, specifically the beach Cabo San Juan de la Guia (which features on the front of the latest *Lonely Planet Colombia* guide), consists of 12,000 hectares of deserted beach, dense jungle and 'eco' accommodation on the Caribbean coast, about a two-hour bus ride up the road from Cartagena.

As tourists bound for the park started to make their way from the nearby hub of Santa Marta to the less crowded base of Taganga, the sleepy fishing village started to wake up. The drug cartels even built some nightclubs, but we'll come back to all that, I'm sure.

Keen for some beach time after a fun but profusely sweaty mulled wine-infused hostel Christmas within Cartagena's walls,

Charlotte and I headed up the coast on a rickety bus to Taganga on Boxing Day. Pre-Christmas, we'd spent 21 December in a sweet local bar waiting patiently for the end of the world — or the awakening at the hands of The *Maestros Ascendidos* — and when it didn't come I said a small pina colada-enhanced prayer for Francisco, probably sitting on the roof of his car somewhere in Capilla del Monte, staring up at the sky, fondling his quartz.

Charlotte, by the way, has had a few adventures of her own since we left each other in Peru, including getting chased and charged twice by a horned bull in a field in Huaraz. Further Googling when we were drunk (and consequently when Charlotte had seen the funny side) confirmed that this happens quite often to hikers on this picturesque day trip through Peruvian greenery, although of course no tour operator will ever tell you.

When Charlotte and I lugged our stuff into Hostel Divanga in Taganga, we were told that we could use the swimming pool at their sister hotel, Casa Divanga, up the road, so we wasted no time in sprawling ourselves on sun lounges and planning our day trip to Tayrona. Here we met another couple of girls, a fun Kiwi and an American, also planning some coastal adventures, but our chatter was interrupted somewhat by the booming reggaethon. The hotel wasn't even playing it. It was blasting instead from a series of humongous, stadium-worthy speakers on everyone's driveways outside.

I noticed this in Cartagena, too. In Cartagena, though, the speakers were placed mostly in shop doorways with microphones attached to them. Men would stand there yelling like crazed DJs at random intervals for people to come in and buy stuff. On several occasions I saw tourists take a tentative step inside these shops and then flee, looking frightened. It must work for the locals, though, especially in the cheap clothing establishments, because there's an awful lot of tight neon T-shirts, printed leggings and garish hooped earrings going on with some of these Colombian women.

Volume plays an integral part in this battle of the speakers in Taganga. Each it seems must be cranked to the absolute max, to the point where the incessant pounding through the cheap mesh is so distorted that you can barely distinguish the tune from the feeling that your head is being bashed in cruelly by the bass.

The funniest thing to me is that the owners of these ear-abusing monstrosities aren't always young men. Sometimes they're really old. Sometimes you'll see five entire generations of one family sitting in front of them on their driveways, on plastic chairs, drinking juice or Aguila or rum quite serenely, munching on their *arepas* as though the throbbing, head-fuckingly loud speaker in their ear is akin only to a fluttering flock of butterflies as they picnic in a quiet park.

Some men even sit in front of them reading newspapers. I don't know how they do it. Just walking up the street had Charlotte and I holding our hands over our ears and speeding up. Perhaps, as someone suggested, it's a keeping-up-with-the-Joneses type mentality that spurs them on here, whereby the family with the biggest, loudest speakers is perceived as having the most money and clout. Who knows? Perhaps they grew up with such things and no longer notice how loud their music is. Perhaps they're all deaf already and don't even know when they're playing music at all. Either way, it was quickly apparent that Taganga is not a place one should come to unwind. We were so wound up after an hour, we decided to head off ASAP.

Being peak travelling season right now, we were warned that there probably wouldn't be any hammocks left for staying over in Tayrona so, whereas the lovely Kiwi Sarah, and the American girl,

Camille, bundled their worldly belongings onto the speedboat the next day, Charlotte and I just took our bikinis and some water.

Good thing, too, it turned out, because the boat trip, which eventually deposited us on the coke-white sands of Cabo San Juan de la Guia, was a thrashing and crashing James Bond-style thrill ride that saw us mounting waves the height of houses to the elated shrieks of our driver and no one else. Had my laptop been on that vessel, I would have cried. Everyone and everything was soaked. One girl was sick in her sunhat. By the time we were approached by the only vendor on the beach, a lady whose homemade cheese-filled croissants were a welcome feast after such horrors, we were all bedraggled, drenched and shaking. I remembered, too, that one of the guys in the book *The Gringo Trail*, Mark, had died in the waves close to here, in Arrecifes — a spot where a fierce undertow and crazy currents claim numerous lives every year.

We'd had the choice between taking the bus along the coast to the park entrance or taking the boat; we kind of wished we'd chosen the bus. Either way, there was no escaping the *muy caro* 'gringo' entrance fee of 37,000 COP (AU $20). No one seems to know what this money is spent on, but by the time you get off that boat and onto land, trust me, you don't give a shit what it costs — you just want to stand on it.

The beach was unbelievably beautiful, like a scene from *Jurassic Park*, all palm-fringed shores and treacherous, galloping waves. At Cabo San Juan de la Guia, the *Lonely Planet Colombia* book cover greeted us — a hut built high on a breezy rock, boasting panoramic views, in which hammocks are so hard to get that, reportedly, backpackers will murder one another over them.

There were a *lot* of backpackers. We set off through the forest on the trail towards the other beaches and even saw people we'd met at other hostels, in other cities! Ironically, it felt a bit like everyone had journeyed to the top of Colombia at exactly the same time in order to spend the Christmas period away from the crowds. The road to paradise, it seems, is a well worn trail. If you need a little time to yourself, bring an iPod.

Our friends finally secured the very last hammocks at Arrecifes, although, as we continued our walk and talked in turn about Mark's death in *The Gringo Trail*, everyone agreed not to swim. Not that we would have anyway. We realised that the sea was too rough for swimming everywhere in the park. It was almost cruel.

The one spot deemed safe enough, a bay called La Piscina, was so full of snorkellers that I'm pretty sure every fish would have left weeks ago. By the time it came for Charlotte and I to leave, we'd taken hundreds of photos but, to be honest, we should have tried to stay over, because we spent more time walking through the forest in order to get to the bus on time than we spent on any of the beaches.

Which is exactly how we came to be in Palomino, two days later, with Sarah and Camille.

Palomino's close proximity to the notoriously unfriendly border with Venezuela makes its stretch of relatively unspoilt beach less of a tourist trap. It's about forty-five minutes further along the coast from Tayrona, and from the sand you can see snow-capped mountains almost 6000 metres high, just forty kilometres away from palm tree-lined shores.

There's hardly anything about Palomino online, or in the guide books, and while most tour operators will advise you not to go — mainly because they won't make any money from you if you head off the beaten track — it's highly unlikely you'll be caught up in Colombia's illegal drug trade or any of the armed conflict that exists between guerilla groups and paramilitaries while you're reclining on an empty white beach with a coconut in your hands. Unless you go off in search of cocaine, of course.

Palomino, we found, was populated mostly by local families all camping out in tents, sitting around blazing fires or paddling in the violent surf. Being the Christmas season, a small cluster of touristic 'hotels' along a small section of the beach was buzzing with gringos drinking beer and burning in various shades of red. We saw a hostel called The Dreamer with shacks for dorms just behind the beach. It had a freshly-painted yellow ring around its brand new swimming pool and we turned our noses up at the obvious blight on paradise. 'How dare they open such a monstrosity here?' we asked each other incredulously, and continued along the sizzling sands. We were desperate for some sort of romance-novel type beach hut to present itself for less than a tenner a night.

It looked highly unlikely.

Soon it was confirmed as impossible.

An hour later, with our backpacks stuck to our skin with our own sweat, we turned around and headed despondently back to The Dreamer.

The blight on paradise welcomed us in with open arms. They'd only been open five days — just in time to save holiday season stragglers like us, looking for a remote, tourist-free slice of sand and sunshine (perhaps also with Internet and access to beer). How absolutely, inconveniently perfect.

Nothing stays off the beaten track for long, these days. At the rate tourism is developing here, it won't be long before Palomino becomes just another extension of Taganga, covered in places like The Dreamer, which, to be fair, is rather a nice place, and great value considering it has a pool and you can't swim in the sea. And yes, it has wi-fi ... when it works. And decent coffee. I hate to say it, but I actually love it. I loved it even more when the barman, Zac, started telling me how he'd been invited to watch 'a donkey-fucking' up the road on his second day of work. Apparently, some young Colombian men out here in the sticks practise the art of sex on donkeys before moving on to women. He attempted to show me proof on YouTube but fortunately this was one of many occasions when the wi-fi was down.

It's still the quiet beach we envisioned would exist up here. Tucking into grilled fish dinners, stargazing from upturned boats on the beach, singing to the guitar around the fire and engaging in the good old-fashioned art of conversation with strangers are all things you can do when the pink sun sets on another perfect day. You don't have to pay an entrance fee, like you do for Tayrona. And better still, you can hear yourself think, relax and unwind, let go of your stresses a while, because, in spite of the inevitable development in recent months, you won't find any stadium-worthy speakers pounding at your ears in Palomino. Yet.

02/01

Stuck-together dogs and other goings-on in Taganga…

2012 was pretty special, but not as good as 2013 started out when we bought some drinks from a cocktail stand in Taganga.

The bartender sets up his little red, yellow and green stall at roughly 5 p.m. every night, though he does take about thirty minutes to make each drink. I'm not sure if this is because there's only one other person helping him cater for the entire waterfront, or because he's incredibly high but, either way, on New Year's Eve, Charlotte, Sarah, Camille and I had a couple of mojitos each and then noticed a Tupperware box full of cake slices on the counter. A sign read 'Special Muffins'.

'You should try, they have spice!' the bartender encouraged.

'What kind of spice?'

'Marijuana,' he winked.

We shrugged and bought a couple between the four of us, never thinking in a million years that they would have any effect. They were only 2500 COP, after all, which is less than $2. Then off we tottered to a restaurant to order one final feast in a year that's been full of the tastes of different countries. It took a while to get a seat.

Taganga's 'scene' still consists of ninety-five per cent locals, in spite of the tourists in high season, and on New Year's Eve the waterfront was crammed full of families in white (worn to usher in a fresh new year), all carrying flowers. Every restaurant was packed. Girls were in their fanciest dresses. Some had clearly been in the salon for hours and most were just simply parading up and down the short main street, looking fabulous. Firecrackers shot off around us, boys on motorbikes tried to dodge the blasts and the boats bobbed gently in the bay in the background.

We ordered steaks and fish, chatting happily, taking in the scene. We waited ages for the food. We waited some more for the wine. It got to 11.30 and we wanted more drinks for the countdown, but waved in vain to every staff member. Vendors approached us with their wares and, in a state of mild amusement, we noted that it's easier to get cocaine, sunglasses and bejewelled, hand-crafted pendants delivered to your al fresco table in Colombia than it is to get a Cab Sav from your actual waiter.

To be honest, we completely forgot we'd eaten the Special Muffins. I probably never would have thought of them again if it wasn't for the fact that my brain suddenly started buzzing on red alert and I found myself thinking obscene thoughts about devouring a chocolate brownie and ice-cream. Looking around, I realised the girls were intermittently staring off into space and bursting into fits of giggles over nothing ... or at least it *was* nothing until we all saw two stray dogs stuck together on the pavement.

One dog, the female, was dragging the other, a male, along on her back, the male evidently attached to her by his penis, which had got wedged in her vagina. I know this sounds gross but it happens sometimes, apparently, and there's really no other way to explain it. If you wanted a more seductive *Fifty Shades of Stray* version, I guess I could say something along the lines of: 'The bitch clasped her ever ready love muscles around her mutt's throbbing member and held on with all her might, until he begged not just for his release, but for his life as she dragged him cruelly, viciously through hell within her vengeful clutch.'

Are you wincing right now? Because I am. Second thoughts, I probably wouldn't say that because, for some reason, all that talk sounds even more dirty when it's about dogs, doesn't it? Forget that happened.

Boys played football with burning fireballs of newspaper and rubbish, which took our minds off the animal kink and had us eyeing children suspiciously as the Special Muffins continued to work their magic. We *all* ordered chocolate brownies with ice-cream. We never actually got any drinks for the countdown, which didn't matter anyway in the end because there wasn't one.

I realised a long time ago that time isn't very highly regarded in these countries. Everyone does what they want, when they feel like it, and the same can be said of New Year. There seemed to be some confusion over the actual stroke of midnight. Every five minutes another group would cheer, or someone else would let off some fireworks. I think midnight lasted roughly half an hour in Taganga, but by then we were all too high and too involved in our brownies to care. We did, however, notice quite a lot of fireworks coming from The Dark Place.

The Dark Place is a hostel I won't divulge the real name of because I'm scared to. You won't find much about it on the Internet or in guidebooks, but once you're in Colombia everyone talks about it. When you walk in, you're immediately overwhelmed by the scale of the place. It looks like a Playboy mansion, complete with a huge swimming pool in the centre of a courtyard featuring a wet table and bar stools. Fancy en-suite air-conditioned dorm rooms open with swipe cards only. Food and drinks are served twenty-four hours a day so you never have to leave. There's a gym, a basketball court and a deck complete with hammocks and a view of the sweeping bay. It's the greatest hostel you've ever seen and rooms are relatively cheap, at just 40,000 COP per night.

But The Dark Place isn't all it seems. The chance to experience the best and purest cocaine in the world is one of the main reasons some backpackers still head to Colombia, and when in Taganga it seems they come *here*. Cocaine is available over the bar at just US $10 per gram. Australians in particular are flocking to it because cocaine in Australia costs up to $300 per gram.

Up to 300,000 hectares of beautiful rainforest is destroyed each year for the production of coca. It's a well-known fact that the farther north you head in Colombia, the better the cocaine gets. The FARC — Fuerzas Armadas Revolucionarias de Colombia — still controls major pockets of the mountains and deep jungle up here, and it's estimated that they alone collect more than US $300 million each year through cocaine production.

The highest coastal mountain range in the world, the Sierra Nevada de Santa Marta, is apparently full of government-sponsored forest watch groups, who've turned over their coca plantations and moved into eco-tourism, although every now and then you'll see a fire burning up high in the hills, which suggests that someone's not happy with something that's gone down.

The other day, Zac the bar man back at The Dreamer told me a cautionary tale. He'd gone tubing on the river near Palomino with a friend, having passed on a tour guide's offer to take them for 25,000 COP. Seeing tubes on the street for just 5000 COP, they'd taken themselves, but the tour guide got very upset when he saw them later that day. Without a local guide, he said, they could have accidentally stumbled upon one of the many cocaine labs operating in the hills and that would have been the end of them.

I met a couple of Australians the other day who told me about a cocaine production tour they did in San Augustin — another popular spot on the Gringo Trail largely thanks to the numerous and mysterious ancient, pre-conquest statues on the surrounding hills. After a phone call made by a man who knew a man, the Australians met with an anonymous bloke in a balaclava at an allocated bar, who then took them deep into the hills. Here they were treated to a behind-the-scenes tour of a coke lab *and* got to keep their own coke afterwards, all for just $40.

I was instantly intrigued, but probably won't be following in their footsteps. No one really wants to come with me, especially not when they can buy the stuff over the counter at a hostel near here *and* not get killed at the same time.

'Ignore us, we're just crack whores,' one girl grinned the other day when a guy called David showed me around The Dark Place.

The pretty Aussie girl was in her mid-twenties, slumped on the floor against a wall with her head on her friend's shoulder. A pack of white powder rested on her lap. Her bottom lip was red and blistered where she'd been chewing.

Her friend was staring into space with her hands resting in twisted, unnatural positions against her body. The bar staff, mostly Israelis, by the looks of it (renowned in town for being unofficially in charge of everything), busied on, oblivious and uncaring. Bikini-clad girls stared at us with glassy eyes in poses around the pool and guys in board shorts grinned behind sunglasses, slumped in plastic chairs. Some looked like they hadn't slept in days.

While I was visiting The Dark Place, I stood on one of the many balconies and watched a deliveryman show up to the entrance on a motorbike. He handed over what looked like one giant, family-sized can of chopped tomatoes to the security guy and then sped off again.

You might say it was just a can of tomatoes. You might say it wasn't.

There are also rumours of prostitutes being brought into the hostel.

I remember once when I was sitting in Casa Nativa with Carlos in Cartagena, a guy came in and asked how much it was for an hour. He wanted to pay for an hour in a dorm room! Imagine wanting that. I mean, not even a cheap hotel room, but a room with up to eight bunk beds in it? Carlos shooed him away but told me it's very common here to enquire about such a thing, especially with prostitutes, because a lot of people live with their parents until they're older and can't be alone anywhere else. The Dark Place, so I've heard, welcomes such arrangements.

On New Year's Eve, we didn't feel entirely safe walking back to Hostel Divanga after ramming ourselves in and out of the nightclub Mirador in a flurry of elbows and dilated pupils. We'd heard that two girls had been mugged outside the hostel while we'd been in Palomino, and it could have been the Special Muffin making me extra paranoid but the drunk boys on bikes beeping behind us as we walked up the darkened street to the pounding of everyone's giant speakers seemed to be zooming extra fast and extra close when they got near us. I'm starting to detect some seriously dark energies in Taganga.

Eventually, back in our dorm, I managed to pass out at roughly 5 a.m., in spite of the pumping music, which didn't actually stop until 8.30. Sarah and Camille then left for Cartagena and Charlotte went shortly afterwards to Colombia's adventure capital, San Gil, so I'm all alone in Scary Town right now, wondering what to do. Moving on is expensive. I left booking my plane ticket to Rio (for the Carnival, wahey!) too late and wound up paying almost $800 one way for the February flight. Right now, everything here on Colombia's coast is double, or triple, the cost! Even getting to Medellín from Santa Marta is over $100, whereas after 31 January it goes down to just over $20.

Tourist season is annoying, if I'm honest — I remember the days back in Argentina in September where I'd have entire dorm rooms to myself. Now it's a struggle to get a hammock in some places, and you can barely move through any dorm without falling over backpacks and discarded Santa hats.

I thought about doing another tour. One of the greatest archaeological finds of the last century was La Ciudad Perdida (The Lost City) and the five-day hike up to it is one of the reasons people come to Santa Marta and Taganga. I was all set to embark on the journey, but wimped out after talking to numerous people who've done it. They've all come back absolutely covered in insect bites.

Allegedly, it's incredible, majestic, mesmerizing, all the adjectives you can come up with for a city that remained lost until 1975, but it's really tough to reach. The entrance can only be accessed at the end of a perilous climb up 1200 stone steps, which take you through dense jungle, teeming with mosquitoes. You're sweating the whole time, sleeping in hammocks and you can't ever shower.

Quite frankly, it sounds awful and I can't be bothered.

Oh, I know. It's terrible, isn't it? I'm here, I might not get the chance to see it again. But I might not get to see Palomino again, either, and I'd much prefer lying on the beach for a few more days with some more yummy Special Muffins, before taking the only affordable transport option away from the coast — my last ever South American night bus, to Medellín.

Well, you can't do *everything*, for goodness' sake.

10/01

The fatties and the Escobars ...

There's a woman in my hostel with bandages around her arms. She's about sixty. Last night she groaned a lot in her bottom bunk and this morning she was very huffy and puffy as she ordered her scrambled eggs. I think the Tiger Paw hostel is a fine establishment, personally, but El Poblado's loudest, most popular party hostel is perhaps not the ideal location in which to recover after surgery on your bingo wings.

Medellín is a good place for surgery, apparently. But it must cost a lot if you have to recuperate in a dorm room full of backpackers afterwards. Perhaps keep that in mind.

Anyway, Medellín is definitely one of the most beautiful cities I've visited in a while. There's a permanent temperature of around twenty-six degrees and the sun always seems to be shining. I particularly like the Metro, too. It smells like freshly baked bread and happiness.

I went to check out the Botero Museum yesterday (also known as the Museo de Antioquia) with a guy called JP. Aside from some suspicious-looking youths sitting under a bridge in various states of slit-eyed intoxication, the Plaza Botero outside with its oversized bronze statues of obese men and women, and vendors selling a variety of weird tropical fruit juices — all of which we tried — was a great place to while away an afternoon.

Fernando Botero is Colombia's most famous artist and you can't escape his work. You'll see reproductions of his paintings of squishy-faced fat folk and sculptures absolutely everywhere. Intrigued as to the meaning of all the plumpness, I was pleased to discover a plaque with his words on it: 'I fatten my characters to give them sensuality. I'm not interested in fat people for the sake of fat people.'

So there you go.

There's something else you have to do in Medellín, by the way, besides photograph yourself under the giant bronzed penis of a fat Botero sculpture. The poster called me from the hostel's pin board: 'The tour that takes you inside of his life. The Escobar family will personally introduce you to their lifes.'

I know something is going to be good when even bad grammar lures me in.

Of course, Pablo Escobar himself is dead. He was shot on the run in 1993 and, in spite of almost thirty years as a narco-terrorist and cocaine trafficker who brought havoc and pain to the people of Colombia, over 25,000 people attended his funeral. This public grieving was a result of the Robin Hood image he created for himself, as a man who relinquished both time and money to the poor, prior to his days as a politician. It seems implausible now, but for a while Pablo Escobar was thought to be nothing but a very rich and generous businessman, who built an entire housing estate for the homeless in Medellín ... and, because soccer was his passion, gave millions of dollars in sponsorship for children's football teams, among other things.

All the while, and unbeknownst to many, Pablo Escobar's drug money was also sponsoring lavish parties held at his ranch in the countryside, complete with hippopotamuses and supermodels. He and his cocaine cohorts were stashing billions of dollars in piles so huge and in places so dirty that rats would eat a percentage of the cash before he could even spend it!

Pablo's brother, Roberto Escobar, is still very much alive and will tell you all these stories and more as you sit in his bullet-riddled living room. At one point, he said, as we all sat around him wide-eyed as if we were listening to grandpa, the Medellín cartel were spending as much as $2500 per month on rubber bands, just to hold all their money together. The most money Roberto has ever seen in one place with his own eyes, he thinks, is $80 million, in cash.

Roberto is partially deaf and blind thanks to a letter bomb exploding in his face, but he's been participating in the tour here in Medellín (Pablo's old stomping ground) for a few years now. If you want to meet him, though, you have to pick your tour carefully, because there are several others that are running without his approval and only one will take you to his house, like ours did. I paid quite a lot for the privilege, I think about $50. But some of this money goes to charity.

Roberto is very into charity now, as you can imagine. I should think if you'd spent so much time in the slammer as the only surviving member of a drug cartel and your dead brother was Colombia's most hated, you'd be quite generous with your resulting wealth, too. He told us how, since 1987, he's been actively involved in finding a cure for HIV. He started to investigate this after using alternative methods to help find a cure for one of his sick racehorses. Roberto firmly believes that his quest to find a cure for HIV is the reason he's the only one of the Medellín drug cartel to have survived. He's supposed to do something great for the world.

The house Roberto currently lives in is the last place Pablo hid before he was killed. To reach it, we rattled up a long and winding driveway that had our van bumping up and down maniacally on stones. Once our driver had pressed a buzzer, a little maid in a turquoise uniform swung a giant gate open to let us in, and there we found Roberto sitting under a canopy on the lawn, drinking coffee, dressed in casual but expensive navy Nautica slacks and a salmon orange Ralph Lauren shirt.

He could have been anyone's grandpa as he stood up to shake our hands in front of the relatively normal-looking, low-level brown and cream house. But an air of knowing and superiority surrounded him as we followed him, as instructed, to the garage. Even without knowing what this man has seen and done, you can tell he's a deep thinker, an introvert, someone whose past plays on his mind like a never-ending movie. You want to fire questions at him instantly, but something holds you back.

In the garage, we saw a small blue pick-up truck from the 1960s, which we were told was OK to take photos in. Roberto bought this truck before he became involved in his brother's cartel, back when he was a regular man with drug-free dreams and a race-winning, professional cyclist in Colombia. I later learned that this truck has a hollowed-out body for stashing cocaine inside; so too, incidentally, does the table in the living room. Once we were all sitting around eating peeled peaches with plastic forks provided by Roberto, our guide, a beautiful Paisa (the name for people from Medellín) pulled the side of a writing desk off and showed us two *casetas* (hollows in the legs).

'Each side is designed to hold one million dollars in cash,' she said proudly. She then swung a nearby bookcase around, revealing a hiding place in the wall the size of a walk-in wardrobe. Poster-sized photos of Pablo Escobar and his family around the house show clearly that he still lives on in his family's memory ... although, when our guide moved one photo aside in the hallway, we were shown a huge bullet hole, reminding us that he was a dangerous man to know. Roberto thinks that Pablo committed suicide. He was shot on the rooftops of Medellín but Roberto told us the two had an agreement, whereby if Pablo ever felt cornered he would end it himself, with a gunshot through the ear. That was exactly how he was found.

Pablo Escobar, as well as being responsible for shipping eighty per cent of the cocaine that made it into the United States, nurtured young soccer players and provided what they needed to improve their game. For a long time it was drug money that funded Colombia's soccer teams and often Pablo and his brother would settle back to watch games as fleets of submarines (all authorised by their allies in the police and military services) sped their goods towards the States, beneath the seas.

In the back of the van, as we were ferried to Pablo's final resting place in the Cemetario Jardins Montesacro, we were shown a documentary entitled *The Two Escobars*, which examines how deadly the relationship between sport and crime could be in this country. It tells the sad story of how the biggest soccer star in Colombia, Andres Escobar (no relation), scored an 'own goal' in the 1994 cup that got his team eliminated, and got him killed. It was Pablo Escobar's money that had turned Andre's team into a team of champions in a time of violent civil war, and because Colombia's national identity flourished along with the team's success and then floundered when they were kicked from the game, Andres, with millions of dollars in gambling losses to answer for himself — mostly to drug lords — was murdered.

The Pablo Escobar tour has become one of the must-do activities on the Gringo Trail and I can definitely recommend it, if only to get a glimpse of how much things have changed in this country over the last few decades. His life and legacy are a story well worth telling … no matter how grammatically or morally incorrect it might be. Some officials are concerned that these tours continue to connect Colombia with cocaine when everyone's trying so hard to keep up appearances of a changed country. But at the end of the day, Roberto won't be around forever to reap the benefits of his former sibling's sins, so I guess it's up to you: would you rather spend $50 on hanging with an ex-convict in his mansion in Medellín … or would you rather put a bit more cash towards sorting out your bingo wings?

18/01

Flamenco, sloths and a cool caffeine fix …

I first saw the trio of frilly men in a coffee shop, but it was only when I saw them again in Exito supermarket discussing the price of cherries that I became properly intrigued. I stopped and asked why they were dressed in such a way.

'We're flamenco dancers,' Ivan told me proudly, gesturing to the other two. 'We have a performance soon. You should come!'

Having become firm friends in the fruit aisle, due to the fact that both Ivan and Fernandez once went to England (though sadly, Don has never been), I agreed to attend their performance a few hours later at a club called Dulce Jesus Mio in Medellín's Las Palmas. Turning up with a few Australians I'd met at the Tiger Paw Hostel, we were all a bit unprepared for the array of neon lights that apparently stay up all year, not just for Christmas. They flickered in an epileptic's nightmare as we were led to our seats by a lady dressed as a whore.

Dulce Jesus Mio, which translates as My Sweet Jesus, is a bit like walking into a toy shop, where everything springs to life after hours. We were welcomed inside by an array of creepy cartoon characters — the sort with eyes that follow you everywhere. Woody Woodpecker nodded and Pink Panther clapped his hands maniacally, close to Bugs Bunny's plastic ears. A red and yellow checked stage floor hurt my eyes and that was before they switched on even more neon. *Jesus* is right.

The place was packed, even at 8.30 p.m. Having paid 10,000 COP each to get in, we were then told we had to buy *una botella por mesa* and then discovered the cheapest *botella* on offer was a whopping 170,000 COP. Begrudgingly we ordered the rum and set about watching the place fill up with even more dressed-up Colombians and people in costumes. We saw several poor Shakira imitators, a few pirates, a couple of clowns, a fat nun in a wig and a rather unsexy town crier, before I spotted Ivan flitting about near a yellow shelving unit that appeared to be full of tiny cars.

By the end of the night (which was still before 11.30 p.m.), powered by the rum and some shots from a clown's bottle of Aguardiente, I was standing on my chair just to be able to dance. There was literally no room on the floor, they'd crammed so many chairs and tables in. After a few awkward twirls with Ivan and friends, and a surprise kiss from a painted man in plastic glasses even bigger than his own face, I was kind of ready to exit the funhouse.

We headed instead to the rooftop bar of the gorgeous Charlee Lifestyle Hotel in El Poblado. You won't find this bar unless you know about it first, if you know what I mean, but head to the penthouse floor in the lift and you'll be swept out into what looks like a sexy, five-star aquarium, with a DJ. Half the room is taken up by a swimming pool with one glass side opposite the bar, giving drinkers the chance to ogle whoever is swimming around in a bikini … or in exceedingly tight, tiny shorts. It's quite pricey, but definitely worth a look for its views. I mean city views, as well as views of semi-naked Medellín folk, who are quite possibly the best-looking people in Colombia. This hotel is gorgeous, too. I got a glimpse of the rooms and they're considerably sexier than my orange-sheeted bunk at the Tiger Paw. Shame the glam-packing days are over.

I should say that I had originally planned to stay at the Black Sheep Hostel while in Medellín (where Farzana stayed before coming to meet me in Ecuador), but the place was recently ransacked for the second time by men in masks, who showed up in a taxi and cut their way into everyone's lockers just before Christmas. According to a Kiwi girl I met who was staying there at the time, they excused two girls in the lobby when they first went in and only mugged the blokes' iPhones, before heading into the dorm rooms for their loot.

I'm not saying don't stay at the Black Sheep if you're in Medellín, as all of this was in no way their fault and I've heard it's a great hostel; it's just that I was a bit nervous already thanks to the attempted mugging in Cartagena, and I really wouldn't have been able to sleep at night if I'd gone there. Plus, Tiger Paw is directly opposite a branch of Crepes & Waffles and you know how I feel about that.

Anyway, after that night out and a hungover morning with JP spent riding the Medellín Metrocable car up the mountain, eating *arepas* and wanting to puke out of the window, the last thing I felt like doing was catching the late afternoon bus to Salento, Colombia's coffee-growing region. But I had the distinct feeling that any longer in Medellín would have been irrevocably bad for my health and a few days spent relaxing in the lush surroundings of La Serrana (a hostel Charlotte recommended on Facebook before she headed home to England the other day) sounded perfect. That was roughly eight days ago. I just can't leave. La Serrana is lovely, and Salento itself is probably the nicest place I've been to on my South American travels yet. I feel like I've been placed under some kind of spell.

As I type, I'm sitting at a wooden table at the back of the bedrooms next to the dining room, looking out at the sweeping green hills and waving palm trees in the distance. Bright yellow butterflies swoop occasionally over my laptop and hummingbirds hover over a nearby hedge. There's a cute little red bird stalking me, too. I have no idea what it is but it's so bright, it looks like a tiny, flapping English letterbox out the corner of my eye.

I have a cup of coffee to my right, which I've been re-filling all morning because they provide it for free — this being the source of Colombia's best — so my brain is buzzing in spite of being quite *tranquila*. A huge black dog called Pablo and a smaller cream one called Salt are sniffing around my bare feet. I could live here, I really could.

It's cooler up here than in Medellín, but not so cool that you can't sit outside feeling the sunshine warm your skin as you lounge in one of the hammocks strung from the veranda ... like Nick, one of the Aussies who's working here to save some cash, is doing right now. He doesn't have to work too hard, to be honest. Not like an elderly man called Howie, who's staying here in order to suss out the price of land in the area. Howie already has two houses in Panama. He told me this when he popped up next to me in the dining room on day three and, between taps to his sparkling new iPad, proceeded to ask me all sorts of important questions, such as, 'What's your favourite drug?'

I almost choked on my chicken curry. 'Um ... I don't know. What's yours?'

'Marijuana,' he replied, almost too quickly.

Howie works desperately hard at being cool. You can't help but feel a bit bad for him because, if he didn't try so hard, he might actually *be* cool. Bless him. Just after we met, I went into my dorm to find an array of freshly pressed shirts on hangers and some dry-cleaning bags hanging from the ladder to my bed on the top bunk. I have literally been sleeping on top of Howie for a week now ... a most unsettling thought, all things considered. Sometimes I hear him unclipping his braces just inches from my face.

Anyway, occasionally it rains here and the whole valley below disappears into thick clouds, making you feel like you're literally on the top of the world. This is also when the magic mushrooms sprout up in the cow fields next door ... but I won't dwell on that because, really, it shouldn't be the reason you come ... even though some people come just for that and it is quite exciting going out to pick them. At night, the fireflies dance in the fields like all the fairies and all the pixies are having a rave in the grasses, waving their tiny glow-sticks in neon swirls and confirming that, yes, you may well be in hippy trippy paradise.

Quite serendipitously, I met two girls on the way here, who I met before in Taganga over New Year. We all shared a dorm room and pool time at Casa Divanga and I had no idea they were heading here until we found ourselves in the same speeding minivan to Salento from Armenia — which is where the bus from Medellín drops you off.

Kelly and Ron (both British) and I shared a jeep, known as a 'willy', to La Serrana itself and, when we rocked up in the darkness, the valley was shrouded by night and all we could see was a bunch of people playing guitar out front and drinking red wine from proper wine glasses. I knew instantly I was going to love it — even more so when we were promptly led from the porch to a blazing fire in the field out back, around which we all sang songs and got ash in our hair.

La Serrana is a hostel but it's also a working eco-farm. It's more like a giant farm house with a few dorms and numerous seating areas, including comfy, squishy sofas and an awesome TV area perfect for folding yourself into a beanbag and watching a movie. Breakfast of fresh eggs or fruit is included. In the day, you sign up on a white board if you want to eat dinner, and in the evening you all enjoy a communal meal around giant candlelit tables in the dining room. These generally cost about 12,000 COP, so it's better sometimes than walking the twenty minutes into town, in the dark, down a long dusty road ... although town has some incredible local restaurants all offering fresh pink river trout lunches and dinners for about 6000 COP, which is probably the best and cheapest food I've come across so far in Colombia.

Honestly, I cannot tell you how much I have fallen in love with this place! All this awesomeness and serenity and it's still only 20,000 COP a night for a dorm, making it by far the best value hostel I've stayed at in South America. We even saw a stray sloth in the tree out front a few days ago, and when he climbed down very, very, very, very slowly and hid in a bush, we were able to sweep the leaves aside and study him up close. I've never seen a sloth in the wild before. He was all fuzzy and had a face like a bear crossed with a monkey. He looked strangely nonchalant in the face of our poking lenses and excited squeals. He must have been extra tired.

A few nights ago, after a day of horse riding and cantering through valleys to a beautiful but freezing cold waterfall, a bunch of us walked into town for the local annual horse show. Everyone was out, standing in the main square drinking shots of Aguardiente (which by the way, means 'fiery water' or 'burning water', i.e., disgusting, but a must if you're in Colombia) and dancing. They were also watching various people do some weird trotting movement on their horses, which made it look as though the horses were actually tap dancing.

Me, Kelly and Ron and two fun American brothers I'll call The Lion and The Crab (like their star signs, Leo and Cancer … they're so different), showed Salento what we were made of by kicking off our shoes and having a dance-off with some friendly locals on a specially constructed stage. Then, an Aussie guy in our group climbed on a horse that clearly didn't belong to him and promptly cantered off around the square — much to the amusement of everyone watching. Honestly, things like this just don't happen anywhere else.

The Cocora Valley is a must-see, too, when you're in Salento. I went with a bunch of American college graduates who were also staying at La Serrana, so I spent the best part of five hours remembering what it was like to be twenty-two. As we wandered the five-hour loop around the valley — part of the Los Nevados National Natural Park — I learned all about kissing boys on acid, teasing ex-boyfriends with slutty Facebook photos, and how best to cook a meal for eight people on just $5.

The same group of girls later tried to share a meal at La Serrana, without realising it was a sit-down affair for everyone at the hostel. It was a bit awkward watching them decide who got to sit in the one seat they'd booked and try to divide a plate of curry into five portions. Gotta say, South America on a shoestring is not as romantic as it sounds.

The walk through the Cocora Valley is quite dramatic, the way flat fields give way to steep hills and looming giant trees. At one point I was so mesmerised by the sheer scale of a towering native Quindío wax palm that I almost lost my North Face trainer in a pit of mud. They were pretty battered by this point, so I didn't really mind too much.

The highlight for me was the little *finca* on a hill, where you can stop to drink hot chocolate with slabs of cheese on the side and watch scores of hummingbirds drinking from special fountains.

Next to visiting one of the nearby coffee plantations and learning all about how they grow, dry, pack and sell their coffee, oh and the horse riding, and hanging out at La Serrana, Cocora Valley has definitely been the best thing about Salento. OK, I like everything. I would stay here forever if it weren't for the fact that Kelly and Ron want us all to head to Cali and learn some salsa in Colombia's dancing capital. Sounds like a good chance for a change of scenery.

The Lion and The Crab will be joining us, too. We've all kind of bonded over sloth-spotting, buzzing on coffee and trying to help old Howie as he looks for the coolest things to do around us 'young ones'. The brothers get the luxury of having him accompany them to the hot springs up the road in Santa Rosa for a few days before they leave the area. I'm happy to let them have him. It'll be weird sleeping without the sound of his braces snapping in my face at bedtime, but sometimes we just have to move on.

The mansion and the wicked witch trip ...

'You have to move your feet, like this,' Alejandro told us as I shuffled with a sweaty, sausage-fingered man from Sweden in the tiny yoga/dance studio in the garden of our latest hostel.

'Like this?' I asked, moving in completely the wrong direction.

'No, like this!'

He pushed sausage-fingers aside and proceeded to twirl me in a series of eight steps I'd never have managed without being encircled in a pair of strong arms, like his. I was breathless and slightly flustered in spite of his apparent gayness. He was wearing lycra shorts and a headband and I was in a bikini top with a flowing skirt. You have to dress the part, you see, even if your two left feet mean you're never going to look it.

Alejandro is a practised salsa dancer who makes every move seem like an act in the Kama Sutra. It's raw sex-appeal, the type that so enchanted me during those first few days in Ecuador when Salvador (oh, sweet, cheating Salvador) danced me around the kitchen with his bottle of watermelon vodka.

I haven't got much better since then — dancing isn't really my strong point — but when the offer of a lesson at La Pinta Boogaloo hostel came up and Kelly, Ron, The Lion and The Crab all signed up, I couldn't very well be the only one standing on the sidelines.

Our latest hostel is more of an old mansion house on a quiet street that we imagine used to be populated by an incredibly rich drug cartel. There's a swimming pool out the back next to the yoga/dance studio, so we've been spending most days lounging around it in the sunshine, drinking beer and listening to each other's music … oh and making friends with the Colombian manager Mario, who's been taking us out in the evenings.

Being fans of the movie *A Bronx Tale*, The Lion and The Crab have taken great pleasure in teaching Mario about the 'Mario Test'. Basically, one of the young guys in the movie talks about a secret test he gives to a girl by taking her out on the highway in his car and seeing if she'll go down on him in front of a passing truck driver. If she does 'she's a pig and she can't be trusted'.

This is now Mario's most-played clip on YouTube and means we're all going around the mansion yelling 'Maaaaaaario' in a Bronx accent. I guess you have to be here (ahem), but anyway, having our little gang all together like this, day-in, day-out, is quite nice right now because, as any solo traveller will admit when probed, when you travel by yourself for so long it's actually quite comforting to find people you can laugh with and share jokes with and be yourself with for a while, like you would with your friends back home.

It's nice on your travels when no one has to pack up and leave again the next morning; when you wake up and know that someone you know and like and trust will still be around. It's really nice not rushing around, having the time to make real connections like this, because it's more about the people than the place, I'm finding. You can be happy wherever you are, in whatever you do, if you're that sort of person. But only by surrounding yourself with strangers for a period of time do you ever get the chance to make new friends. It's been especially comforting here because my gran died a few days ago, and it made me feel quite far away from home.

Over the past week I've discovered that The Crab, in particular, and I have tons in common. We read the same books. We like the same music. We can sit in silence or talk for hours about everything under and beyond the sun. Maybe it's the Scorpio me and the Cancer him, two water signs floating along on the same wavelength? We went to the zoo the other day, just the two of us, and I have to admit when we walked through a garden full of butterflies I couldn't quite tell which ones were real and which were in my tummy.

Cali is the kind of mysterious city that, while being exceedingly large and hectic, is not particularly full of 'things to do'. You can pretty much do all the touristy things in one afternoon, leaving the rest of your days free to learn salsa and then exhibit your new skills at night in a series of dance venues. At a club called Zaperoco we were instantly shown up by a crowd with similar skills to Alejandro. Luckily, though, everyone seemed only too happy to dance with us gringos. All people want to do in Cali is dance, it seems. Or head out of the city altogether for something completely different … like the brothers and I did yesterday, when Maaaaaaario recommended a day trip to San Cipriano.

Now *that* was interesting.

As Jesus, our driver, shot around another corner with the velocity of an astronaut attempting to launch us horizontally into the side of an alien planet, The Lion and The Crab and I grabbed at what we could in the back — namely each other — and said a small prayer that we'd make it to San Cipriano alive. We only wanted to go tubing, for God's sake, but it was looking highly likely we'd end up nose-first in the back of a cattle truck, or speared *Final Destination*-style onto a lorry-load of wooden poles we saw hurtling along the motorway at the speed of light.

Almost three hours later, having made it in one piece, we rearranged ourselves and boarded our *bruja*. A *bruja* — a word that means 'witch' in Spanish — is a motorbike niftily attached to the side of a long, open seat made of boards with wheels underneath it. This runs magically fast along the old train tracks, making you feel a bit like a kid on a fairground ride — or a wicked witch on a broomstick.

With the wind in our hair, the guys and I, and a German girl called Rebecca, soon put the car ride from hell behind us and were promptly deposited in a tiny village, whereupon we were led to wash away the last of our worries in a crystal clear river. 'One of the top five clearest rivers in the world,' Jesus told us proudly. He gestured to its shimmering greatness, already playing host to numerous local families, most of whom had set up tents on the pebbles close by.

Rebecca and I swam in the shallows. The Lion and The Crab both jumped from rocks roughly ten metres high into the twinkly depths. Jesus rewarded his questionable driving skills with a ginormous spliff. And then another one.

San Cipriano is a tiny town of 500 inhabitants, predominantly of African descent (though there were just ninety-two people living in the part Jesus took us to), close to Buenaventura in western Colombia. To live here you have to be born here, apparently, but in spite of this, there was a disappointing lack of people with six toes and hunchbacks in the vicinity, proving that incest isn't practised quite as much as pumping iron appears to be, here. Most of the men we saw (or ogled at, in my case) were bare-chested hulks with bulging forearms and six packs so impressive it was difficult not to reach out and stroke them. Are *these* the hottest guys in Colombia? I did wonder.

After a lunch of fresh fish cooked on blazing coals, we were led down a dirt track beside the river. As we approached the rapids with our giant tyres, we tried not to think about the fact that, beyond the fluttering yellow tails of endemic 'mochilero' birds making hanging basket-style nests from the trees, and the fleeting rainbow streaks of toucans' beaks, lurked members of the FARC with machetes in one of the most dangerous rainforests in the world.

We had no reason to fear the *guerrilleros* in our midst, anyway. Jesus is a well-respected man. Not only can he drive a car like Michael Schumacher on acid, in his spare time, when he's not tubing stoned and bleary-eyed down the river, he practises paragliding, kite surfing, kite boarding and was once even pretty famous in the soccer world. It's all about who you know, in the rainforest.

On the river rapids we were swept along on alternating wild swirls and calmer currents for at least two hours, maybe even longer. I kind of lost track of time (as well as my sunglasses, which are now clinging to the bottom of the river somewhere), imagining a million unseen eyes training on me from the treetops: monkeys, parrots, snakes and more sleepy sloths all peering out from their hidden homes. The jungle world unfurled around us as we spun in frothy circles and, once I'd successfully stopped my tyre from squishing a few sunbathing spiders splayed out in eight-legged abandon on the rocks, it was hard to think anything other than 'Wow!'.

Wow. This is the real Colombia.

Also, I couldn't help but think, as we drifted along in the quiet, of my gran, who recently died. Being away from home made me feel a bit useless at the time, and sad, and sorry, and I thought of the last time I spoke to her and how she told me to take care and have fun. While I said goodbye, I never knew it would be for the last time.

I couldn't help but think of how it probably didn't matter if I screeched like an excitable child on those rapids, or tilted my head upside down over the back of the tube to feel like I was floating in the sky, or yelled at the brothers to do the same in case they missed the parallel world I'd created for us all inside my head.

These are the moments, spinning through the elements with eyes completely open to every wonder (albeit bruising my arse on every hidden rock) that I love this gypsy lifestyle and I realise I'm changing for it. Who cares what other people think, really? Life is short, and it's a gift.

As it was, my bruised arse was soon numbed by the peanutty potency of a local drink called *bicho*, which The Lion liked to call 'a gypsy moonshine.' This is made locally (in a woman's house, I think, as that's where we were taken to buy it) with nuts and sugarcane. We bought a bottle for the *bruja* ride back to the car. It tasted a bit like a peanut butter smoothie with vodka in it.

Thankfully this moonshine also served to lull us into a false sense of security as Jesus rocketed us all the way back to Cali, managing to get stuck in the blessed calm of a huge traffic jam for at least an hour — in a tunnel. Hmm.

Getting to and from San Cipriano isn't the most tranquil experience, really, but take it from me, it just means you'll be even more glad of a homemade smoking contraption fashioned from an apple, or a semi-naked salsa-dancing pool party, or a bit of drunken freestyle rapping when at last you make it back to your friends in Cali (I confess, all of the above has commenced within our mansion walls).

I'll be a bit emotional leaving Colombia after all this time, especially as only Kelly and Ron are coming to Rio for the Carnival and The Lion and The Crab are going off to Peru to zen out in the Sacred Valley. I never got to go to the Sacred Valley, apart from Machu Picchu of course, but I've heard the landscape and spiritual energy there is pretty special. I'm sure I will see the brothers again, though. You meet people all the time when you travel, every day. But there are those who really do leave their mark on your heart. Sometimes you know it instantly … the ones who'll be friends for life.

It's hard to imagine Brazil can be any more incredible than some of the stuff I've seen and done here, but I'm about to bus it to Bogota where my friend Zac from The Dreamer in Palomino is now working as a teacher, and then I'm flying into the frenzy on my ridiculously overpriced one-way ticket to Rio.

Hopefully seeing my old friends, Russ, Koulla, Charlotte (another one!) and Sara again will fill the void. They're coming all the way from London and I've not seen them in years, except for Russ, who came to see me last year in Bali. Russ and I will be going on together afterwards on a trip with Dragoman Adventures, which is an overland trucking company. It's the only way we could find of getting through the Brazilian Pantanal (one of the world's largest tropical wetlands) and through Amazonia back into Peru. It will take us through some of the least visited and hopefully more interesting parts of this massive country. We're boarding after Carnival and will travel until 8 March with a group right through to Cuzco. Apparently the oldest traveller is in his seventies, the youngest is just twenty, and the trip involves long, long, looooong drives and a lot of bush camping. Things could get interesting.

For now, though, we've hired an apartment via Airbnb in Copacabana overlooking the beach, so I'm imagining — or at least hoping — that a few caipirinha cocktails and a week spent dancing on the streets will sweeten the transition between countries. Colombia, for all of its craziness, sexiness, weirdos and yes, even the attempted mugging, has been my favourite leg of this incredible journey by far. I know without a doubt that I'll be back.

12/02

Carnival carnage...

If the planet earth was a giant, dancing, naked body, Rio would be its throbbing penis. I've never felt so much sexiness in the air in one place! Entering Colombia was different in that, compared to the russet-toned, wrinkled faces of the stocky Andean people in Bolivia and Peru, it finally felt like the real Latin America. Suddenly there were tall, bronzed or black and dazzlingly handsome humans everywhere. But it's nothing compared to Rio in Brazil. Most people here don't even wear clothes.

I just lost a bunch of my friends, including JP, who I first met in Medellín, Kelly, Ron, Koulla and Russ, in a heaving huddle the size of a Wembley Stadium evacuation. I think the point at which I found myself in the armpit of a transvestite in a peacock headdress adorned with plastic penises was kind of the final straw, especially as his/her pit was a little bit fuzzy and more than a little bit sweaty. I don't mind when people don't wear clothes, I just mind when they rub their bits against me in a juice bar. Plus, the deaf ear that troubled me in Bolivia and cleared in Iquitos after the ayahuasca camp has blocked up again. I don't know why, but not being able to hear out of one ear is throwing me even more off balance than all these caipirinhas.

I was just forced to abandon ship and flee in fear, so I'm now holed up in my apartment waiting for the noise to stop. You have no *idea* how crazy it is on the streets right now. One million people in one place is not normal, no matter how prepared Rio claims to be a year ahead of the 2014 World Cup, not to mention the 2016 Olympics. And apparently, I've not seen the half of it.

'I went to a blocko last year with two million people,' Ron told me the other day as we all sat sipping said caipirinhas outside a restaurant called Arab in Copacabana.

'How did you cope?' I asked. Blockos are street parties held all over Rio during Carnival. I find these things suffocating.

'Oh, I'd just arrived so I wheeled my suitcase right through it and danced as I went,' she said. Ron's hardcore, if I haven't mentioned. Personally, having spent the last month or so in quiet Colombian havens, most of the time here in Rio I'm walking around with eyes wide as saucers, not sure whether to be enchanted or petrified.

Still, I can't deny that this city is impressive. Two days before Carnival started I found myself with JP and a rock-climbing champion from Illinois with the biggest arms I've ever seen, watching the *cariocas* (Rio residents) and tourists from a beach towel by the sea in Ipanema. I thought to myself, well, how crazy can it actually get? I mean, look at this place, look at the lolling blue waves and the smooth white sand and the grinning coconut sellers. Look at the circling, swirling cormorants, the jutting brown rocks poking out of the turquoise water like ten-storey buildings in a fantasy movie. Look at these waxed to perfection women, sporting bikini bottoms invisible from behind, eaten up by pert, luscious buttocks standing firm in a way that make my own droop even lower in misery … How can a simple thing like a

An abandoned feathered headpiece on the top of a
mountain? Only in Rio.

party change any of *this*? *This*, that has to be the most spectacular
cityscape in the whole wide world?

On day one, a couple of cable cars took me, Russ and co up
to the infamous Pão de Açúcar, or Sugarloaf Mountain. Here
we snapped a million photos of a glittering sunset and donned
some abandoned Carnival costumes, for kicks. These were truly

289

spectacular, complete with huge pink feathered headpieces. Whoever left them must have been mad. I wore mine for at least an hour and I would have worn it for longer if an Aussie bloke hadn't literally stolen it off my head and run off with it. The swine.

There are monkeys up here, too, which made up for my loss. They're so small that they'll sit on your hands, reminding you that behind the concrete and glitz, and the rundown *favelas* on its outskirts (in which a staggering twenty per cent of Rio's people reside), the city is in actual fact a paved over paradise by the sea, which once teemed with wildlife far more wondrous than the jaguar-printed swimsuits that prowl its beaches today.

Equally impressive was Cristo Redentor, of course, Jesus the Redeemer, who stands tall on Corcovado with his arms outstretched in an eternal pretend airplane pose for the city … although I was a bit shocked by the size of him up close, to be honest. He seems smaller than I'd imagined, and he's not very detailed. Almost half-sculpted, in fact. Not that I could have done better, but I guess I was expecting something huge. Apparently it's more impressive from a helicopter, but we couldn't afford that. Personally, I think it's more thrilling to spot Christ hovering in a cloud of afternoon mist from elsewhere in Rio, like a distant reminder of heaven.

Two nights into Carnival, much of Rio was hell. Having ridden the Metro round all day with old women in sparkling hot pants, and men dressed as women dressed as semi-naked sexy Spongebob Squarepants/court jesters, I was sitting on the same beach in Ipanema watching a stream of blokes pissing up against the wall, unashamedly making a public urinal out of paradise. A group of teens in harlequin masks were puffing away in a cloud of marijuana smoke on the sand, an array of speakers were blasting samba in all directions, and strolling along the beach was not unlike I imagine wading through a landfill might feel.

Still, the waves rolled in and out like a pensioner struggling for every breath, clearing the filth as it did so and harboring some vague hope that, soon, things in Rio would return to normal.

'I've never seen streets that have to be cleared by a JCB before,' my mate Russ observed the next day as we made our way from the apartment over to the beach at Copacabana. The JCB (or digger as you may know it) was pulling half of a shipping container full of trash along behind it and the smell of piss and shit was clinging to my nostrils like a tiny, invisible homeless man.

We were nursing hangovers from our night in the Sambadrome, which, incidentally, was insane. If you can imagine 85,000 people screaming, drinking beer, eating terrible 'Bob's Burgers' of the sort you'd usually only find in vending machines, and attempting the Mexican wave, you've only pictured a portion of it. The floats that made their way down the catwalk of the Sambadrome for almost seven hours straight in a constant procession by fourteen of Brazil's samba schools came surrounded by marching bands, semi-naked dancers in heels the height of buildings and thousands of people in costumes the likes of which I've never seen anywhere else in my life ... not even at Disney World. Your average man in a Mickey Mouse suit has nothing on Rio during Carnival. If birds had to die in the making of all these feathered headdresses, there would be no birds left on earth.

At AU$130 each for the tickets, a seat in Sambadrome is not cheap, but if you're going to Carnival, you have to go. It's essential, the very essence of the celebration itself. Each samba school has an hour and twenty minutes to make it down the walkway, accompanied by their own *samba-euredo* (or theme song) and this procession makes even the most riotous blocko seem tame … almost.

It was one such blocko that had made a proper mess of things outside our apartment in Copacabana. These blockos are basically moving parties that start at a designated spot and follow a live band on some sort of float, or truck, around the block. Sometimes these parties are stationary but more often than not you're moving with the crowd, very, very slowly, squished up against pirates, or pineapples or just naked men covered in paint, creating one huge, sweaty ocean of people who can barely put one foot in front of the other. Some blockos have themes. For example, there's a Beatles one soon, during which the band will play samba versions of all the Beatles songs and people will sweat profusely into smelly Sergeant Pepper outfits.

Generally it's expected that you'll dance at these things and, believe me, we've tried. But dancing is kind of hard when you can't physically move. I'm not usually claustrophobic but just now, during a particularly crowded blocko, I had what I can only call a panic attack and found myself squeezing my way back here for some personal breathing space and an anti-oxidising açaí berry smoothie (a super food, don't you know?)

While it's totally great being here with my friends … when I can actually locate them … I can't help but think I'm perhaps a bit too old and boring for Rio Carnival these days. It's one big hen and stag night gone awry and there's just no escaping it.

I'm kind of excited about joining the Dragoman tour now with Russ and making my way through the more serene regions of Brazil, and back to Cuzco. If anything, it will be good to drink something other than caipirinhas for a while. There's another reason why Jesus watches over Rio above any other city. It's positively sinful, I tell you.

Alien visitations and ear probing ...

This morning I decided I should finally get my deaf ear sorted out. It got worse again after I slept on a particularly hard pillow, and Dave and Daniele, our Dragoman truck drivers, said it would be best to get it fixed now, rather than risk going totally deaf somewhere in the Pantanal or the Amazon, where I wouldn't be able to hear their cries of 'tarantula!' or 'anaconda!' or 'fanged sloth!' or whatever else lives out there in the middle of Brazil.

While everyone else in the group was out splashing in a nearby waterfall, seeking out capybaras (sort of like giant guinea pigs), and exploring a landscape forged of quartz crystal and multi-coloured sandstone in the Parque Nacional da Chapada dos Veadeiros, I took myself on foot to the local hospital here in Alto Paraíso – a town they say lies on the same energetic lines as Machu Picchu. This makes it one of the most powerful and spiritual places in South America, a fact the hippies have certainly bought into.

Numerous fake spaceships are erected on driveways and an abundance of boutique stores sell nothing but nuts, crystals and incense. Shops here have names like Doors of Perception and Serendipity and Gems of the Earth. There's even a restaurant called Astral Sushi, although I haven't seen it open since we arrived, so perhaps they simply operate on another plane.

Indeed, barely anything is ever open here. It reminds me of Capilla del Monte back in Argentina, where for most of the time it was just me and the stray dogs hanging out on empty streets. I'm not sure why hippy towns don't open their shops very often, especially when they see a giant orange and white truck sporting fifteen camera-toting tourists rocking up, but perhaps they're all just too busy clutching their crystals and discussing when the *Maestros Ascendidos* will arrive, seeing as they never made it in December. It must be a worrying time for them.

Anyway, the hospital. I wasn't sure if it was a hospital or a Rotary club when I first walked in, as the building had both signs on the front. I managed to find the reception and held up my phone with a Portuguese Google translation on it for 'ear plug stuck in ear, needs unblocking, please' to a lady who looked about sixteen. She had braces on her teeth and was dressed in a neon yellow T-shirt so loud my deaf ear almost imploded. I was hoping she'd understand that it was time to get it syringed, and if the members of a Rotary club were the ones to do it, so be it. At this point, I really didn't care.

After filling in a form, she and her colleague sent me back to my bench seat and, as I sat, I noticed a model of Jesus with his arms wide open standing on a shelf behind them. The woman in the yellow top stood up to shove a thermometer under someone's arm right there in the waiting room, just as a dreadlocked man holding a tray of handmade earrings sauntered in and stood there looking pained. For a moment I thought he was going to try and sell me something. A bearded man beside me was told to stand on some scales so old they had one of those measuring bars at chest height with weights on it, and I noted a water cooler held together with masking tape was struggling to stand up in the corner. A guy in a purple shirt with acne sat with his head in his hands on a bench behind mine, and a chat show featuring three glossy-haired, pearly-toothed Brazilian ladies blasted from a TV on the wall above a row of dilapidated wheelchairs.

Three windows appeared to have been painted black to stop the sun streaming in and, as I sat there with one eye on Jesus and the other on the earring-seller now motioning to a wound on his leg, I hoped that the money they'd clearly saved by skimping on curtains had been spent on ear-unblocking equipment.

The woman in yellow was looking at me in bewilderment at this point. I tried to see things from her point of view. I was a freak who'd come in with no ID except an outdated driving license, no understanding of the native language, tapping into a strange gadget and miming swirling movements around my head. Of course, I was indicating how I was slowly going deaf and could barely hear the world around me, but for all she and her colleague knew I could have been claiming to have been abducted by aliens.

I realised then that quite possibly I should have had this problem addressed somewhere more touristy, like Cuzco, but back then I was too busy listening in on sobbing, hippy alien worshippers droning on about alternate dimensions in Starbucks. The irony of this does not escape me.

Eventually I was led through to a consultation room, where I spoke in English and the female doctor — a very kindly-looking, but very, very short lady who could have actually been a Hobbit — spoke in Portuguese. We both pretended to understand each other and somehow came to the conclusion that something was indeed stuck in my ear. Then she walked me through to another room and told me to sit on a bed. Before she left, I thought she indicated for me to take my top off, which I thought was a reasonable request, because no one wants to get earwax on their clothing. Luckily I was wearing my bikini top underneath, so I obliged. A few minutes later she came back in with a male doctor and shot me a look of utter disdain. I realised she hadn't told me to remove any clothing at all — I'd simply chosen to take off my top and arrange myself on her bed. No wonder these people get upset with gringos.

The male doctor unwrapped a series of instruments and arranged them on a tray and then looked at them in confusion, which wasn't a good sign. Then his mobile rang and they both left the room again, leaving me sitting there on the bed noting how *these* windows were painted *blue* to stop the sun coming in. I thought maybe they'd run out of black paint and couldn't afford any more, which in turn made me wonder what ear-unblocking equipment they'd been meaning to order but hadn't and whether that was why the guy had looked so confused and left the room.

I continued to sit there for almost forty minutes with the tray of instruments beside me. Various people wandered in and out collecting items from metal drawers and tubs and other containers but no one looked at me. Not knowing how to request a timeframe in which I was likely to be attended to, I busied myself with counting the large brushstrokes on the blue windows (there were twelve on one) and then attempted to translate a sign with a photo of what might have been a poisonous scorpion on it. I was just about to blow up a rubber glove and create a chicken head with a crest of five puffy plumes when both doctors came back in with what I assume was the missing item and proceeded to clear my ear. It took all of five minutes, after which the Hobbit lady took great delight in showing me a clump of silicone, the very one that had, of course, been stuck in there since the salt flats tour in Bolivia.

I could have hugged her as the noises from the street and the waiting room and the fridge in the corner flooded my eardrum once more, but I didn't because she was only little and she might have fallen over. The joy of hearing is something I will never take for granted again. Oh, and she didn't charge me a penny, either. She simply sent me off with what I assume was a warning in Portuguese, to never, ever wear ear plugs again, or at least not the teeny tiny ones of the sort she'd just sucked out of my ear with a probe she could well have borrowed from the aliens.

I decided after that to stroll into town and buy myself a rose quartz, as you do. It's my 'I'm not deaf anymore, hurrah!' rose quartz and it's now hanging around my neck to help open my heart chakra and make me feel more positive and loving. Feeling very much full of love and appreciation for my working ear and for Hobbits, and for sunshine and towns full of aliens, I also bought another açaí berry smoothie (an addiction you *will* form in Brazil, no matter where you go) from one of the only places that was open, which is when I met Ivan.

Ivan is a Brazilian–German tour guide who also welcomes travellers into his home, on the assumption that they will smoke copious amounts of weed with him and talk about crystals. He has ginger dreadlocks and perfectly even teeth. We got chatting over our smoothies, and Stef and Ladina, two other girls from my Dragoman group, turned up. After a while, he invited us all to his house because he wanted very much to show us the place in his garden where he holds campfires, with room for a hundred people to gather round. Not having anything else to do, seeing as nothing was open, we followed him and spent a good two hours oohing and aahing over everything he told and showed us, which, as well as the camp fire spot, included various gnarled branches he'd picked up from the nearby forest and given names.

'This one is the whale,' he said, pointing to a lump of bark he'd strung from the ceiling. It had a vague hump on its back. 'This one's the ballerina, and this one's Jesus.'

Jesus, which looked to me a lot like a stick pinned across another stick, was nailed to the wall above the door and I concluded that Ivan must have a lot of time on his hands to think very deeply about a lot of things. And a lot of weed.

Before we could think about escaping, Ivan's friend showed up — a man with the biggest dreadlocks I've ever seen. These ratted, matted tufts of hair were as wide as tree trunks, and it did cross my mind, as he swept me up into an inescapable hug that lasted at least five minutes and sucked me into a dark, dark vortex of BO, unwashed hair and the vague smell of incense, that if I stayed somewhere like this too long, my hair might actually start to dreadlock itself. Perhaps that's how it happens. Or is that what the aliens are doing as they hover over this spiritual town, emitting some sort of strange frequency that only dogs and hair can hear?

Ivan and his friend decided they were going to show us some videos on YouTube of a dance and theatre group they belong to. These videos were very impressive the first time we watched them, but when they played them again and sang along with their online-selves at high volume, we started to feel a bit trapped. This feeling intensified when the computer was turned off altogether and we were treated to high-speed freestyle versions of tracks by Cypress Hill and House of Pain as we all sat cross-legged on his woven mat. These tracks helped Ivan to learn English before he learned it properly from couch surfers and Quentin Tarantino movies.

Finally we made our exit, but not before we were hugged again and kissed goodbye on the lips. I'm starting to like Alto Paraíso, especially now I can hear again, but alas, we're going to have to move on soon. We've still got a long way to go before we get to Cuzco, and I guess it will be better for our hair if we go, anyway.

28/02

The Pantanal and a public flogging ...

'I'm seriously PMS-ing over here,' Russ said in frustration as he smeared the window of our bouncing truck with another coating of sunscreen from his forehead.

Russ started taking anti-malarial pills somewhere between Alto Paraíso and Brasilia and has since been struck with sudden emotional bursts that he says are opening his eyes to what it must be like to be a woman. I have to say, dark-mood inducing anti-malarials are dangerous at the best of times, not least on a long-distance truck journey with fifteen people you may or may not exactly get along with.

Travelling in a group after all this time going relatively solo isn't always easy. There are strict schedules to adhere to, whingers to deal with, muddy tents to erect and a strange rule about 'flapping' your dishes after each camp meal, meaning we must all stand in a field like raving scarecrows waving plates and spoons about until they're dry. Towels are full of germs, you see.

We are also not allowed to call the Dragoman truck a bus. If we do, we must perform five press-ups. This was funny the first time, but after the ninth mistake or so my arms are starting to burn. In fact, *all* of it is fun, until you're knackered and sweaty and haven't showered in four days and the Indian girl is still asking if she can upgrade to a hotel while the rest of you sleep in tents surrounded by crawling, hairy, black tarantulas (this really happened!) — then it's just a bit of a stupid idea you wish you'd cancelled.

Ah, I don't mean that. See how knackered I am? It's just that travelling overland like this is not for everyone and there will be moments when you hate it. There will also be moments you'll remember forever that make it all worthwhile. I guess because Brazil is so frickin' huge we're spending a lot of time trundling along dirt roads and highways in the truck just to reach each point of interest. We're getting a great insight into what it's like to be a lorry driver, though, eating only indistinguishable foods that have been deep fried to within an inch of their existence along the way. Brazil offers free coffee, too, in every service station.

Gearing up for the jungle with the Dragoman crew.

This excited me greatly until I tried to drink some and discovered it was ninety per cent sugar.

I will say that one seventy-something-year-old guy on the truck, Ken, is fantastic. He was on the hunt for Che Guevara in the sixties, used to own a baby food factory and has all sorts of cool stories, confirming my previous statement that old people are awesome. I call him Khaki Ken because, since we left Rio, he has worn only beige hunting outfits, as though we might deposit him at any moment in the jungle and leave him to fend for himself.

A two-night stop in a colonial gold mining town called Ouro Preto was a welcome break — it's like a Brazilian Cotswolds, if you can imagine that. Very quaint. Dave, our chirpy British driver, loves it particularly because it has a shop that sells the best hot chocolate in the world.

'It's like real melted chocolate!' he enthused and hurried off quickly along the cobbled streets to buy some while the rest of us went to see two mines. He's been to Ouro Preto before, of course, so I guess the highlights are different for him now.

A guy called Billy, who sounded American and looked like a weathered George Clooney, took great pleasure in showing us round Brasília the other day. As the capital of Brazil, this city is all but sixty years old and, to me, it feels a bit like England's Milton Keynes crossed with Canberra — a concrete jungle where nothing seems to make sense, in spite of having been purportedly designed for convenience.

Brasília consists of a montage of concrete blocks and weird, white sculptures deposited at random. The significance of each one was explained and instantly forgotten as Billy gesticulated enthusiastically in all directions, a human beacon in his fluorescent yellow vest, complete with his own name on the front in giant letters. Between spouted facts and figures regarding social demographics, he told us proudly of the time he showed Obama's people round the city, and how he came to be in the *Lonely Planet*.

Underneath his vest, Billy wore a Dragoman T-shirt with a Rio to Cuzco map on it, which he'd drawn himself in marker pen. He'd had these T-shirts printed for all of us and charged us $15 each for them. We paid up rather begrudgingly because no one had the heart to tell him they were a bit shit, and Stef (who, incidentally, is twenty-four and a circus performer who climbs silk ropes — how cool is that?) hacked hers up creatively with my nail scissors, so it's now a bit more wearable. The rest are bunged in the overhead nets in the truck till we can get rid of them. Bless Billy.

We did see a rather nice church with a million blue windows, and a cathedral shaped like a crown, before he took us to an all-you-can-eat pizza restaurant on a strip of fast food outlets that looked like Las Vegas. I couldn't help but wonder if he'd taken Obama there, too.

Three days of driving and several bush camps later, we arrived in Poconé, the small gateway town to the Pantanal. There, a group of us found ourselves in a pool hall surrounded by local guys who stared at us girls slack-jawed and blinking, like they'd never seen a woman before. It wasn't long before one particularly amorous man in his sixties started dancing around our pool table. He was swigging Cachaça from a plastic bottle, grinning with teeth so lopsided he looked like he'd been struck in the face with a baseball bat. At one point he spilled some of his Cachaça on the floor in a cross-shape and said a small drunken prayer over it, before lifting his shirt in an effort to make one of us fall in love with his beer gut.

Seeing that he was being annoying, the pool hall manager came over and asked him to leave us alone. This worked for five minutes, until the drunk recommenced his dancing and slurring. The manager asked him to leave again ... and again ... and again ... but each time he'd come back in and wobble around us, singing.

After maybe five or six evictions and re-entries by this drunk, the manager appeared again with a whip. But not just any old whip, mind you. It was one of those whips with numerous tassels on it, creating one long leather weapon of fear. He grabbed the annoying man by his sweaty shirt, hauled him outside and proceeded to whip the living shit out of him. We watched in horror as he struck his face with the same force you'd apply to a growling werewolf about to eat your baby, over and over again, until eventually the poor man burst into tears and ran away to the park over the road, where he sat on a bench and continued to drink his Cachaça. We assumed he'd wake up in the morning wondering why his face was whiplashed, and concurred it was probably better he didn't remember. We also realised why his teeth were probably so wonky. You wouldn't want to piss anyone off in Poconé.

So anyway, here we are now in the Pantanal, finally, at an eco-lodge called Pousada Rio Claro. On our first boat trip into the murky river waters this afternoon, we were surrounded by inquisitive otters and circling caiman. The engine died in the middle of this wildlife display and our drivers were forced to tie our two boats together with what looked like a skipping rope, but we survived and made it back to the lodge triumphant, having learned that caimans are afraid of otters. Did you know that? Apparently otters will always win a fight.

With 100,000 square kilometres in Paraguay and Bolivia and the rest in Brazil, the Pantanal wetlands is by far this country's number one destination for bird watching and wildlife spotting. It covers an area nearly half the size of France, and in the far north merges into the Amazon, which, surprisingly, is where most tourists will still head first.

Russ and I just watched the most sensational sunset I think I've ever seen. The brooding sky was reflected in the wetlands as billowing clouds turned from white, to amber yellow, to pink, red and blue, creating a 360-degree wonderland that stretched to infinity. Giant Jabiru storks, toucans and hummingbirds, kingfishers, parakeets and macaws all fluttered happily around in trees resembling gnarly hands poking up from the water, as we stood there in the changing colours, wondering if we'd died and gone to heaven.

The Pantanal is one huge nature documentary in action, twenty times the size of Florida's Everglades and home to even more birds than the Galápagos. You won't find many flowers here, but it boasts the biggest concentration of fauna in the New World and, whereas many animals hide in the dense Amazon forest, here in the open wetlands they're all on full display. There are also more insects here than I've encountered anywhere else, ever. When we first pulled up at the eco-lodge, having driven the 145-kilometre Transpantaneira Highway — a dusty, orange, lizard-infested dirt road from Poconé, so beautiful for its emerald surroundings that, at one point, we all sat on the roof of the truck and counted the birds in awe — I noticed that it, too, appeared to be bordered with flooded grass and stagnant pools.

'Oh wow, it's soooo pretty, look at all the water!' Stef enthused. But I caught the glint of recognition in Khaki Ken's eyes, and my instincts, too, were primed. Top mosquito real estate by the acre stretched before us: a nursery for malaria carriers birthing killers by the millisecond. We were right. Sure, the Pantanal is all so pretty in the day, what with its preening birds and glistening caiman and white horses wading through the swamps like mythical unicorns missing their horns, but come nightfall we're forced to make a mad dash between our rooms and the dining hall through what can only be described as an insect blizzard. You can tell when Stef's on her way back to our room because you can hear the screams.

Still, it's definitely all worth it … the whingeing companions and the bad truck-stop food, even the enforced 'flapping' and press-ups. Because I can't even begin to explain how incredible that sunset was tonight. If Pachamama blesses everywhere in South America, as I've witnessed over the past eight months, the Pantanal, at the heart of it all, is surely the place she must call home — the place she keeps her rocking chair and comfy slippers and comes to have a chuckle at tourists screaming in an insect blizzard.

Lucky escapes and new beginnings ...

So, I was going to leave you there, my friends, at the very centre of this fascinating continent, humbled and enchanted once again not by another South American city, but by the vast expanse of nothing and everything in between.

I was going to leave you there, high on natural wonders with yet more travel ahead to God-knows-where-exactly ... but I should probably tell you what happened on the truck ride back to Cuzco at the end of our intrepid Dragoman expedition.

We were trundling up the road with steep cliffs and deep valleys on either side when we saw a white car parked, a blue pick-up truck on its side in a ditch and a motorbike in the middle of the road. I caught a glimpse of a man standing between the motorbike and the car, leaning in towards the car window. I thought there had been an accident. Daniele, our Spanish-speaking driver, was at the wheel and he pulled to a stop, at which point we heard a gunshot. *Holy shit*! My heart literally slammed into my ribs and I almost puked. The guy was so close-range to the car, there's no doubt whoever was in that car had just been murdered in the middle of the road.

'Guys, get down,' Dave told us then from his place in the passenger seat up front. He didn't have to tell us twice. All fifteen of us threw ourselves to the floor just as I caught sight of both our drivers throwing their arms in the air. I was huddled under a table with two other girls, looking at Russ under the table opposite, fully expecting the man with the gun to get on the truck. I've never been so terrified in my life — I thought that was it, quite frankly. Everyone's face was drained of colour, in spite of our tans and insect bites.

'*Tranquilo, tranquilo*,' I heard Daniele say then, as whoever it was with the gun approached him. I later found out it'd been one of three guys all wearing balaclavas. Another shot went off and I hugged my knees on the filthy truck floor, not caring about the mud, the smelly shoes, or the possibility of stray tarantulas on board. Every part of me was trembling. Stef, who'd been asleep with her iPod on, woke up suddenly and was yanked to the floor by Russ before she knew what was going on. Daniele was speaking hurriedly in Spanish at the front. I later learned that the people who'd been in the upturned pick-up truck were lying on the road and one had been shot in the knees. The white car had stopped to help and, unfortunately, the driver had been shot at point blank, no doubt as a result of having seen too much.

I have no idea what it was all about, or how someone on our truck wasn't shot at, too, but apparently, while the shooter was pointing his gun at us and urging Dave and Daniele to look away, somehow Daniele found the presence of mind to calmly ask if they could just let us pass like nothing had happened. The guys with the guns were obviously panicked at having already shot so many people, and probably didn't want to risk doing anything else, although I guess they could have got on board and taken our valuables, if they'd wanted.

I think Daniele staying calm saved our lives, or at least stopped us getting robbed. Eventually we were allowed to drive off untouched and unhurt, thank God, although further up the road at a tiny village we saw another white car parked by the road with at least fifty people crowded around it. A bullet hole was clearly visible in the windscreen but we never saw any police about as we high-tailed it as fast as we could to Cuzco, without stopping.

I've heard worse stories than this over the past eight months —

people who've been held at gunpoint on the street, kidnapped, mugged, stripped, raped. You never think anything like that is going to happen to you. But the truth is, this is the real world. Calling a 'path' The Gringo Trail doesn't necessarily make it safe. Shit happens when you grow complacent, and I guess there's a lesson in that for all of us.

There is so much more to see of this daunting continent, so many places I didn't go, but I guess in going with the flow I've still seen so much more than I ever dreamed I'd see, good and bad. I, along with numerous other people who've crossed my path, have been floored by the wonders of the world and changed irrevocably by standing small in the face of so many miracles. The mountains, the sweeping grassy plains, the sequined southern skies at night. The jungles, the beaches, the wetlands, deserts, scrub and snow, each setting as different and inspiring as the passionate, proud people who inhabit them all.

It's kind of hard to decide which specific part of this trip has been my favourite, or my least favourite. In retrospect everything looks different and my eyes have been opened to so many new things. You can't help but grow and expand spiritually (as well as width ways) when you're travelling out here and, if I'm honest, I feel that this experience has shaped me as a person more than living in Bali last year ever did.

Opening my mind always seemed like something I was trying to *learn* how to do. But somehow, in exploring South America, I've found it has come naturally. A connection with nature, and to something else. To the divine perhaps, at times? Even without ayahuasca running through my bloodstream, I can still appreciate now how we're nothing but energy, flowing like rivers from mountains into the fields of other people. This continent is as beautiful as it is frightening, as vast as it is part of a ridiculously small world (as exhibited when you meet a friend from home in the middle of Machu Picchu).

Excitingly, it looks as though The Crab and I are meeting up again when this truck reaches Peru, and there's talk of us travelling northern Chile together once The Lion goes home to work on new projects … a thought that makes me smile even when my head is bouncing off the window on a dirt road and Russ is acting like a woman on his period. I'm ready to go out and face the future, whatever that might be. All I know is that, when it comes to travelling, there's no such thing as going the wrong way. Every time I've thought I've made a bad decision, I've made a new connection that has ultimately led to something else.

Of course, I've also learned to be extremely careful with earplug insertions, to never put a date on the expected arrival of extraterrestrials, and to never, *ever* fall for a Latin American man. Especially not one who lives in the Ecuadorean jungle, plucks bats from thin air and doesn't even have a Facebook account.

Epilogue

Poor Eduardo, we thought, as The Crab steered the car over the rocky salt flats back towards San Pedro. Our fabulous Chilean guide had been pointing out the natural habitat of a pretty pink flamingo when he tripped over a concrete bollard in the viewing area and dislocated his shoulder, so instead of learning more about the harsh desert environment, we were speeding through it on the way to the hospital. Poor, poor Eduardo.

After working our way down from Cuzco, back to Arequipa and into Chile's northernmost city, Arica, The Crab and I had headed south via Iquique – a really pretty coastal spot (although the sea was way too cold for swimming) – to spend a few amazing days in beautiful Valparaiso. Imagine a city by the sea that looks as if first a rainbow was splashed all over it, then a crack team of graffiti artists armed with spray cans hit it. Valparaiso is crazy cool and expensive.

After dining there on some of the most ludicrously priced food and wine I'd had in South America, we'd found ourselves in the harsh, cowboy town of San Pedro in the Atacama Desert, where we'd taken Eduardo up on his offer of a tour – and that didn't end well, obviously. After depositing him in the emergency ward we headed back to the Aatacamadventure Wellness & Ecolodge, a sandy, windswept resort consisting of a few rooms and a hot tub in the middle of nowhere. This place offers quite possibly the most rustic desert experience you could ask for outside of living in a Bedouin tent and plodding around on a camel.

We also stayed a few 'romantic' nights at the ridiculously chic Alto Atacama Desert Lodge & Spa, which spoilt us rotten; something The Crab and I felt we deserved after time spent in a hideous granny flat back in Arica, which was so much worse than anywhere else I've ever stayed I'm struggling to describe it. We couldn't even get into that place without ringing a bell and waiting ten minutes for a decrepit old woman to hobble down the stairs and open the door.

Perhaps we should have booked somewhere in advance in Arica, but The Crab and I have kind of been winging this whole thing, and we're not the best-organised people, we're discovering. I think travelling alone makes me get off my arse and get things sorted but when you have a travel buddy somehow it's easier to leave more to chance. Sometimes that can be amazing: you can have such unprecedented adventures, like the time we smoked some local produce (ahem) with a guy we met on a beach in Arica and ended up first in a skateboarding park attempting Spanish with his teenage friends, then back in the dreaded granny flat talking to dead people. (Don't ask.) But most times you really should prepare.

I've been travelling with The Crab for a few weeks now, but I have to say nothing tests a friendship like spending twenty-four hours a day, seven days a week with someone. He's become my best friend, husband, wingman, sidekick, all in one go with no room for 'gradually getting to know each other' whatsoever, but that's travelling, I guess. It's all or nothing on the road when you team up. You're going to see each other at your best and worst, when you're hungover, sick to the stomach, sunburnt and grouchy … but to compensate, you're going to have the time of your goddamn life and you're never going to forget any of the eye-opening things you'll witness together.

I thought the stars in the Galapagos were incredible, but the Atacama Desert is known for being one of the best places for stargazing in the world and it didn't disappoint. A trip to the observatory the other night had us standing inside a huge glass dome, which moved around us like some kind of space pod, allowing us to see the craters on the moon in such close up clarity it felt as if I could touch them.

I've never actually travelled with a guy before, but we get along surprisingly well. I guess we wouldn't keep going if we didn't. Plus it's really great to be stargazing and desert trekking with someone of the male species. Not only do I have someone who can appreciate the wonders of the world with me, but he can also help carry my bags, ward off creepy local men, apply sunscreen to my back and keep me on the ball when it comes to shaving my legs.

We still have two more months to go, as we're planning to carry on to Santiago and then back to southeast Asia to see some of Thailand, Vietnam, Bali (The Crab has never been) and Japan. Who knows what the future holds after that, but I guess the point of this epilogue is to show that the journey never ends; it just goes on as you bust more doors down and open yourself up to opportunities. I never thought I'd end this South American trip by travelling even further with an American guy, but then a year ago I never thought I'd be in South America at all.

Actually, the more I hear about the US from The Crab, the more I want to go back there. I lived there once, from 2001 to 2003, and I never quite got it out of my system. If we're supposed to meet people for a reason, perhaps one of the reasons I met The Crab was to kick-start another process; to take me back to where it all began; to where I first started believing in lands of opportunity?

We are changing each other day by day, second by second and, even when it seems like there isn't a plan, things are falling into place, just as if everything was planned all along.

For now, though, being in the moment is all that matters. I'm just going to enjoy looking up at the stars some more, and wishing on one or two that Eduardo's OK in his hospital bed.

Aww.

Poor Eduardo.

Printed by RR Donnelley at Glasgow, UK